COLORFLOW

Discover Your Perfect Colors
Experience Life's Easy Flow

Patricia Kay Lebow

For all those
who share in my awe
of the sweet sorcery of color.

CONTENTS

Note: In order to offer this book to my readers at a reasonable cost, illustrations throughout appear in black and white. For full color illustrations listed by chapter number go to <u>www.gardenroomdesigns.com</u>.

Illustration Credits

Each illustration with a file # is used with permission from !Stockphoto.com, a royalty free image website.

> **"Each friend represents a world in us,**
> **A world possibly not born until they arrive.**
> **And it is only by this meeting that a new world is born."**
> **Anais Nin**

My mission is be that friend, midwife to new worlds for all those who choose the gentle path of ColorFlow.

My belief is that for each of us there are specific, unique color harmonies that deeply nourish our spirits. These hues are vital in the creation of an environment that enriches our lives with unimagined abundance and ever diminishing stress. Because this set of colors is exclusive to each of us, think of them as your "color fingerprint." Considering that the eye can perceive seven million hues, it isn't difficult to imagine that every human being on earth possesses his or her own distinct set of colors. In the ColorFlow course we call your personal color palette your "*ColorPrint.*"

Once you have discovered your ColorPrint, the unique combination of hues that lifts and indeed heals your spirit, you begin to experience a gentle rhythm to your life, a flow. As you incorporate the colors from your ColorPrint and those of your family members, the atmosphere in your home grows more tranquil and untroubled as the décor becomes ever more beautiful and increasingly in tune with your spirit. Your home, now saturated in authentic hues, undergoes a gradual metamorphosis emerging a healing retreat from the frenzied world that lies just beyond the front door.

The pages that follow are not meant to help with the simple redecoration of your home. Rather they are a careful guide to the manifestation of a mindful interior design that profoundly affects mind, body and spirit. It is a journey of transformation culminating in the most natural state of flow we call ColorFlow.

Together let's create a new color struck world!

"True life is lived when tiny changes occur."
Leo Tolstoi

Chapter 1

LETTING GO
Cleansing Your Color Palette

I have always been extremely focused, orderly about my surroundings and exceptionally hard working. My "To Do" list had for years been carefully compiled an evening in advance with pen and paper on my nightstand for last minute additions. This nose to the grindstone mentality became a deeply ingrained habit. Eventually though, I began to notice that the completion of a task brought me greater satisfaction than any of life's leisurely delights. A relaxing cup of tea on the deck at sunset or taking an afternoon to simply window shop with a friend were things I believed only others enjoyed. I needed to stick with the constructive, important stuff. Certainly, something was out of kilter. My life was off balance and worse, I was no longer the captain of my own ship. I instinctively knew that introspection and change were needed if a peaceful, richer, more joyful life were to be mine.

Gradually, almost imperceptibly, over the last decade or so, a deep sense of melancholy had permeated a region beneath the surface of my being. On the thinnest, outermost veneer, to others and even to me, it appeared as if nothing were amiss. I went about my daily routine of keeping up with responsibilities, enjoying my garden and spending time with family and friends. I knew, however, that there was a facet of myself that was fading. The facet was, until this sorrowful turn, a part of me since the beginning of memory. I tried to dismiss the feeling, reasoning that it was simply a normal part of life's changes as one matures. But if this missing piece were, in fact, natural, then why was the sense of loss so profound, so unshakable?

That which had quietly slipped away while I was industriously making lists, completing chores, and basking in my accomplishments was my delightful capacity for head over heels enchantment for the breathtaking beauty that surrounds us. As a child and even as a young woman I had the gift of paying attention, of delighting in every small, yet precious wonder. Kneeling in last autumn's decaying leaves in search of the first, pale green shoots of spring's snow drops had been more uplifting than a vitamin B shot administered directly into my veins. The smell of summer's moist earth and fresh air at my windows revitalized my senses. And when days grew shorter and the air frosty, I looked forward with childlike anticipation to the perfect winter day for adding warmer colors all around my home. The cozy hues would support my creative spirit in a period of physical rest and mindful reflection and introspection.

Lately these sweetnesses were an increasingly rare part of my existence. I suffered now not from a mid-life depression, but from a treadmill life anemia. My lackluster spirit had not resulted from a deficiency of blood cells, but from a lack of breathing in the beauty around me. I had become ensnared in a web of achievement and perfection to the exclusion of the simple treasures of life that had once supported me. But this web had been of my own making. Surely I could undo what I had unwittingly done myself.

And so my journey began. I set out to recapture the bliss I once knew when the beauty that is ever abundant in our Universe was an integral part of my existence. What I knew for certain was that I needed to change my balance of priorities. I would find a healthy rhythm of work and rest. And I would begin again to nourish my aesthetic essence. What was beyond any expectation was the extent to which the Universe would enhance, support and multiply my efforts. As I reflect upon my period of emptiness, I see now, that it was not a dark time in my life, rather an incredibly fortunate, albeit misguided chapter that served to catapult me to even greater bliss than I had originally known.

I became a lovely melange of my younger essence, the one possessing energy and stamina to both keep up with her industrious lists and to bring beauty into her life and the older essence who now craved only the beauty. But alas an older, more enlightened feminine essence, a portent of my future self, had a luscious secret she so generously revealed. "Take time to truly know yourself, to find your unique aesthetic spirit, and *give up the struggle.*" If an endeavor is inordinately difficult, it is not your path. Engage your creative breath and discover your unique aesthetic sense. Bathe yourself in beauty; your beauty. And for me there was nothing more beautiful than color! I immersed myself in a journey of color and resurfaced with great confidence to pass on what I've learned about of the abundant, blissful life I now call ColorFlow.

What I know now about color has to my knowledge never been printed in a book. I will explain my complete theory about color here in Chapter One. Please be prepared to reread because everything that follows builds on this foundation. Upon completion, you may think it too simple. It is my hope that you do see simplicity in the concepts for two reasons. The first we've already touched upon. That is the ease, the flow, with which I believe we're meant to live within this Universe. Our work ethic has taught us that hard work yields the best results. ColorFlow seeks to shift our mindset to a gentler effort over a longer, less prescribed time frame.

The second reason is that we've tried complex. Decorating and design dogma has had many rules, ideas, formulas, myths and opinions regarding the use of color in our homes. How are we doing? Aunt Doris still doesn't know what color to paint the family room. Uncle Jack says he's only going to paint it once so Doris just better decide. My friend, Dana, wonders if perhaps she were possessed by aliens when she chose the color for her sofa. We continue to hear, it's only paint, you can paint over it. And every couple of years there seems to be a new set of color trends, while some poor soul is still back on blue and mauve. I think we may be ready for simple.

My belief and in fact the premise upon which all of ColorFlow is based is that each one of us has somewhere from five to seven colors that *perfectly* resonate with our unique spirits in the most profound aesthetic sense. These are the colors that I refer to as your ColorPrint because like your fingerprint they are unique to only you. You were born with these colors already in place and the hues will not change as you age. Your unique ColorPrint hues are specific shades of color. It would be rare for someone to have simply blue, red, orange, yellow and neutral white as his or her ColorPrint. A person will have, for instance, a specific shade of blue that tends a bit toward blue-green or maybe very much toward blue-green. Or perhaps their ColorPrint blue would tend toward violet and be expressed as a periwinkle blue. Another person may be nourished by a similar periwinkle, but recall that the eye can perceive seven million different colors. The chances of that person having the identical remaining combination of hues on his or her ColorPrint palette are all but impossible.

When we are attracted to a certain hue for awhile and then grow tired of it, we sometimes say, "My tastes are changing." I believe we say this because it's the only plausible explanation that easily comes to mind. However, to my way of thinking, this is evidence of a person who's searching for colors that "feel right." This individual senses that color can elevate the spirit and intuitively knows that seeking the *right* colors is a valuable endeavor. The old favorite color was never an authentic hue. It was not a part of his or her ColorPrint. The reason for growing tired of it was because there was finally a clear sense that it wasn't right. The color didn't bring joy, calm, warmth, creative energy, whatever was needed by this individual.

Most times a new color, *any* new color will uplift us temporarily. However, we are responding more to the *change* than to the color itself. It is like the old adage, "a change of scenery will do you good." Paint a room a new hue and you will feel uplifted, but if it's not a color that resonates with your core aesthetic essence, the enchantment will be short lived. Its allure has no staying power because it was never right in the first place.

How your ColorPrint hues came to be connected to you I cannot explain just as I can't explain why one person, for instance, feels restored and refreshed after a quiet day at the beach, while another abhors the sand and the sun. Some have a preference for living with an abundance of possessions around them, while others bask in the starkness of bare minimalism. We just each of us are who we are.

Perhaps our colors have something to do with our complex emotional make-up and our ColorPrint is a type of environmental nourishment to help us remain stable and balanced. Maybe the precise wavelengths of our ColorPrint colors are imprinted onto the strands of DNA. Or one may choose to believe it has something to do with the alignment of the planets and the stars at the moment of birth. It truly doesn't matter how they came to be. What does matter is that our journey begins with the knowing that the colors that belong in our homes are not in a book or magazine. They are not the latest color trend, nor are they in any interior designer's file. Your ColorPrint hues are only found deep *within you*.

Once you discover your authentic colors, you will learn to use them in the perfect environments and ideal quantities to match your individual taste and needs. It is only then that you will see the enormous power of the life flow that I call ColorFlow. Your treasured hues will begin to nourish you spiritually as if they were a vitamin for the emotions. You will be drawn to your color harmonies like a plant reaching for the sun. You will see that colors, if they are *your* colors, uplift you like beautiful music. Particular harmonies from your ColorPrint move you in a way that until now only painting or sculpture has.

ColorFlow teaches restraint and the judicious use of color. Not every hue from your ColorPrint will appear in every room. All of your ColorPrint hues together do not make up a traditional color scheme you have become familiar with. Color harmonies vary throughout your home and as your mood changes you will be drawn to different areas because, in fact, you need a different kind of nurturing at varying times of the day. But it is all there. Your home has become a perfect retreat through color.

Recall that your unique ColorPrint is made up of five to seven colors. All of these colors together or any combination make a perfect harmony. The color harmony of your Print is sheer perfection because it comes from the Universe, from within, as part of your make up. I am often asked, if there are so many colors on one person's print, how can they all go together? My answer is that every color can make a harmonious match with every other color on the wheel. Red goes with yellow. Blue goes with green. Orange goes with purple and so on. The key is that there are thousands of reds and thousands of yellows. Which red goes with which yellow? Nature does not put clashing colors together. And the Universe has not put clashing colors on your spiritually nourishing ColorPrint. My book guides you to find the exact colors that will enrich your life with unimagined abundance and ever diminishing stress.

Additionally, many have inquired about the time required for the self-discovery to unearth your authentic color palette. You will find that the time required becomes unimportant. My color exploration was fascinating and enjoyable. The time spent seemed secondary. Moreover, I emerged from my journey knowing both the colors and the style of décor that is truly mine. I can furnish my home now with complete confidence. Costly decorating mistakes are a thing of the past. Design magazines have in the last ten or so years been using and indeed overusing the word "haven," but my home has truly become a haven of rest and rejuvenation since I have come to know ColorFlow. My wish to have home feel like a bowl of hot soup on a snowy February day has been realized.

Now, changing the color of a couple of rooms every few years, getting rid of a perfectly good piece simply to update, or redoing a decorating project gone bad just doesn't happen. Instead, during my personal ColorFlow journey there was a time when my home looked a bit sparse. It was a period of cleansing. I may not have known what I wanted, but I was beginning to see what I didn't. Gradually, I introduced pieces that resonated with my true aesthetic spirit. They were quite different in style and color than anything I had ever imagined in my home. I removed old colors and brought in genuine hues that spoke to my subconscious, elevating my mood and supporting me spiritually, emotionally and physically. Now, decorating my home was becoming a gentle layering over time rather than a frantic task of making it all work, fixing mistakes along the way. This type of layering is achieved only with the confidence of being deeply attuned to your design spirit yielding a genuine, domestic patina.

In the search for your perfect colors, you will look not at hundreds of color chips, but to your preferences in design styles, patterns, shapes and textures. You'll consider life experiences observing how your décor developed into what it is today. The inter-connectedness between who you are and what you prefer is undeniable. As you explore, what will surface will be more than your authentic color palette. Additionally, there will be an emerging style and design aura that is more congruent with your unique, spiritual aesthetic than what you currently see in your home. These are clues to your ColorPrint, the precise colors that will perfectly support the mood you wish to create. Be prepared; your travel log may have unexpected twists and even a surprise ending.

In a nutshell then . . . each of us has a "fingerprint" of colors. These are the five to seven specific colors for each person. These hues are yours for life. They are unearthed through a process of self-discovery detailed in this book. Once discovered, surround yourself with your unique and deeply nourishing colors. As you bring these hues into your home, there will be quite perceptible changes in your life. My own personal journey has led to both spiritual and financial abundance, a joyful and more peaceful everyday existence and an enchantment for beauty like never before. In short, I have manifested a flow to my life. Although I'm still a hard worker and enjoy accomplishing much, there is a gentle rhythm, a flow to my life that I have come to call "ColorFlow."

We have all heard it said that necessity is the mother of invention. I think of my ColorFlow philosophy as an invention of sorts because necessity is how I developed the concepts you'll explore. At the outset of my journey I believed that I knew the colors that I loved and wished to use in my home. Additionally, I was so certain of my style that it was something to which I never gave an ounce of thought. Yet even with my colors and style in place, my rooms were pretty, but just not truly me. I would grow tired of furniture and accessories. I'd rearrange and freshen up, but my contentment was temporary. In short, my spaces were beautiful, but they didn't "fill me up." Remember I wanted my home to nourish me, to feel like hot soup on a winter's day.

Because ColorFlow is an invention and rich with yet unconsidered concepts, I've found it helpful to create a set of terms unique to ColorFlow theories. By the end of this book, you will be able to "speak" ColorFlow. You've already been introduced to the ideas of ColorPrint and ColorFlow. These two terms appear along with their definitions near the end of the chapter for easy reference. As new terms are introduced, they, too, will appear in a section entitled Color Speak near the end of that chapter.

Two additional and essential Color Speak terms are *simply beautiful space* and *deeply genuine place*. A *simply beautiful space* is any space in which all design elements including furnishings, color, pattern, texture, scale, and light are at least pleasing and balanced, but may be breathtaking. A *deeply genuine place* is a particular space created by one person or family who resides there. This space is saturated in authentic colors and styles creating an environment steeped in life-giving energies which bring lasting contentment, joy and abundance to those embraced by the surroundings.

In other words, imagine a *simply beautiful space* as the incredibly gorgeous bedroom you might stay in at a bed and breakfast on Cape Cod. Think of the *deeply genuine place* as your bedroom, the personal haven you're creating. Last summer's getaway was wonderful, but there's no place like home.

As my own ColorPrint was revealing itself, with no additional effort I began to turn away from the traditional style of furnishing and patterns that I had used my entire life. My preferences were leaning in the direction of contemporary and, in fact, quite avant-garde designs. It wasn't a conscious decision. It would be rather unsettling to tend toward traditional decor all of one's life and suddenly decide to purchase a contemporary sofa. But my shift wasn't the least bit uncomfortable. To the contrary, it felt quite natural. That's because for me it was the natural choice. Contemporary/avant-garde or whatever I would choose to call this authentic style that was revealing itself, is and was the real me all along. And so it felt right.

And my colors? They are not only harmonious in varying combinations, but they look especially fitting with the style that is authentically mine. I can recall a point along the way when I realized just how much I adore hand woven, raw silk pillows in natural, pigment dyed colors. Some of them have an Asian feel with embroidery and beads. I knew they didn't fit with a traditional room, but they are fabulous with my authentic style. I'm grateful that I noted this as a relevant clue to the style and colors I so wished to discover. You will observe, as I did, seemingly unrelated clues to your emerging style and ColorPrint all along the way. Heed each one no matter how insignificant it may appear. There will be that "tipping point" when all of the information begins to align in a way that makes sense. You will know your style and you will know your colors. And then your life, like mine, will begin to flow.

Keep in mind as you read and experience the activities here, that self-discovery is best not hurried. It occurs in tiny, advancing increments with what seems like down time in between. These periods of creative rest are as critical as the forward thrusts. Until now, for many the time and effort invested in choosing an interior color has been perhaps no more than a few days spent pouring over paint strips from the local home store. Some who have been more diligent purchased a few quart samples and painted several areas before deciding. Then, armed with a tiny paint chip, matching or complementary furniture and accessory choices were made.

I've also experienced this challenging and potentially frustrating task and let's be truthful, at best, the results are usually mixed. Unearthing your authentic ColorFlow palette, that alchemy of hues capable of enhancing your life, healing your wearied spirit and transporting you to a relaxed, yet energetic state of flow requires a gentle, deliberate introspection and investigation into the core of your artistic essence. Come with me on this most unusual journey culminating in the discovery of your unique, spiritual aesthetic along with the palette of colors that are yours and yours alone. Be patient, and let the journey unfold before you.

Let's assume for the moment that you've put together a "pretty good" color harmony. It is the intention of my ColorFlow philosophy to guide you to discover combinations that are not pretty good, rather those that *perfectly* reflect your genuine essence and innate appetite for your slice of the rainbow. For a first glimpse into the potential value of perfect colors, imagine that you've had a particularly trying day, followed by a long wait in the grocery store line, topped off by heavy traffic driving home.

Entering the front door, grocery bags in hand, you unconsciously scan the space you've seen daily. There on the piano is the cherished photo of your son on his 18th birthday. In the far corner is the green velveteen chair that was once a crisp, springy shade. Now faded to a sumptuous, subtle sage, its cushions, too, have lost their spring allowing you to be cradled into their incredible softness. The seascape over the mantle is a remembrance of your youth and those glorious summers up the coast.

8

In this precise instant of visual contact with these and other objects for which you have a profound, visceral connection, your stress level drops, your mind tunes out the chatter of the day and tunes in the loves of your life. In much the same way, colors you choose for your home can embrace you in your most personal spaces providing calming, restorative, and yes, even healing vibrations. Your ColorPrint colors have this effect because they are equally as personal and unique as your family, your memories and beloved possessions. These hues are, in fact, a part of you.

You may have considered hiring an interior designer to help with color choices. An experienced decorator will spend a great deal of time with you exploring color preferences. Then he or she will create several palettes and help you to decide. Because they are professionals and know their craft, the results will most times be stunning. However, even if the results seem quite successful, when you enter the completed room, does it fill your spirit with uplifting energies? Are the colors calming and nurturing? Or are you responding to what I call the wow factor? "Wow, this room is beautiful!" If the room is beautiful *and* a nurturing space, great! If, however, it is *only* drop dead gorgeous, its appeal won't be lasting. In a few years it will begin to look a bit dated and in several more you'll be ready to redecorate. It was just a pretty face, but not authentically you.

In these examples either relatively little time and effort had been spent on color choices yielding results that were in proportion to those efforts, or energies had been directed on methods that were not satisfying for the long term. What I propose is that you make a generous investment of time for self-exploration to unearth those colors that will lift your spirit and sweeten your life for this moment and for years to come. It is not each of your authentic hues on their own but the myriad color marriages you will create throughout your space that is the true alchemy. These color harmonies eventuate in a timeless, profoundly beautiful environment steeped in life-giving energies bringing you and your family lasting contentment, joy and abundance. So in order to realize the rich rewards that certain colors can generate in our homes, let's slow down, save the hunt for the perfect paint chip for much later in the process and prepare to embark on a powerful journey of self-discovery.

As we move forward, keep in mind that the early stages of ColorFlow work deal as much or perhaps more with your home's current interior style and your lifestyle needs as it does with color. You see, your authentic style, your shelter needs and your healing colors are inseparable. It would be impossible to unearth your ColorPrint without exploring the other two. As the journey

9

progresses, focus will shift increasingly away from design style and lifestyle and move exclusively to color.

So let's begin by observing and considering colors already present in your space in a new way. Imagine for the moment that you are able to place all of the colors in your home, all of your color preferences both present and past and everything you have ever believed about color, on a make-believe artist's palette. It is the sort of kidney shaped wooden palette with a hole cut out for the painter's thumb. Once everything is there, let go of any judgment you have about the items on the palette.

The blue bedroom walls that you painted last Spring … it certainly is not the blue you envisioned from the magazine clipping. But your negativity only adds to daily unease. Those feelings transfer to others and then back to you. You will not feel suddenly giddy about your blue bedroom. Instead, you are completely neutral on the subject. Pretend that the catalyst for this change has been the palette itself. This is your artist's palette where one day your ColorPrint will emerge. The palette itself is such a powerful harbinger of favorable changes that it neutralizes all previous color mishaps!

Be aware that the colors you love or have loved are also on your imaginary artist's palette because at this point in your journey it holds everything. It is essential to understand that at least for the moment your judgment of these colors even though favorable must now become neutral. You neither love nor detest any color. These hues may or may not appear on your final ColorPrint. A yellow that is a current favorite may reappear with a bit more green in it. Or you may be surprised that it will fade from your favor completely and a new favorite will replace it. But there is no free pass to the end of the journey. Recall that your mission in this chapter is to let go and cleanse your palette. So for the moment, simply stop and observe where you are presently and where you've been. And for the time being, judgement toward everything that is current reality, everything on your palette is neutral.

It is only by becoming non-judgmental with regard to all color that we give ourselves the gift of *infinite selection*. Someone, for instance, who clings tightly to a distaste for brown has narrowed his or her color selection considerably. Now there is no opportunity for a stunning bronze accent wall whose role it is not to stand alone, but to enhance a collection of blue and white Asian pottery. Bronze *is* brown.

Your current judgements affect colors for which you have a distaste as well as those that you have always been fond of. I had clung tenaciously to a particular blue-violet. But wherever I used it, something just didn't feel right. By journey's end, I found that the violet more fitting for me was warmer one that tends toward red rather than blue. But I had to first let go of the blue-violet in order to find the red-violet that now resonates so perfectly with my aesthetic spirit. *Infinite selection* then, is literally every color on earth and is available only to those who are able to fully suspend judgement whether favorable or unfavorable of all hues.

In ColorFlow, it is crucial that the discovery of our colors come with neither a struggle nor an imposed time constraint. The successful unearthing of our authentic hues is manifested most easily if we view ourselves not as travel guide, but as travel partner with the Universe. We are ready now for our first *Imprint,* or meditation. A key component of meditation, a deeply relaxed yet mentally alert state, allows us to clearly see and understand concepts that remain obscure in our normal preoccupied state. Further, in meditation our subjective mind becomes pliant and accepting of alternative ideas presented in the ColorFlow course. In each chapter there will be an *Imprint*. You may read through it and then sit and meditate, paraphrasing or simply considering what you have read. Alternatively, you may tape the *Imprint* and play it back as you sit quietly and listen. Use each *Imprint* as many times as you choose.

Imprint, A Meditation
Silver Palette

Sit comfortably with your feet flat on the floor, your back upright, and your palms resting upward in your lap. Close your eyes. Become aware of your breath. Relax and breathe more slowly and deeply as you give yourself well deserved permission to take a moment's respite from the day's chatter. For the first time today, just be.

Mentally count backward from ten to one. Ten nine eight seven six five four three two one. You are totally relaxed and ready to imprint alternative ideas for your décor into your mind. These new thoughts bring you fresh perspective and renewed joy for life.

Now imagine yourself at home. Everything appears to be just as you left it, but in reality everything has changed. Each object from the heaviest armoire to the lightest slip of paper has become nothing more than vibrating energy. Take your hand and pass it easily through a solid wood furniture piece just as you could pass your finger through a flame. Each item is feather light. You differentiate the objects by color or size, but no particular object stands out as being more or less attractive.

Envision a silvery artist's palette on your lap. It is the palette from where one day your treasured ColorPrint will emerge. Once again scan the items in your room. Then in your mind's eye see them floating effortlessly onto your palette. Recall that they are feather light. And no matter how many objects in your space, they are a perfect fit. Notice now a change far more important than weight or density. There is no longer anxiety over the planned décor that didn't work out, no embarrassment about the chair upholstery that has needed redoing for years, and perhaps a bit surprising is a lack of attachment and a dissolving attraction to items to which you were once devoted.

This is your palette. You are poised for one of the most joyous and energizing essentials of ColorFlow. . . Cleansing Your Palette! Now mentally counting from one to ten, return from your Imprint refreshed and anxious to cleanse. One two three four five six seven eight nine ten.

Cleansing, as the chapter title suggests, is the first tool you will use to uncover your authentic color palette. At this point in our journey I will ask you to cleanse, but as ColorFlow techniques become second nature, clearing and cleansing will come naturally to you.

In order to cleanse, the first thing I would like you to do is *stop*. Stop shopping or bringing anything new into your home. Stop thinking about shopping for your home. Stop planning about the day when you will begin to shop for your home. Stop accompanying friends as they shop for their homes. Even with no intention to buy, cease looking for interesting items on eBay, at yard sales or auctions. And my favorite . . . there can no more curling up on the sofa with a couple of luscious home décor catalogs. Simply stop. Your focus needs to shift to what you *currently* have and how these things make you feel.

You are about to take a hard, critical look at your possessions deciding whether or not they bring pleasure by their aesthetics or perhaps by providing welcome comfort at day's end as in a favorite, comfy chair. Some items are held onto with great tenacity only because you've had them for such a long time. Perhaps they bring neither beauty nor comfort. In any case your plate, or shall we say your "palette" is full, so this is not the time to acquire yet more. Further, anything brought into the home will have color and you are yet unsure of your most nurturing hues. Once you truly know your preferences, shopping will be an experience more gratifying than you can yet imagine! Your living space will develop its own personality, an aura, that will make decorating mistakes a thing of the past.

Next, I'd like you to consider a concept I have come to call *design chatter*. It is simply the ever changing plethora of colors, patterns, styles and opinions that bombards us on a daily basis. Whether reaching us consciously or subconsciously, *design chatter* deafens our genuine sentiments about design.

One example of this unending and unnerving prattle is the limited color palette that designers and merchandisers choose for each new season. Say that the design powers that be decide that this year's fall palette does not include the rich claret red that is genuinely yours. In its absence you are more easily lured to the incredibly popular greens, violets and golds that do appear in every home décor magazine, show house and linen collection. The attraction occurs so subtly that you may believe your own tastes are changing. But in reality you are experiencing a sort of merchandising propaganda that we refer to as *design chatter*.

By contrast then, our *authentic design voice* is that visceral or gut feeling that draws us to particular colors, patterns, and styles, regardless of current trends, fashions or anyone's opinion but our own. Our *design voice* is always there. It is unwavering. The ColorFlow philosophy is merely a set of tools to help you become still, tune out the chatter and allow your *authentic design voice* to be heard.

It will prove valuable to become aware of *design chatter*, so that you can separate it from your *authentic design voice*. In other words, separate everything you see and hear about what looks good in your home from what you believe looks best. If you do nothing but take a break from shopping, the *design chatter* will be reduced considerably giving your authenticity a voice.

So advertising, whether it is television, magazine, store flyer or in-store display, is a major source for *design chatter*. Until now your single *authentic design voice*, the voice that articulates what is genuine for your inner self, has been no match for advertising. Your awareness will become your second, most valuable tool to quiet noisy advertisers. Your first will be the discovery of your authentic aesthetic self. However, until that occurs, look out for the media!

Perhaps less powerful, but still part of the *design chatter* is the way your home looks presently. The décor of your space at this very moment can act to restrain your authenticity by the simple phenomenon of inertia. An object at rest tends to stay at rest and we all to some degree resist change. For instance, if your living room has always been decorated in shades of green, it may be easiest just to keep the status quo. It may not look great, but it also doesn't look too bad. The risks associated with change are more distasteful than the comfort in avoiding change.

The sum total of our visual impressions from childhood through early adulthood make up a third part of *design chatter*. The way our parents' house was decorated made us feel a certain way. If we had a strong sense of shelter and nurturing, similar décor may have some appeal to us even if it is not our own true style. If, for instance, we grew up middle-class in the fifties as I did, our childhood home may have been no-nonsense Early American. My childhood living room was avocado green and gold and the family room was deep red and blue with pictures of Minutemen on the love seat fabric. How do these memories affect us, if at all? As much as we say we aren't going to become our parents, as a young woman there was a suspicious amount of traditional furnishings in green and gold in my own home.

It took me until the age of 53 to be able to purchase an avant-garde, Japanese platform bed. It is 180 degrees opposed to anything I would have ever in the past chosen for my home. I realized that I had been noticing contemporary platform beds in magazines for 20 plus years thinking they were beautiful, but not for *my house*. Before my personal design journey, that alone may have held me back from the purchase though in my gut, I knew it was me. I have learned that it is safe to listen to my *authentic design voice*.

Step one of the cleanse then, is to imagine yourself detached and feeling neutral about every household object in your home. The second is to stop acquiring any additional objects. Step three is to become aware of *design chatter* which comes from three major sources. They are advertising, our desire to hold on to the way our home currently looks and the way we have always decorated. Remember, you are seeking design solutions because to some extent you're not satisfied with your décor. Your surroundings cannot become more life enhancing without change!

Now let's get physical! Choose a room. Don't mull over the decision forever because once you do a bit of ColorFlow work in this room, the spirit may move you to work in another. What you need to know at the outset is that the "work" of ColorFlow is just as much mental as physical, both subjective and objective. And everything I say to you is a suggestion, a jumping off point for you to run with in your own way. When we discuss clearing and cleansing there will be no rules such as "If you haven't used an item in 2.5 years, toss it." I will not come to your home with an organizational system of baskets that *I* have chosen for *you* to use. You're getting my drift.

Sit comfortably with a good view of most of the room you've chosen. Relax and move your eyes slowly in a clockwise direction around the room from one object to the next. Pause as you recall where you acquired a certain vase. Are you attracted to the color of it? Now to the top of the TV. Stacks of magazines. Wouldn't a lazy, rainy day with time to clip recipes and dream about decorating be a luscious treat? There's the floor lamp that your mother-in-law gave you two Christmases ago. You smile at the pleasant memory. Along side the lamp is the lounge and ottoman. "What was I thinking when I chose that hideous gold fabric? It certainly doesn't go with the tweed on the sofa that I do so love."

You wish to have a deeply genuine living room, but if you are like most of us, our lives are so busy that we don't ever carefully look at what we have, at our starting point. The exercise above of simply taking fifteen minutes or so to look around may be all you need to begin. For an even clearer picture, I suggest taking photographs of your room. About four or five shots from different angles of one room will suffice. Viewing them on the screen of your digital camera won't give the full effect. Print them. Seeing your room in photographs is like seeing it with new eyes. Nine times out of ten your room is not as attractive as you thought. I believe you'll be surprised.

Now I'd like you to find one object that you will remove from the room. It should not be a transient item of clutter like yesterday's paper or the loose change under your sofa cushions. For that sort of clutter you don't need my help. It also should not be anything that simply needs replacing because it is worn or in disrepair. A good example of this might be a set of threadbare pillows one of which has a broken zipper. Further, the item you choose will not find a new life in another room. This piece is leaving permanently. Before protesting too rambunctiously, remember that you wish to create more uplifting, life enhancing surroundings. Change cannot occur if all things remain the same.

Think back to your artist's palette, the one that embraces all of your belongings. The article that you will release from your palette today is a *simply beautiful* object. It does not belong in your home because it is not a *deeply genuine* object. It may be lovely, but it is just not you. If you are having difficulty deciding whether a certain object is appropriate to remove, it may be helpful to apply the following litmus test.

Try to remember how much you paid for the item. If you don't remember, estimate the price that it might reasonably bring in a furniture or department store. Now imagine that you have saved a little extra cash and it's time to splurge. If you didn't already own it, would this article possibly be your splurge purchase? Would it be in the top five? Top ten? Beautiful, but not on the list at all? If you wouldn't repurchase the object, you must not feel strongly about it. Can it possibly be nourishing to you in any way?

Just before I removed the first item from my living room, my house was on a garden club Christmas House Tour. Because I am a florist, my home was literally drenched in fresh greens and unusual floral arrangements. As I greeted tour goers, many commented on my floral designs, but by far what sparked most commentary that day was a small, metal toleware table. The occasional table was made to look like a stack of books and actually opened to reveal a box for storage. Nowadays there are inexpensive knockoffs, but mine was a handpainted Italian import and had been with me for about 25 years. It had cost $450 new.

Today if given $450 to splurge on anything I absolutely loved for my home, the book table wouldn't even be on my radar. Further, if I saw this piece in a store for considerably less, I still wouldn't be interested. The lovely books were purchased at a time when I was searching for my authentic style. I've enjoyed the table and it's been useful. The delightful stack of books was a *simply beautiful* piece, but not an *authentically genuine* one for me. Now it was time to let it go, to cleanse my palette.

After having carefully settled on the piece to release from the room, decide whether it will be sold, donated or given to a family member or friend. Clear it away from the space as soon as possible. Now, in essence, your room is a new palette slightly less muddled by the *design chatter* of *simply beautiful* pieces that don't resonate with your *authentic design voice*. What may appear to be a small step is in Universal terms monumental. You have created a chink, a space, in the solid, frozen energy that has kept your room from feeling alive, from being a living breathing, vital part of the gentle existence you crave. It is through this opening that the first whisper of your *design voice* will be heard.

Staying in the same room, it's time to clear a bit of clutter. Before clearing, however, it's essential to know what clutter is and how much of it to clear just now. The best definition of clutter I've found is very succinctly anything that does not bring comfort, convenience or joy on a regular basis. For now clear just a small, well-defined area of clutter. Please do not allow this to become an enormous project. Recall that nothing in ColorFlow should be difficult or overwhelming. It is best that your activities occur in small, measured increments. Amazingly, you will find yourself effortlessly revisiting the issue of clutter as ColorFlow becomes integrated into your life.

Perhaps there are bookshelves in your space that hold not only books, but knick-knacks and videos. Shelves notoriously become overcrowded and disorganized. If, for instance, there are ten shelves, you may choose to focus on only a few. In a dining room, there may be a display cabinet for china and assorted art glass. Over the years we all manage to accumulate. There can come a point when the displays lose aesthetic impact either because there are too many items in a given space or because the pieces don't relate well. Choose to sort out one or two display areas according to their size.

Once you've identified the clutter spot, clear everything away. Scrub surfaces and polish objects sparkling clean. Reorganize, put things away, toss what isn't used and put back the rest. It's invigorating!

Rearranging comes next. Just like your work with clutter, limit yourself. This is not the time to redesign the entire space. Two upholstered chairs with contrasting fabrics may simply switch places. A silk floral that has always been on the coffee table moves to the mantel. A luminous pewter tray poised to reflect a group of candles can now move in from the dining room. The object here is to affect just enough change to stimulate the eye. You are stirring up energy to combat the effects of inertia and stagnant air space.

Now you're ready for the final touches. I feel the excitement just writing about it; you should be feeling in the groove, experiencing the first tinglings of being in the state of "flow" with your home. A thorough vacuuming now will further cleanse and energize the room. Open the windows for several minutes. Yes, Northerners, even if it's winter! All the more reason to rid your space of stale air and energy. Finally, bring life into your room. In the north, a few tightly budded forsythia branches will open beautifully inside in a vase of clear water. In warmer climates, float a single flower clipped from the garden in a small saucer. I would like you to make the assignment of bringing life indoors especially simple as a reminder of the simple, yet amazing splendor of nature.

Following is a concise list of your first cleanse.

- Stop
  Stop acquiring additional items for your home.
  Become mindful of *design chatter*.
  Honor your emerging *authentic design voice*. We *all* have one.

- Take time to carefully study the room of your choice.
  Photograph it from several vantage points to see it more candidly.

- Choose one *simply beautiful*, but not *authentically genuine* item.
  Sell, donate or give that item away making your room a new palette slightly less muddled by the *design chatter* of *simply beautiful* pieces that don't resonate with your *authentic design voice*.

- Clear a limited amount of clutter. Scrub and polish this small area.

- Rearrange to stimulate your senses.

- Vacuum.

- Open windows filling space with the vibrant energy of fresh air.

- Bring life into your room.

Color Speak

Authentic Design Voice: That visceral or gut feeling that draws us to particular colors, patterns and styles, regardless of current trends, fashions or opinions of others. Our design voice is innate and unchanging.

Clutter: Anything that does not bring comfort, convenience or joy on a regular basis.

ColorFlow: A mindful creation of interior design that incorporates your ColorPrint together with styles and arrangements unique to your personality and lifestyle. This genuine atmosphere clears your mind, exhilarates your body and lightens your spirit transporting you to your most natural state of flow: *ColorFlow*.

ColorPrint: The specific colors and color harmonies which when used in our homes act to nourish our spirits creating an environment that enriches our lives with unimagined abundance and ever diminishing stress.

Design Chatter: The ever changing plethora of colors, patterns, styles and opinions that bombards us on a daily basis consciously or unconsciously deafening our own authentic design voice.

Imprint: Connection to the pliant, subjective mind easing acceptance of alternative or unfamiliar concepts into our personal realms while in a deeply relaxed yet mentally alert state.

Infinite Selection: Literally every color that we can perceive expressed in all ranges of value and intensity. It is available only to those who are able to fully suspend judgement whether favorable or unfavorable of all hues.

Simply Beautiful Space: Any space in which all design elements including furnishings, color, pattern, scale and light are at least pleasing and balanced, but may be breathtaking.

Deeply Genuine Place: A particular place created by one person or family who resides there. This space is saturated in authentic colors and styles creating an environment steeped in life-giving energies which brings lasting contentment, joy and abundance to those embraced by the space.

Color Study
The Color Wheel

*"The purest and most thoughtful minds are those
which love color the most."*
John Ruskin, 19th Century Art Critic

The color wheel is a standard way that painters, gardeners, decorators or any artist use to show relationships among colors. Color theory related to the wheel provides a common language for the discussion of color. The wheel helps to visualize how colors will harmonize, aides in choosing combinations with bold contrast to excite and surprise or more subtle harmonies to relax and calm. Understanding and using the color wheel is likely the most powerful tool for choosing color for your home. Knowledge of the wheel helps predict how colors will play off each other. At the same time color choice remains a creative process and one for self-expression. Note that the words color and hue are virtually interchangeable.

The color wheel is made up of 12 colors. Actually, the wheel is little more than a graphic depiction of the rainbow, but instead of the linear configuration we see in the sky, the hues are arranged in a circle to better show their relationships. We'll begin with a round white disk and build one color group at a time. In the illustration that follows only the group containing red, yellow and blue are represented. These are called the primary colors because they are pure hues on their own. Pure color pigments cannot be obtained by a mixing of any other colors. Red, yellow, and blue, along with black and white, form the basis for all other colors. Notice that these primary colors are located in a triangle. Specific arrangements will become important as we move ahead.

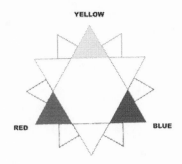

PRIMARY COLORS

Clear bright red, yellow and blue are perhaps not colors many of us choose for our homes. However, cranberry, mustard and navy may be quite attractive in the study. Pink, maize and robin's egg are cheerful in the baby's room. All of these are simply tints and tones of the red, yellow and blue, the primary colors on the color wheel. That which we learn about the qualities of the primaries also applies to these subtler hues. Therefore, as we study the basic wheel, bear in mind that each of the twelve colors represents literally hundreds of tints and tones in that color family. And this myriad of possibilities is just one of the attributes of color I find so irresistibly intriguing!

The secondary colors, arranged in a triangle reversed from the primary colors, are orange, green and violet. Each is produced by mixing two primary colors.

Yellow + Red = Orange   *Yellow + Blue = Green*   *Red + Blue = Violet*

Notice that colorists call the color made by mixing red and blue "violet" and we will do the same.

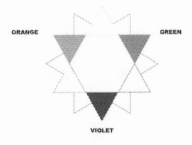

SECONDARY COLORS

The remaining six colors on the wheel are called tertiary or intermediate colors. Each is made by mixing together one primary with one secondary color. The six tertiary colors are yellow-green, blue-green, blue-violet, red-violet, red-orange and yellow-orange. Notice that each of their names begins with the primary color followed by the secondary color name. The color wheel system will work regardless of how the wheel is oriented. However, I have found it easiest for teaching purposes to consistently place primary yellow at the top. Think of the sunshine high in the sky.

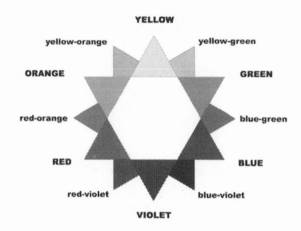

THE BASIC 12 COLOR WHEEL

With all of the colors in place, this wheel is called the basic 12 color wheel. Don't worry if it seems a bit confusing just now. It becomes easier when applied to design.

Now you are equipped with an introductory knowledge of the basic 12 color wheel. You've had a taste for the bliss that cleansing can bring. And perhaps most significant, you've taken the first steps toward loosening your grip on long held beliefs concerning color and design. Some have served you well, while others have not. The only thing that remains perfectly clear is that you are ready for change. You are poised now to partner with the Universe to unearth your true design spirit. Although what you discover will seem new, in reality it is your innate, authentic aesthetic. It has been with you all along. With each discovery no matter how small, a portion of stagnant energy dissolves. These realizations make way for the vibrant, sparkling energy that more closely aligns with the unique rhythms of your spirit.

*"Being an artist doesn't mean you can draw;
being an artist means you can see."*
April Cornell, <u>Decorating with Color</u>

Chapter 2

EMBRACING THE ARTIST WITHIN
Your Abundant Creativity

In Chapter 1 attachments to colors and styles began to dissipate by cleansing both your living space and your mind making way for the first utterances of your authentic design voice. Now self-exploration continues as you embrace a second, critical tool that we will call *Color Bridges*. We'll embark on this yet deeper journey; connecting with your abundant creativity. Whether you've realized it or not, there *is* an artist lurking within.

Human beings are by nature creative. You will need to call upon this creativity, that which you *already possess* within, to design the perfectly hued, deeply genuine living space that will enchant your life and bring you to a tranquil state of flow.

Many of us have adopted rather serious misconceptions regarding creativity. One is that creative people are only painters, sculptors, novelists and actors and actresses. The rest of us have regular jobs and aren't all that creative. However, consider researchers working to solve the problem of our limited energy supply, a landscaper experiencing a rough economic year attempting to devise a plan for saving each of his employee's jobs, a teacher whose methods succeed for every child but one or a single mother on a fixed income making her monthly check stretch into thirty days worth of nutritious meals. All of these people need to call upon tremendous reserves of creative thought. Indeed, there isn't one of us whose lives would not be enriched by using his or her creativity. It is a grossly overlooked skill that is well worth developing.

Second, we have acquired the notion that creativity has been handed out in unequal portions. If you believe that creativity means that you can paint a landscape, then certainly French impressionist painter Claude Monet had more than I do. Or if you believe that creativity means that you can act, then chances are that Reese Witherspoon is infinitely more creative than you. But something that is creatively executed is truly characterized by no more than originality and imagination. And we all started out with plenty of both. Just listen to any five year old! Perhaps we're merely out of practice or plainly too busy to use such skills these days. In this chapter, you'll begin to reconnect with your abundant creativity.

There is a marvelous book called <u>The Artist's Way</u> by Julia Cameron. Many have missed out on her work because they were put off by the word "artist" in the title. It is a book about creativity. I was fortunate enough to have not only read it, but to have participated in an <u>Artist's Way</u> workshop with Ms. Cameron. She emphasizes the amazing power inherent in the acceptance of creative help from the Universe. This support often manifests itself in the form of something called synchronicity which means that when we change the Universe furthers and expands that change.[1] Cameron continues:

> "Once you accept the idea that it is natural to create, you can begin to accept a second idea that the creator will hand you whatever you need for the project. The minute you are willing to accept the help of this collaborator, you will see useful bits of help everywhere in your life. Be alert: there is a second voice, a higher harmonic, adding to and augmenting your inner creative voice. This voice frequently shows itself as synchronicity. You will have the experience of finding things - books, seminars, tossed out stuff - that happen to fit with what you are doing. Expect the universe to support your dream. It will." [2]

Synchronicity by its very simplicity appears to be a minor detail in our color study. If the concept is new to you, think of it like interest on your savings. Only this is interest on your creative dreams and the Universe is much more generous in its help than any bank I'm aware of. One of the paradoxes that makes life such a breathtaking mystery is that our experience here on earth can be so deeply enhanced by looking to the simple rather than the complex.

When the mind dwells in possibility rather than skepticism synchronicity flows most freely. Recall that during my color journey, I realized that many of my possessions were neither nourishing nor healing. Their colors, finishes, shapes, styles or in some cases simply the sheer number of items were diminishing my energy levels, clouding my mind and blocking the zeal for life I once had. Looking back, I realize that the changes in my surroundings have been enormous. Each ounce of my energy at the crucial beginning stages of transformation needed to be positive in order to attract ample support from the Universe. The first small step was made into a substantially larger step by the Universe. Success begets success and confidence builds.

1. Julia Cameron with Mark Brown, *The Artist's Way*, 2
2. Julia Cameron with Mark Brown, *The Artist's Way*, 119

As we move through the ColorFlow course the concept of synchronicity will become second nature. For now, let's consider one example and realize that it will appear to be nothing more than a small coincidence. It will become increasingly apparent, however, that these "coincidences" are suspiciously frequent and that their cumulative effect on life is remarkable.

It is Easter and my friend Kay enjoys setting an eye catching table for her annual spring buffet. She scours her china closet, the piles of linens and her knick knack collection to come up with an interesting combination. She's chosen pale green salad dishes atop pristine white dinner plates. Not having enough of any one color pastel napkins for everyone, she decides on a cheerful spring mix. Because the food will be served buffet style, Kay will be able to have a floral centerpiece. Something low will allow for easy conversation, but isn't quite as showy as a taller, more dramatic piece. With time to decide, she'll calmly tuck away the idea of a centerpiece having unshakable trust in her own creativity.

Several days later on a long, restorative spring walk in the woods, Kay notices the most graceful tree branch that has been blown down by the wind. Holding it out in front of her, she studies how it would appear from several angles and knows that this is her centerpiece. It is a bit taller than she would have originally chosen. Yet the tracery of branches are sparse enough to allow an unobstructed view for her guests. On Easter Sunday Kay's branch is further enhanced with clear florist tubes filled with several varieties of daffodils. The tubes have been loosely covered with moss making the branch resemble the lovely live oaks seen throughout the deep South.

Had Kay not been relaxed and confident in her uniquely creative spirit, she may have made a beeline to the yellow pages and ordered a perfectly beautiful, fresh centerpiece. It would have been yet another item on the "to do" list and an additional expense. However, with Kay's trust in her abundant creativity, her life was enriched with her genuine aesthetic. Placing the daffodils in water, affixing the moss, breathing in the life vibrations . . . all of these became a meditation, a respite from the unrelenting hustle and bustle that has regrettably become our day to day existence.

Synchronicity can and does assist and support you in virtually every area of your life. However, the degree to which you choose to foster the abundant, synchronous magic that permeates the Universe is directly proportional to the ease and the level of success you will experience as you set out to unearth your life enriching color palette. In short, synchronicity is paramount. It must become second nature. For it is only then that you can freely connect with your inner design spirit. And there in the depths are embedded your nurturing colors, those perfect hues, the treasured colors that have the power to bring you abundance and flow.

Although synchronicity and its incredible powers are frequently mentioned particularly in New Age literature, I have rarely found more than a definition followed by a few life examples. Over the years I have internalized synchronicity and have made several observations that may be helpful to those new to the idea. The following list is one that I share with ColorFlow students. You may wish to consider it your "User's Guide" to synchronicity.

In order to fully embrace the concept of synchronicity one must:

1. **Unequivocally accept the existence of synchronicity.**

2. **Freely consider the enormity of Universal abundance.**
   It is as equally possible for your efforts to be magnified 100 times as 10 times. Expect generosity. Reap generosity. (On the other hand, expect scarcity and you will surely reap scarcity.)

3. **Relax. Work *with* the Universe instead of striving to gain control *over* the Universe.**
   Sometimes in our zeal to be industrious, we set arbitrary time limits for our goals. We solve a concern or finish a project with the primary intention being to gain control of our "to do" list. Keep in mind that we have a different perception of time than does the Universe. Sometimes just giving ourselves a little more time, stepping away, brings new insight to an existing issue.

4. **Be aware that synchronous gifts may be discovered in unexpected places.**
   We tend to think of information in a linear fashion. For instance, if we want decorating answers, we tend to look *only* in decorating books or talk to interior designers. The Universe, on the other hand, works in concentric circles. Answers or help for *any* topic may be found literally *anywhere*. Further, it seems once you find aid in one place, it begins to pop up in additional, unrelated locales.

5. **Be aware that synchronous gifts appear with little fanfare.**
    Because synchronicity is so valuable, we've come to expect that it will arrive with a drum roll. It doesn't. The ingenious answer to something you've been working on for weeks might come in a casual statement a co-worker makes at lunch. Something clicks and you've got your help. Keep you eyes and ears open.

Imprint
Starfires

Sit comfortably with both feet flat on the floor, your back upright and the palms of your hands turned upwards resting on your lap. Give yourself permission to be alone with yourself, to have nowhere to go, to have nothing to do. Let go of your immediate responsibilities and the places you will need to be later on in the day. Bring all of your attention here. Bring all of your focus to this beautiful, present moment.

Mentally count with me slowly and rhythmically from ten to one. As you do, notice your breathing. Take deeper breaths only as necessary to slow your breathing to a relaxed, gentle pace. Ten nine eight seven six five four three two one.

Still breathing gently and rhythmically, turn your attention upward and know that your energy radiates skyward into the infinite Universe. It commingles with the collective consciousness of millions of creative ideas that were on earth but for a fleeting moment in comparison to the earth's ancient existence. See each of these creative thoughts as stars in the night sky. Now they float above for eternity and are there for all to share should we decide to embrace our rich, creative spirits.

Upon more careful inspection notice that these stars have unearthly qualities. Should you take one, the creative spark it holds is not unavailable to others, for each is like an astral tablet with infinite thin sheets ever replenishing. Further, these creative stars demonstrate fantastic alchemies. There appears to be a chemistry within every star that reacts with each of our unique chemistries. What I can manifest with the blending of a certain star will vary greatly with your astral alchemy. While supported by the same star, my creation will be colored by my spirit and yours by your spirit.

Finally, these celestial gems have a cleansing effect on our bodies. Each time we relax into and trust the enormity of our creative spirit, our bodies are further cleansed and cleared to accept yet more creative generosity from the Universe. We become like open vessels for the creative energy of the Universe.

Yes, these stars are unlike ordinary stars. They contain within the burning creative passion of all of humankind from the beginning of time. And so we will not call them stars, but starfires, the stars that hold all creative thought that is deservedly ours. You are an open vessel for all creative energy held in the starfires of the night sky.

It is your nature to be a singular creative spirit. This will become a daily mantra for you. Say aloud now ...

> *"I am an open vessel for all creative energy held in the starfires of the night sky. It is my nature to be a singular creative spirit."*

Mentally count with me slowly and rhythmically from one to ten. One two three four five six seven eight nine ten. Return from your Imprint mentally refreshed, eager to claim your creative spirit.

When most of us enjoy a work of art, whether an oil painting, a sculpture or a passage of music, we tend to dwell for those moments fully in the present. We are looking, listening or feeling, in other words becoming engaged with and responding to the art, in the here and now. And therein lies much of the magic of art or of beauty. In those invaluable flashes of suspended time we are able, if only temporarily, to unclench our stressful grip on yesterday's parking ticket and the bills that must be paid tomorrow to become serenely entranced in the beauty of now. It is a quieting of the mind. In essence, it is the same stilling of the mind we seek to achieve through meditation.

The fundamental goal of ColorFlow is that your home becomes a personal work of art, a healing, meditative atmosphere enabling you to savor life's rich treasures moment by moment. Being present and stunningly conscious for each of life's small yet wondrous gifts is the forgotten essence of our existence.

While enjoying these works of art many of us don't consider the deeply personal journey that led to each creation. Imagine, for instance, an artist who works in pastels. She has become quite well known for her seaside scenes which often times depict children playing at the beach. Her work hangs in the homes of the most discriminating collectors. If we were lucky enough to see her pieces in a gallery, our thoughts would likely not center around the scribblings she did as a child or her art training at the University. We wouldn't be privy to the fact that she began in still life oils with little success. And we would have no inkling of the many twists, turns and synchronicities in her life that brought her to pastels and to the sea and to her passion. It is only when we discover our passions that each of us illuminates . . . as brightly as the stars in the Universe of which we indeed are a part.

And so, it is all of what lies beneath, the totality of an artist's life that culminates in the brilliant creation that becomes the gift to those of us who embrace the legacy of their passion. These experiences are the sum total of formal education, self study, trial and error, experimentation, self-exploration and discovery, and perhaps most importantly, the unique path of day to day experience each has lived.

It is the perfect time now for you to become the artist who creates the deeply genuine place we've been discussing. It will be colored by your ColorPrint, the unique combination of hues that enriches and heals your spirit allowing you to experience both greater abundance and the gentle, rhythmic flow of life each of us deserves. Like the artist in the example, the finished creation emerges only after following a path of self-exploration to unearth that which lies beneath. I have imagined the ColorFlow journey as activating that which is already within in total perfection. The analogy for me that most closely relates is a bed of campfire embers appearing to have completely cooled, but if one were to blow ever so gently, the smoldering embers would once again alight. As children our creativity burned red hot. As adults we may feel that creativity has been lost, but indeed the glow remains.

This is the point when students love to tell me, "There's nothing really very interesting about my childhood." Or, "I've never been very creative. I don't think I can make my home my work of art." Everyone's past whether it was happy or sad, privileged or underprivileged is a combination of experiences seen and felt only through his or her unique senses and known to no other human being on earth. That alone makes it a treasure and a place you must journey to peel away all that has been obscuring your connection with your authentic colors. Dig down. You will find, especially if you begin to share it with others, that your past is far more interesting than you ever imagined.

You are an artist, so I'll ask you to do much of your exploration in an artist's sketchbook that can be purchased at most craft or art supply stores. The ones I use are 9 by 12" and contain 160 empty white pages. They are wire bound so that they lie flat when opened. Anything similar or more to your liking will be great, too. In this book you will be making lists, writing thoughts, creating color schemes and pasting magazine pictures. Although I call it preliminary "work," I've found these exercises to be relaxing, rewarding, and most of all, your certain path to self-discovery. From this point forward, we'll call this book your *Studio* because it is in fact the artist's studio where your color palette will be kept and from where your final creation will emerge.

The activities you'll complete in your *Studio* are called *Color Bridges*, or simply *Bridges* for short. They are meant to serve as "bridges," or connectors helping you move past current knowledge of self, design and color over to the vast internal wisdom yet to be unleashed. Consider that for most of us, each time we have redecorated, the starting point has virtually been the same. In other words, we have set out with the same body of knowledge and set of tools at our disposal for carving out a personally supportive space. Perhaps in the interim we had read several interesting articles in *House Beautiful* magazine, visited a few Design Show Houses, perhaps even taken a class. But had their truly been a connection with the core of our aesthetic spirit since the last redo?

Any design knowledge, experience or expertise that is currently part of your consciousness is what we'll call your *existing design repertoire*. The intent of the ColorFlow course is to facilitate the expansion of your aesthetic sensibilities, free the flow of natural creativity and ensure intimacy with your innate sense of style. The scope of your potential design repertoire is limitless. A more desirable outcome can be achieved once tools have been honed and knowledge broadened. *Bridges* transport you from your *existing design repertoire* to your expanded, authentic design potential.

In simpler terms, your *existing design repertoire* is the bag of decorating tricks you've been using for years because they're what you know. In order to move beyond your *existing design repertoire*, a conscious and deliberate effort must be made to broaden it. *Color Bridges* are specifically designed to guide you toward that very goal.

Color Bridges can transport you to the very deepest core of your artistic soul. It is a place possibly unreachable if you were to approach your journey with a similar plan of attack as say cleaning out your garage. For mundane chores such as a Saturday garage clear out, high energy and specific goals are necessary. For instance, all gardening paraphernalia will be stored at the back right. Trash cans and recycling will go near the kitchen door. Bicycles will be hang mounted on the wall. By 3:00 PM everything needs to be organized, the floor swept and room for one car in the garage. Although each *Bridge* is presented as a separate activity with an apparent beginning and end, think of them more as explorative adventures that may continue indefinitely as long as they are valuable in your journey of self-discovery.

There are four guideposts that will help you turn away from the high energy, work oriented mindset we saw in the "garage clear out" example. That method works well for cleaning and similar jobs, but not for journeys of self-discovery. First, it is crucial to relax and let your mind float and wander. Let go of rules and become playful. For instance, there will be *Bridges* that require choosing and cutting magazine pictures. When I first present *Color Bridges* in a class, there is a flurry of questions. "Do all of the pictures have to relate to interior design?" "Can I put more than one picture on a page?" "What if there's one item in the photo I dislike?" By mid-session, no one asks such questions and students are dazzling me with unique compositions, collages and wonderful insights about themselves. Relax. Save rules and time frames for tasks that call for them.

Second, embrace all possibility. Restrain your judgmental mind and simply play. Recall the concept of infinite selection and realize that once you begin to analyze and judge, you've limited the possibilities. Say, for instance, that during a particular *Bridge* yellow-orange comes onto your palette. Without a thought you strike it from possibility. All of us have been trained to see, analyze and judge almost instantly. But Color Bridging *without* judgement is a rich, creative gift for which you'll need to retrain. Does it mean that yellow-orange will be among the hues on your final ColorPrint? For now you don't know. But yellow-orange has surfaced in your playful, imaginative mind. And for this reason alone, it is worthy of further consideration.

Third, analyze and set aside. Imagine that a *Color Bridge* were to require the listing of furnishings in your home that you dislike. If you didn't analyze your list, it would have no value. But supposing that you did analyze your list seeking emerging patterns and clues to your color and pattern preferences. Say that a large number of the objects on your list have a flowery pattern.

There is the floral sofa in the den, the floral guest room comforter and the color splashed, daisy love seat in the living room. It would be easiest to draw the simple conclusion that you don't care for floral patterns. You could get rid of them all, never to purchase another blossom printed fabric.

Surely there is something about these blossom strewn prints that repels you But what if the flowers are merely too large or exceedingly bright. Maybe sofas, comforters or love seats are simply too large for your taste in florals. Your preference may tend toward using them on smaller ottomans and pillows. And perhaps you really don't like florals. For now, be content that you have a clue, but don't quite know the end of the story. What's important at this stage is to analyze the information and set it aside. It isn't time to draw hard and fast conclusions. In short, analyze, set aside, but don't decide.

Finally, let it go. Once you feel rather satisfied with a *Color Bridge* you'll need to free your creative thoughts. Let them float among the stars in the Universe. All creative thought requires what some have called an incubation period, time to evolve and expand. Recall the concept of synchronicity and know that your efforts will be enhanced and magnified. Learning to relax is key. It must become natural to partner with the Universe, rather than to seek control over it. Once this becomes your customary way of operating, the auspicious changes in your life will astound you. The "REAL" and colorful you will surface most easily once you learn to . . .

Relax and let your mind wander.
Embrace all possibility.
Analyze, set aside, but don't decide.
Let it go.

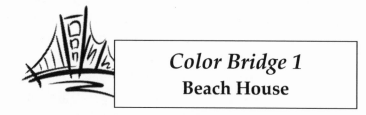

Color Bridge 1
Beach House

If you are anything like me, you may have occasionally wondered if you have multiple design personalities. I had mentioned earlier that my style had always tended toward traditional. Light, airy colors with minimal clutter and accessories were my signature, that is until I would see a photo of a jewel toned room layered with interesting patterns, textures and objects d'art. I could fall particularly hard for anything ethnic country. I loved the exotic aura of all things Moroccan. But then there was mid-century modern with its sculptural shapes and clean lines. Yes, I was a child of the sixties. Perhaps Eames style furniture would nurture me. However, redoing the entire house in the style I loved at any particular moment was an impracticality. And so I would dream. I'd say, "If I had a beach house, my décor would be completely different from where I live throughout the year. It would be …"

And so this is your first *Color Bridge*. You will be scouting out magazine pictures of all sorts of colors and attractive interior design. However, for this *Bridge* stick to styles and perhaps colors quite different from what is currently in your home. To get started, decide what sort of second home you'll have. Remember we're dreaming. Our bank accounts are limitless and our imaginations have no bounds. If you love the sand and the sea as I do, then you might also call this Color Bridge, "Beach House." Or do you have a ski chalet or an upscale, urban loft? Perhaps a secluded cottage deep in the forest is more to your liking. You may even want to leave it open ended and simply call it "Dream Home."

Now tear out pictures you love. Remember that this is just for fun. If your home away from home is a ski chalet, your photos need not be appropriate only to a winter's hide away. One photo may show a bear rug by the fire while the next features bamboo furniture and tropical fans. This is one time when you do *not* want to remain focused. Your mind, in fact, should bounce from style to style and color to color. You may even include pictures that have nothing to do with interior design. Magazines are full of professional photos with breathtaking color harmonies you may wish to analyze.

As someone who has always had a passion for interior design, I have for years continued to add to my now bulging files of magazine clippings. I would see an extraordinary design or a particularly beautiful color harmony that spoke to me. I'd tear it out, file it away and that would be the end of it. It was not until I discovered a marvelous and quite unusual book entitled <u>What Color is Your Slipcover?</u> by Denny Daikeler that I knew I was missing out on a crucial piece of the design puzzle. According to Daikeler, I needed now to analyze this mountain of pictures. Only then would I discover key elements of my authentic design style. "You're gathering your story through pictures that attract you. . . . When your journal is done carefully, it becomes a primary and rich representation of so much that resonates in you."[3]

3.   Denny Daikeler, <u>What Color is Your Slipcover?</u>, 96

Here, in your first *Color Bridge*, once all of the pictures have been collected and pasted into your *Studio*, you'll go back and see what information can be gleaned from the selections. In order to make later analysis a bit easier, leave space under each picture to jot down some notes. What is key for now is that judgment and analysis are reserved for later in the process.

Work on this activity when you have leisure time. Don't feel like it must to be finished in one sitting or at any particular time. And there are no certain number of pictures required especially since this is not the only time you will be collecting pictures. Five, for instance, may be too few to give sufficient insight into your preferences. Fifty pictures may prove confusing.

The most critical aspect here is that you allow your mind to float and wander. You see a picture. You like it. Cut it out. Done. We have been trained to have critical minds and we wish to please. Students are much more apt to see a picture they like and say to themselves, "I wonder if this is what we're supposed to be looking for." "This picture is really neat, but it doesn't have the colors I've always loved." Too much thinking. If you are truly attracted to something, there will be plenty there to analyze. If you are relaxed and playful and savor this time of revelation, the magazine pictures you choose will be rich in a melange of information relevant to your aesthetic spirit.

Open your fresh, new *Studio*. On the first page write the following heading. Under the heading paste your selected pictures into your *Studio* with ample space for analysis under each.

Color Bridge 1
Current Date
"If I had a <u>*beach house*</u>*, my décor would be completely different from where I live through the year. It would be ..."*

Analysis
Color Bridge 1 Beach House

Now that you have selected, cut and pasted a variety of pictures for the first *Color Bridge*, you'll need to go back and carefully examine the photos both individually and as a group. Recall that during picture selection it was important that your mind be relaxed and free floating. Now, in the second half of the *Bridge* your mind becomes analytical in order to gain enlightenment from the wanderings of your visual attractions. Quite simply you will study your work and answer two questions. What do you see? And where do you see it? The "what" in "what" do you see simply refers to any pattern, any outstanding feature in the picture.

It is important that you give equal consideration to both questions. Say that ColorFlow student, Leigh, has pasted thirty five pictures in her *Studio* for this activity. After carefully paging through her selections, she finds that at least twenty of them contain a clear, Mediterranean Sea blue color. What does Leigh see? She sees blue. Off she goes to the local paint store to purchase that gorgeous, coastal blue for her bedroom walls. Much later in the course she finds that it is actually part of her authentic color palette.

Once the room is painted, Leigh loves it. Of course she does. The color is deeply authentic coupled with the fact that change, most any change, will at least temporarily lift the spirit. Then in a couple of months, surprisingly she grows tired of the Mediterranean blue walls. They feel oppressive and already she longs for a change!

You have guessed by now that the missing piece here is that consideration was not given to "where" the sea blue color appeared in the *Color Bridge* selections. Once Leigh examined her magazine photos more carefully, the mystery of the objectionable painted walls unraveled. There wasn't a single photo in which this color appeared on a wall or on any other *large* surface.

The pictures indisputably showed that Leigh had an affinity for neutral walls from creamy whites through beiges to chocolatey browns. She loved the watery blue-green on smaller surfaces such as fabric and furnishings. Leigh had cut pictures of blue pottery with a matte finish. There were blue-green pillows in a lustrous sheen of raw silk. Leigh was willing to explore texture with her favored color, but not the environment where it would be placed. Had Leigh addressed both what she had seen in her *Color Bridge* and where she had seen it, the wealth of information about her core aesthetic essence could have been much greater and a decorating mishap averted.

To help get you started, let's look at the three sample pictures that follow. By answering the questions "What do you see?" and "Where do you see it?" we learn much about the color and design preferences of the person who selected this group of photographs. Recall that as this student cut each picture, she was relaxed and non-analytical. She embraced all possibility. In other words, she didn't look at a photo and say to herself, "I love this, but it would never work in my house." During Color Bridging everything is possible. The point is that the specifics of the design may not work in your space, but the essence or the underlying aura may be attainable.

Note: For full color illustrations listed by chapter number, go to www.gardenroomdesigns.com

Each note should include both what is seen and where in the composition the item appears. This picture could have come from Leigh's Color Bridge. Certainly she is attracted to a particular blue. But should she run out and purchase a couple of cans of blue wall paint just yet?

- *two color "batik look" prints on pillows*
- *vibrant blue solids on pillows and other small accessories such as a teapot and small bowl*
- *creamy whites on both large surfaces like the comforter and smaller accessories such as florals*
- *rustic brown woods on furniture pieces*

- *neutral creams/browns on large surfaces of floors, walls, cabinetry*
- *brilliant saffrons and oranges on fabric and floral accents*
- *organic elements of wood, flowers, motifs in fabrics and chairs*
- *mix of casual and elegant throughout the space*
- *tropical, island atmosphere*

- *lots of cream and bits of brown/gray in a large expanse of background*
- *brilliant red-orange that's almost a focal point accent*
- *metallic gold, a smaller supportive embellishment*
- *primitive nature is a pervading aura punctuated by the finer, fancier silk dress and metallic pot*

The student to whom these pictures belong completes the exercise by writing a *Bridge Summary*. It is a handwritten paragraph that sums up the discoveries with regard to authentic colors and styles for the completed *Bridge*. Content, not spelling or grammar, is important. Further, it's critical to include even the smallest discovery because the theme of emerging patterns will continue.

Here, in a single *Color Bridge* you are searching for patterns, colors and styles that attract you. Much later you will be able to search for patterns and recurring themes among all of your *Bridge Summaries*. It is only then, that the tiniest detail may become consequential. If a seemingly insignificant discovery occurs many times, it becomes significant. Following is an example of a *Bridge Summary* for this set of pictures.

Beach House Bridge Summary

What stands out is a love for neutrals, mainly cream and brown. I knew that when given a choice between cream and stark white, I would choose cream. But I didn't know that the neutral cream looks to be a favorite for me. It appears that I like splashes of bright colors against expanses of neutrals. I see red-orange, orange, and blue. There's a tropical island feel that I've always liked and there's something more subtle here. It's the pairing of opposites. It shows most in the third photo where the woman's silk garb and metallic pot sparkle against the rough, dull stone walls. I'd love to create these pairings in my home. For now, I don't have any idea how to fit that into my décor, but it's something to tuck away. Like the course says, for now I'll just analyze, set aside, but not decide.

Before moving on, an observation regarding the above *Bridge* example may prove as helpful to your journey as it did to mine. Design elements including color, style, pattern and texture all work together in a way that either attracts or repels us. The magazine pictures I chose for this *Color Bridge* were similar to the example above in that I had numerous examples of pale, neutral furnishings accessorized with brilliant pillows, throws and area rugs. One day I would see a cream sofa and chair accessorized with brilliant blues and violets. I believed then that this was an authentic combination for me. Days later I'd notice neutral pieces together with bright orange pillows. Then I would flip-flop my opinion thinking that perhaps the warmer oranges and yellows against cream were genuine hues on my ColorPrint. But wait, fuschia paired with ivory ... that's a color marriage that really speaks to me. What was going on?

In reality, I was not responding to any certain color. My strong attraction was simply in response to the *combination* of any brilliant clear color against ivory. Now I would need to dig deeper to find the particular brilliant hue that for me was most genuine in the nourishing *combo* I had discovered. In other words an innate attraction to a certain melange, in this case brilliant hues against cream is a separate preference from an intrinsic attraction to a particular brilliant hue.

You have now the first clues, the initial pieces of your color puzzle that will lead to your genuine color story. Because I have found that any spiritual journey unfolds more fluidly when the destination is clearly visible, I want you to be able to visualize where you're headed with these newly found discoveries. You know that the goal of ColorFlow is to excavate from deep within those colors that perfectly resonate with your unique spirit. These are the hues that will transport you to a more abundant, increasingly stress-free life. These colors make up your ColorPrint.

Let's look at a specific example of a final ColorPrint so that you will have a good idea of its ultimate physical form. Currently, you have various preliminary clues to your colors drawn from your first *Color Bridge*. Now you'll see how your colors will ultimately be listed in your own ColorPrint. Recall that a ColorPrint, like a fingerprint, is quite unique and deeply personal. For these reasons I have chosen to share my personal ColorPrint.

First, you'll name each of the colors on your ColorPrint using one of the twelve color names from the wheel plus black, white, gray, cream or any of the browns. Recall that the color wheel colors are yellow, yellow-green, green, blue-green, blue, blue-violet, violet, red-violet, red, red-orange, orange and yellow-orange. Refer to page 22 to review the wheel.

In the ColorFlow course I refer to *color families*. There are *primary color families* and *secondary color families*. Each primary color and its neighbor color on either side make a family. Memorization of these is unimportant. For instance, blue is a primary color. On either side of blue is blue-green and blue-violet. So blue, blue-green and blue-violet make up a *primary color family*, the blue family. Orange is a secondary color. On either side of orange is yellow-orange and red-orange. Thus, orange, yellow-orange and red-orange is a *secondary color family*, the orange family. It is a way to effectively communicate about color. For the purposes of ColorFlow you'll be identifying colors more precisely than simply saying, "I like green, orange, purple, and white." You may instead say, "I like yellow-green, red-orange, violet and cream." You are merely becoming much more specific about the hues that are attractive to you.

Even with this level of explicitness, you will need to go one step further. For instance, a color on my Print is yellow-green. There are yellow-greens that tend more toward yellow, those that lean almost to clear green, yellow-greens that are quite grayed or muted, and those that are brilliant. As I moved through the exercises, accepted synchronous help from the Universe and allowed my true colors to float to the surface of my consciousness, I became aware of the precise yellow-green that was mine. You, too, will experience such a phenomenon. When this occurs, the hue will remind you of something because at that point in your journey there will be a mood or aura surfacing that you'll want to express in your space.

The exact nature of the aura is yet a second treasure that comes effortlessly on the wings of your authentic colors. The aura you'll create will perfectly resonate with your inner artistic essence heightening your spirit and elevating your mood. My yellow-green leans heavily toward yellow. It is clear and light. The aura that heals me is minimalist and Asian primitive. I have named my yellow-green, Bamboo. Give each color on your Print an authentic aura name. My ColorPrint looks like this . . .

Color Wheel Name	*Authentic Aura Name*
Violet	*Japanese Iris*
Red-Violet	*Distant Kii*
Green	*Jade*
Yellow-Green	*Bamboo*
Blue	*Export China*
Cream (neutral)	*Rice Paper*
Brown (neutral)	*Teak*

The column at the left shows my five authentic colors identified with their color wheel names. The two additional hues are the "neutrals," cream and brown. Later we will learn that cream and brown are not true neutrals, but what we will call popular neutrals. The corresponding authentic aura names to the right are very personal and should when viewed as a group portray the desired mood. No one else needs to either understand or approve of your color names and the more deeply personal, unusual and specific, the better.

It is an appropriate time to reiterate the fact that a ColorPrint is *not* a color scheme. These are hues that sustain us like vitamins sustain the body. Your authentic colors are simply nutrients for the soul. And each color provides a different sort of emotional sustenance. Carry the vitamin analogy further and consider that spinach is high in beta carotenes which our bodies need. However, we don't eat spinach at every meal. Although orange juice is rich in vitamin C, we don't normally drink it each time we eat. It is the same with our nutritive colors. You'll use them in varied quantities and combinations throughout your home according to your individual needs in that space. Although a topic for further discussion, for now it is only important that you make a clear distinction between a ColorPrint and a color scheme.

And so my ColorPrint is Japanese iris, distant Kii, jade, bamboo, export china, rice paper and teak. Distant Kii is an extensive mountain range in Japan. Initially, I had chosen to call my reddish violet hue "distant mountain" for the hazy violet color that appears at the top of a far off mountain. It would have been a lovely and unusual descriptor, but recall that these terms should exude the mood you're creating. I'm a spiritual person drawn to objects of Asian origin. During my color exploration I read about a breathtakingly beautiful mountain range in Japan. It is a sacred place where it is said that the gods of Shintoism and Buddhism reside. The mountain range is named Kii. The hue is now imbued with special significance.

"Japanese Iris" conjures up for me a violet vastly different from Distant Kii. It is a rich purple standing on its own with no undertones of red. Near my water garden the color is ephemeral. A particularly graceful Siberian iris blooms at pond's edge in June. It is the precise shade of violet that is warming and relaxing to my spirit. On those treasured spring days when the irises are in blossom, I bring them into my living room for their healing color. For the remainder of the year, I am nourished by their color memory in fabrics and accessories.

Also on your final palette may be a snippet of paper, fabric or dab of paint that most nearly represents the hue you have in mind by the colors you've discovered. Although your final ColorPrint contains five to seven precise colors, don't be concerned that everything in your home be perfectly coordinated. If that were even possible, it would yield a cold, antiseptic atmosphere. We'll discuss variation in color palette hues in more depth in later chapters.

Now you've completed your first *Color Bridge* which has hopefully yielded the first valuable clues to the colors that are yours. You've examined in detail my final ColorPrint for the purpose of making clear your journey destination. Just when ColorFlow concepts are looking rather simple, comfortably straightforward, I'd like to introduce you to what I call the *creative paradox*.

In the writing of this book, I have noticed a curious phenomenon. It is that many projects or ideas come to fruition with the greatest artistic success if approached in the exact opposite way than one would believe to be most logical. The paradox idea emerged for me actually within the premise upon which ColorFlow is based. We have all for years been busily searching everywhere for the best colors to put in our homes, everywhere, that is, *outside* of ourselves. However, the best colors, so it turns out, are *within*.

The *creative paradox* that may have been the most freeing for me has to do with the order in which a room is decorated. When most of us approach a room that needs redoing, say a masculine home office, we decide first on the wall color. "My husband likes green. He enjoys golfing and actually looks great dressed in green," you might say. So you choose a wonderful green for the walls. With the room now freshly painted, the decorating can begin.

While shopping for furniture and accessories for the new office you see a stunning leather desk chair. It is amazingly comfortable and would be a real luxury for your husband because he spends an incredible amount of time seated at his desk. The chair is in stock in brown and black, but can be special ordered in hunter green! Of course, you'll wait the extra few weeks for the special order color. And so your shopping and decorating goes. You've found someone to make drapes in a divine fabric that has a fleck of the green paint color and the carpet is going down next week. Finally, everything to the last detail is complete and the room looks good. It is an attractive space, but something is not quite right.

Think now about which elements of a space are more important to those who dwell within. Does greater importance lie in the furnishings and the accessories or in the color of the walls? Of course the answer is that what makes our lives comforting, what cultivates us is that which is inside the room, not in the walls that surround it.

Let's assume that the green of the leather chair is a color that is attractive to your husband and will elevate his spirits daily. Further, the high quality, luxurious leather will provide years of comfort. Isn't the chair, then, one of the most important purchases of the room? If so, it should be among the first considerations in your design. After the chair should come anything and everything that will make the workday flow more smoothly. These include items such as a desk, proper drapes to allow sunlight to brighten, but not too much as to produce a glare, file cabinets within easy reach and personal mementos to sweeten the mood of the day. And it is with these items within the room that you need to be most mindful of the nourishing green.

Once these concerns are addressed, step back and consider a background color. In other words, what wall color will best enhance each of the key design elements chosen for the purpose of creature comfort and ease of livability. Now there will be little stress over matching. Having settled on key elements, there are literally thousands of paint colors to coordinate. Now it becomes clear that if the walls were to be any shade of green it would be too much of a good thing. Additionally, the focal points of green would lose importance fading into the background.

Even with green no longer a possibility, the range of selection for wall colors remains quite broad. A neutral gray, for instance, with green undertones to relate may be an appealing choice. It serves as a lovely back drop to *showcase*, rather than *match*, your creation. And the green leather chair? Now instead of disappearing into the background, it is enhanced by rich, yet gentle contrast.

And so our first ColorFlow *creative paradox* is to be mindful first of the elements within the room whether they be purely functional, purely aesthetic or hopefully a balance of both. Only when these pieces are in place, is it time to consider a background hue, a color for the walls that will best showcase your creation. Gretchen Schauffler, creator of the Devine Paint Color line and author of <u>Devine Color</u> says, " Wall color has a job and the main one is to make all of the rest of the colors look good."[4] Although some may point out that it's much easier to paint first when the room is empty, the true goal of decoration and design must be considered. Is your objective ease of painting? Or is it to create a space that will heighten your mood and help cultivate your dreams each day for many years to come?

4. Gretchen Schauffler, *Devine Color When Color Sings*, 90

Color Speak

Bridge Summary: A handwritten paragraph that sums up discoveries, clues, patterns or any additional significant bits of information with regard to your ColorPrint and genuine design style. A *bridge summary* is written directly into your Studio after most Color Bridge exercises. Content, not spelling or grammar, is most important in a *bridge summary*.

Color Bridges: Design activities completed with your most creative, playful, non-judgmental mind. The purpose of a *Color Bridge* is to discover the unique ColorPrint that will reawaken your spirit enabling you to celebrate life's bounty.

Color Family: A primary color on the 12 color wheel and its neighbor on either side make a primary *color family*. A secondary color and its neighbor on either side make a secondary *color family*. An example of a primary *color family* is red, red-orange and red-violet. An example of a secondary *color family* is green, yellow-green and blue-green.

Creative Paradox: A design phenomenon wherein projects or ideas come to fruition with the greatest artistic success if approached in the exact opposite way than one would normally believe to be most logical.

Existing Design Repertoire: Any design knowledge, experience or expertise that is currently part of your consciousness is your *existing design repertoire*. It is the intent of the ColorFlow course to help expand your aesthetic sensibilities, free your flow of natural creativity and ensure intimacy with your innate sense of personal taste and unique style thereby expanding your *existing design repertoire* many fold.

Studio: The artist's sketchbook for making lists, writing thoughts, creating color schemes and collecting magazine pictures. The sketchbook from where the final ColorPrint will emerge.

Color Study
The Qualities of Temperature and Value

"Color makes me happy. I've got to have it. I simply couldn't work as hard as I do without home. This place restores me."
Bonnie Relsas, Chef and Owner Soho Café Savannah

Temperature seems to be the most popularly discussed quality of color. We know that the warm colors are yellow, orange, and red along with each of the tertiary colors associated with them. The cool colors are green, blue, and violet and each of the tertiary colors associated with them. The generally accepted dividing line delineating the cool half of the wheel from the warm is a line running from yellow-green to red-violet. Although technically correct, the difficulty is that this is far from the full story. A small amount of additional knowledge regarding color temperature will profoundly expand your expertise in the use of color in interior design. It is well worth exploring.

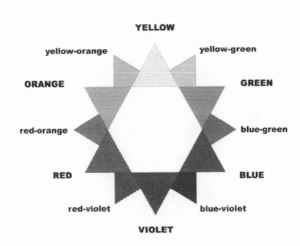

Imagine bisecting the color wheel in half with a line that runs from yellow-green and continues through red-violet. The cooler colors fall to the bottom right of this imaginary line while the warmer ones fall to the top left.

First consider that temperature is not always absolute. For instance, until now, you may have believed blue and violet to be equally cool as they both lie on the cool side of the wheel. Consequently, if a proposed color scheme were in need of a cool accent, blue and violet could be interchangeable choices. However, recall that blue is a primary color not made from a mixture of any other hues. As such, it is wholly cool. Violet, on the other hand, is a secondary color, and is a mixture of red and blue. Because violet is created by combining one warm and one cool hue, it is actually less "cool" or a bit "warmer" than blue. Knowing this could potentially affect your final choice and finesse your color scheme from just striking to sumptuous. Further, this kind of refined color knowledge may result in the difference between a *simply beautiful space* and the *deeply genuine place* that has become your goal.

Second, color temperature is relative to the surrounding colors. Consider yellow-green which is on the cusp, or at the point of transition between the warmer and cooler colors. Place yellow-green next to warm orange and it will appear cool. This is because yellow-green actually contains a touch of blue. You know this because the green is made up of yellow and blue. Now place the yellow-green next to pure, primary blue and the yellow-green will appear warmer. Of course, this is because the yellow-green has the warm qualities of yellow, but the primary blue is wholly cool. Again, enhanced knowledge of these relationships serves to further refine your color choices.

There are two secondary colors that are sometimes referred to as "bridging" colors because they are each a perfectly balanced combination of one warm and one cool hue. Green is a mixture of cool blue and warm yellow. Violet is a mixture of cool blue and warm red.[5] The eye naturally looks for balance of warm and cool so these colors are many times good choices as they are naturally balanced on their own. On occasion, if you are searching for an additional color to add to a scheme, consider one of the bridge colors as it will not upset the temperature you've already created.

Value

A second quality of color that is important to our study is value. If you stop to consider the fact that color has always been a part of your existence, it will seem obvious that you already know the meaning of color temperature and value. I am merely attaching names to the familiar concepts. Then once we have a good means to communicate our ideas, we can discuss how best to use these qualities of color in our homes.

5. Christine E. Barnes, *Sunset Color for Your Home*, 9

Value refers to the lightness or darkness of a hue. Each color has a wide span of values ranging from light-value through medium-value to dark-value. The violet on the color wheel may be expressed as lavender which is a light-value violet. A darker violet, say a rich amethyst is a medium-value. Eggplant would be considered a very dark value, but still in the violet range. Note also that each pure color on the wheel has a natural value. Yellow, for instance, is a color with an inherently lighter value than violet.

Value is the artist's term for that which we normally call a "shade." If, for instance you wanted to paint your shutters green, you might choose the particular green from a small paint swatch. What many don't realize is that when a large surface is painted with the exact hue from the small sample, the color will appear brighter and many times darker on the larger surface. Once the shutters are painted, you say, "I had hoped for a lighter *shade* of green." The concept of *shade* that we use in everyday speech is what *value* is to an artist and to the study of ColorFlow. It is simply the lightness or darkness of a particular color.

A color that occurs on your final ColorPrint can and in fact, will, feed your spirit in varying values, or in shifting degrees of lightness or darkness. Recall that one of the colors on my print is red-violet. It is the one which I have chosen to name Distant Kii after the Japanese mountain range. Although I have a favorite "shade" of the plum color, the hue appears in my living room expressed in a rather light value, one that has lots of white mixed with it, a very dark value, almost an eggplant along with several values in-between.

The color itself, though, is what is our nourishment, sustenance for the spirit. Whether it is diluted with the neutral white or darkened with the neutral black is more a function of design. When I use a fabric with a very light red-violet hue, the red-violet is still there. It is akin to ingesting a vitamin encased in some sundry, inert ingredients and fillers. The added ingredients have purpose apart from the main nutritive objective. However, the main reason for taking the supplement is the vitamin itself. Pale red-violet pillows were chosen for my room for the support that the violet hue affords me. That the hue is immersed in neutral white, is purely a function of design. And what is that design function? Why would we want to add white making values lighter or black making values darker? The reasons are simple and twofold.

The first is to add variety and the second is to enhance what is in the foreground. Imagine that on your ColorPrint is red-orange. Your favorite red-orange is a mid-value hue that you've chosen to name "Sunset Over the Casbah" and the aura of your space is turning out to be exotic, Mediterranean, Moroccan with earthy spice colors. First, if you used the same value of red-orange each time it appeared, your surroundings would become boring and lackluster. There would be little visual interest, nothing to attract the eye from one place to another. Second, because of so much sameness in hue, there would be a blending of one object into another. Think of a camouflage suit. It is green and brown to blend with the green and brown of the surroundings. Your objects would blend into the sameness of their surroundings.

When I teach I don't like to use notecards, but wish to remember everything. This makes it necessary to have a few pneumonic devices, those little memory tricks we all became familiar with in elementary school. Some are clever enough to share and one of these is the memory tease I use with regard to value. The word "value" begins with a "v" and ends with an "e." Those are the beginning letters of the two, simple, design reasons for varying the value of colors within your space. The first is to add *variety* and the second is to *enhance* what is in the foreground. V is for variety and E for enhance.

"Every time you don't follow your inner guidance, you feel a loss of energy, a loss of power, a sense of spiritual deadness."
Shakti Gawain

Chapter 3

RUSHING TIDEWATERS
Creating Space for Authenticity to Swell

Even during these initial stages of your journey, it is not uncommon to begin noticing the first audible sounds of your authentic design voice. By letting go of deeply ingrained notions about color, beginning to cleanse and completing the first exploration of Color Bridging, you have whittled a narrow yet significant channel connecting your ambiguous conscious mind to your genuine subconscious. It is through this ever widening passageway that enlightenment of your aesthetic spirit surfaces. The title of this chapter, *Rushing Tidewaters, Creating Space for Authenticity to Swell* comes from a vivid childhood memory. We'll use it as an analogy to support our current topic.

As little girls, a favorite beach project for my sister and me was to carve out a huge depression in the sand as deep and wide as possible. Clamshells and upturned sand buckets were our excavating tools. When finished, we had what resembled a dry pond bed. Next, we would dig a channel leading from the huge hole to the water's edge. Then it was time to sit back and watch the tide come in.

Sticky ice cream bars in hand, we giggled as each succession of incoming waves crashed shoreward inching the tidewater further up the channel. Finally, the much awaited moment arrived when the tide pushed the water just far enough to flood our cavernous impression. No longer did we have a sun parched crater, but a cool, swirling pool of ocean salt water. My sister and I had seized for our own, a piece of the mighty ocean. The sea, however, would not have flooded our pool without the creation of a void ready for filling. Had we looked beyond our own sandy encampment in either direction, there would have been no other swirling pool that day, for no one else had made space to draw in the ocean.

It is the same with authenticity in color and in design. Imagine the vast ocean as infinite possibility. The tidewater is authenticity, the colors and designs unique to each of our aesthetic spirits. Like the tidewater rising up the channel, your genuine artistic soul becomes increasingly palpable when space is cleared allowing it to swell up from within. When this passageway leading to your waiting abyss is created, innate artistic expression floods into your consciousness.

This void or space so necessary to your journey is in reality an opening of the mind. In Chapter 1 you began to let go of your beliefs and biases about color. Many of these you had tenaciously clung to simply because there was no more favorable replacement. Now you'll begin to conceptualize how a new idea replaces an old. Think of it as the sparkling ocean water washing over your dusty, conscious mind. Most of us strongly resist change, but visualizing such a positive graphic image as bubbly water cleansing your mind can help. A valuable example of how this occurs is the manner in which I discovered the vivid blue on my ColorPrint.

Since childhood, delicate, sky blue has been "my color." As children my mother liked to dress my older sister and me the same, but in different colors. My sister, Mary, had very dark hair and eyes and loved red. I had lighter hair and blue eyes, so I became the blue sister. Since no one would paint a young girl's room deep blue, nor order a birthday cake with dark blue icing, pale blue became my shade. I didn't recognize this shade as a preference myself. Instead, it was sort of assigned to me. Little ones thrive on compliments and my blue dresses with eyes to match garnered many. So at this very impressionable time, I came to believe that sky blue was genuinely "me."

Naturally, when I began to decorate my own home I used a generous amount of sky blue. However, each time I included the color on my palette, it proved a disappointment. On its own, I'm strongly attracted to the color. The first pale blue hydrangea that appears in my summer garden still takes my breath away. Inside things were quite different. Once I painted my bedroom the most gorgeous celestial blue, only to grow disenchanted with the color in a month. I tried the hue on smaller surfaces like pillows, but still there was something askew. Pale blue is simply not the potion that heals my spirit. Time and again I decided, "Okay, no more blue. It just doesn't work for me." But I was unwilling to let go. My frustration was like a bad love affair. I couldn't live with it and I couldn't live without it.

After working through the ColorFlow journey, rekindling the artistic embers that glow within, contentment and healing has replaced frustration in the matter of my blues. During my most active period of self-discovery, I came to embrace the idea that the world is a much gentler place if you give up the battle of "either or." Either I can use the sky blue that I so love or not. Either or is both harsh and frustrating. Furthermore, it tremendously limits our connections with the truth.

I ultimately realized that I could use blue without disappointment. It would simply need to be a different shade than the sky which I had been unwilling to give up. The first clue that there was a particular yet unconsidered blue that would perfectly resonate with my psyche came from something I noticed about patterns, not colors. I discovered it among the magazine pictures I had cut in the first Color Bridge.

After paging through my photos several times, I detected a recurring style of pattern on fabrics and pieces of pottery and porcelains. The motifs were quite ethnic in feel. On fabric, it resembled batik or hand done block printing. After some research I found that some of the fabrics were batik while others were something called "ikat," a fabric in which the yarns have been tie-dyed before weaving. The pottery and porcelains were mainly blue and white Asian designs on Chinese export pottery.

This design thread was so strong that I decided to photocopy only these pictures thereby isolating the repetitive theme among my preferences. Then, I created a simple collage with this group on a single page. When complete, the aesthetic message of similar artisanal patterns along with like color combinations moved to the forefront. Almost every element depicted in the photographs featured a vibrant, mid-value blue. Thus, the observation of a certain type of appealing pattern ultimately led to the unearthing of the genuine blue that would appear on my authentic ColorPrint.

For all of these years my authentic blue that I now so love did not appear in my artistic consciousness. I was unable to see it because my mind was otherwise filled. It was occupied with the ongoing dilemma of using either pale blue or no blue at all. I had left no "space" for an additional possibility. Eventually, in the free wheeling world of ColorFlow thought, I became willing to create a clear mental expanse thus inviting the possibility that there may exist something between pale blue or no blue. In the instant that the "space" in my consciousness materialized, the genuine nourishing blue was on its way up the channel and into the waiting pool. Just as the ocean of my childhood had washed over the dry and barren cavity of sand, my consciousness for the first time was awash with my genuine, sparkling spirit.

The particular hue that emerged as my ColorPrint blue, I named "Export China." Recall that ultimately you will give each of your ColorPrint colors a unique moniker that expresses the mood you wish to create. Chinese Export is the color blue that appears on Asian porcelain and pottery exported from China to Europe between the 16th and 20th Centuries. The name supports the Asian essence I desire. Upon even closer analysis of my Studio pages, Export China blue without exception appears in combination with white. Hence it is not the blue alone that resonates with my aesthetic spirit, but the marriage of this blue with white that so enchants me.

Even though the point of my anecdote was the manner in which my "true blue" appeared, the commonality of patterns proved an equally important discovery. The primitive ethnic motifs are "aesthetic tonic" for which my spirit thirsts. For years I had timidly clung to solids after some early decorating disasters with multi-color prints. But solids just didn't have the panache I craved. On the other hand, when I chose prints, I tired of them quickly. On the bolt I would feel confident in my cheerful print purchases, but once at home the print would always appear too busy for my taste. It was here in my journey that I realized I was simply using the wrong patterns. "My patterns" had begun to reveal themselves.

As unearthing of true self deepens and knowledge of the artist's color wheel broadens, you will experience a phenomenon that we'll call *color sophistication*. Being *color sophisticated* means that one can discriminate within and among colors based on value, intensity, quantity and environment. Similar to my discoveries with the mid-value blue, developing a sophistication or finesse in the use of color includes using tasteful restraint with regard to where a certain hue is placed.

Continue to focus on the creation of space in both the mental and physical realms. Colors and styles in your existing design repertoire begin to appear at best "nearly there" and at worst impersonal and non-descript. Further, colors and designs that in the past you would have dismissed may now spark your interest. Your grip on your present taste in décor and preferences in color has relaxed almost to the point of release. The challenging Color Bridges, Imprints with the most divergent thought to date and continued cleansing that follow act as a final clean sweep in the manifestation of a pristine canvas poised to attract more of your nourishing ColorPrint.

Imprint
Rushing Tidewaters

With relaxed eyelids, close your eyes and sit comfortably in an upright position. Imagine yourself alone on a pristine beach. You are unaware and in fact uninterested with the details surrounding how you came to be here on this shore, utterly alone, with no belongings, on this particular sparkling day. You are content and unconcerned with how the afternoon will unfold.

It is natural for you to be near the sea. You face the ocean watching the waves rhythmically rise, curl, then break, each getting smaller until finally at water's edge there is no more than a gentle ripple before retreat. Together let's imagine that in each succession there are ten waves. The first ascends tower-like out of the briny depths crashing with millions of bubbles in foamy fanfare. As it does we will draw in a deep breath. As each wave diminishes in size, our breath too, will diminish. And so we'll breathe in partnership with the sea. As I count from ten to one, imagine each breath mirroring the strength of its sister wave.

Ten   *Breathe most deeply and hold your breath as the wave near the horizon line rises skyward and hurls itself against the rushing water below.*

Nine   *Take quite a deep breath, a bit more shallow than the last.*

Eight   *Deep breath. This wave is lower and crashes less forcefully.*

Seven   *Still breathing from your abdomen, relax precisely as much as the sea relaxes into its entry to the shore.*

Six   *Your breath now is closer to normal. Watch the wave curl effortlessly and gently to meet the water.*

Five   *Breathe in perfect rhythm with the gentle sea.*

Four   Three   Two

*One   The water swirls gently and playfully at shore's edge. You are
                  serene and have at your disposal infinite creative possibility
                  for colors and styles. The rhythm of the tides brings you the
                  precise color notes that vibrate in perfect harmony with your
                  inner essence.*

*Your color harmonies are a treasure from the sea, a gift from the Universe
should you choose to accept them. Reach unprepared lacking profound belief
in the power of the Universe with merely outstretched arms, and your soul
colors will fade and disappear in the sea breeze. The Universe makes a
condition of its generosity that you remain patient yet prepared with a vessel
or chalice in which to collect your treasure. Once contained, your soul colors
swarm helter-skelter like fireflies caught in a jar. They glimmer with
increasing brilliance allowing you to recognize each hue.*

*When we look to powers beyond ourselves for help in discovering our true
artistic spirits, there is no person to whom the Universe is more or less giving.
It is so bountiful in all things that our vessels are spontaneously filled. A
tiny chalice attracts small, yet precious rewards; a large goblet signals the
Universe that we consider ourselves deserving of greater riches and the goblet
fills to capacity.*

*Remain patient and prepared with a substantial, empty vessel. At the perfect
time, the Universe will reveal your soul colors, your ColorPrint for a
soothing, healing home.*

*Mentally count with me slowly from one to ten. One Two Three Four Five
Six Seven Eight Nine Ten. Return from the sea mentally and emotionally
refreshed and eager to clear both mental and physical space in your life.*

This chapter's Color Bridge will require you to create space for the existence
of fresh thought processes and significantly expand your existing design
repertoire. Briefly introduced in the last chapter, your existing design
repertoire adds to the already powerful apprehension many of us have for
considering anything that varies greatly from the status quo. It acts like a
shut-off valve in our minds.

I can already hear a few of you saying. "Well, that's not me. I love change in
my home. I'm always repainting, reupholstering or buying new furniture." If

this applies to you, try to recall several of the enhancements you've made. Consider whether they have profoundly altered the character of your space transforming it into one that more deeply feeds your soul and supports your dreams. Or were many of the changes simply *substitutions*, a new chair similar to but a step up from the old. Perhaps your changes have represented a bit of both. Even so, I would venture to guess that most of us could benefit from the broadening of our design horizons.

Clear evidence of your attachment to your existing design repertoire many times surfaces when purchasing upholstered furniture. The store has piles of fabric swatches on large metal rings. It's a daunting task. Here, your automatic shut-off valve works like a charm. You leaf through swatch after swatch mindlessly saying "no, no, no." Every once in awhile, something catches your eye and you bookmark it. The marked page is most often a pattern or similar facsimile of something you already had in mind upon entering the store. Perhaps you had imagined what might work in that particular room. Or maybe you had clipped a few magazine pictures or had seen something attractive at the home of a friend.

Whatever the case, selections made in this manner are based on a rather narrow set of past experiences. Any design knowledge, experience, or expertise that you currently possess is part of your existing design repertoire. So, in fact, the pages are marked more because they are *recognized*, not because you have carefully judged them best for both the surroundings and your deeply personal aesthetic. Your existing design repertoire may be rich, but thus far has not been adequate to provide you with the environment for which you thirst.

Meaningful and life changing design can only occur when we are willing to widen the pool of options to include those elements of decor we once would not have considered. In the example above, you were out in the marketplace where selection abounds. This is one example of the generosity of the Universe. Take advantage of it and don't discount anything. In short, each of us needs to be willing to consider any one of the upholstery, paint, or *any* design option that we skip over while saying "no, no, no."

The way to begin sorting out any yet unexplored design territory as an even remote possibility for your home is to use what I call your *"artist's eyes."* It is akin to what I asked you to do during the Color Bridge activities. You were to relax and let your mind drift embracing all possibility without judgement. A person using his or her *artist's eyes* observes the environment without judgement or bias, using the visual sense to its fullest in a joyful, child-like manner. When the eyes are freed to become *artist's eyes* the viewed object is actually seen for the first time. Hence, limitations are removed and possibility becomes boundless.

Just before setting out on this chapter's Color Bridge, it will be helpful to discuss a second paradox. Recall that in previous discussion we examined the wisdom of first selecting colors for objects of both function and aesthetic pleasure within the room before choosing a wall color. This is the reverse of the order in which room colors are commonly chosen. In this paradox, we'll once again approach something in what appears to be 180 degrees from logical reason. This time our paradox has to do with your feelings of distaste for particular elements.

If you hear yourself repeatedly saying you "hate" a particular color, pattern or style, record that feeling in detail in your Studio because nine times in ten it's a clue to something quite authentic within. At the very least, further investigation is warranted. I have a great "hate" story that both illustrates the paradox and has taught me an enduring lesson.

Over the years, I have countless times said the words, "I hate anything primitive." In younger, more narrow minded days, I can even admit to saying "How can people live with that decrepit stuff?" Now, near the door to my garden hangs a primitive hay rake that I consider a prized possession. In the great room is a primitive Chinese rice measure for corralling all of my magazines. I could list several additional primitive items that perfectly resonate with my deepest design spirit. The artisanal nature of these objects and their connection to peoples who lived in rhythm with the seasons of the earth exude an aura of peace and belongingness that fills me with a sense of truly being at home in the Universe.

I first began adding primitive items to my home after noticing them as a recurring theme in my decorating files. Key here is that these photographs would have never made it to my files had I not consciously cleared my mind thereby opening all channels of possibility. Had I relied only on my existing design repertoire, I may have unconsciously sailed right past the primitive elements in the photos. As I was gathering the pictures, there was no awareness of the specifics in the room that had attracted me. I simply was drawn to the overall feel of the space. It became apparent only after analyzing my work, that primitive objects were, indeed, a common theme.

Because of my insatiable curiosity with regard to the how's and why's we enhance our spaces the way we do, I needed to investigate further. How could I have such strong negative feelings toward a certain design element only to discover that, in fact, it is one that I need in my personal space? I began to look at primitive elements in home décor everywhere I could possibly find. I observed these rooms not casually, but with my *artist's eyes*, as if I were looking with childlike wonder and scientific curiosity. And one day the answer just came to me.

It wasn't "primitive" that I didn't like. It was the "package" it came in. Most times primitive objects such as hay rakes and other gardening tools, rusty cookware, hand carved wooden bowls and antique tools are displayed in homes of people who are attracted to country décor and love to collect. They spend long summer afternoons scouring flea markets to find an even more interesting tin strainer than the three already hanging on the wall at home.

You've seen the photos in *Country Home* magazine. There's a dramatic twelve foot stone wall literally filled with a life's collection of primitive artifacts. Don't misunderstand, this type of décor is nourishing for the person who craves it. For me, the sheer quantity of items is suffocating. I have a strong affinity for minimalism and space. *Hence my aversion is not for all things primitive, it is for the busy environment in which we most often see them.*

Place a hay rake on the stone wall surrounded by an entire collection of antiques and you can keep it. Hang the same the rake in a contemporary setting *alone* against a shimmering bronze wall with soft light emanating from the beams above and for me, it's pure sculpture. So it's not quite so simple as saying, "I like this but I don't like that." We need to create space within ourselves for the possibility of most anything being attractive if only we could see it anew, with our *artist's eyes* engaged.

Become mindful then, that the things we have repeatedly said we "hate" are elements that may actually end up on our "love" list. You've noticed this particular element and have chosen to talk about it because intuitively you sense something personally magnetic about it. Consider other distasteful styles and colors that you've never mentioned. Could it be that they're not worthy of comment because there's nothing in your "gut" that even renders them noticeable?

Color Bridge 2
Luminesce

As you begin this Color Bridge, recall the importance of both the functional and aesthetically pleasurable focal points within the room becoming a priority before choosing the wall color for the space. Instead of painting your living room a luscious coffee color and then searching for a sofa that looks great against the coffee background, it is far more logical to do the reverse. Shop for a sofa considering color, fabric, ease of cleaning, size, shape, style, price and most of all comfort. Now, what color sets off the sofa? The background paint or paper follows. This method is both easier and leads to a better result.

We tend to think of backgrounds as mostly wall colors. They are perhaps one of the most important backgrounds you will consider, but keep in mind that walls are not the only backgrounds. Any element that lives behind another is a background. Recently I purchased a pair of vintage, Henredon slipper chairs and had them reupholstered in a gorgeous, cream mohair. The wall behind them was builders' white since we had just moved into our new home.

The white chairs against the white background made them simply disappear. I painted the wall behind them the "teak" brown from my ColorPrint. The teak has become the background to the chairs. Now I'm shopping for a pair of pillows for the cream chairs. Here my background is the chairs because the pillows will be against the cream of the chairs, not the brown of the walls.

In this Color Bridge you will be looking at color marriages, how one hue looks when layered on another. You will move from the known to the unknown. Go to your home decorating magazines to select one picture of something that has a color to which you are attracted. The item you choose should be large enough that you can get a good feel for its relationship to the background colors with which you will pair it. Also, try finding a photo that depicts basically one item without many other distracting elements. If the picture is rather busy, the myriad hues may confuse your judgment about color relationships. In other words, try to choose something simple.

Good examples of picture selection for this Color Bridge are an upholstered chair, a vase of yellow roses, a sky blue, velveteen headboard, a bowl of granny smith apples, a piece of sea coral or a painted wooden box. It is important that you have an affinity for both the color and for the object itself. It should be something that you would consider a treasure for your home. However, treasures need not be objects of high monetary value. Consider the vibrancy of color and life that a few lemons placed in a wooden bowl can bring to time spent in the kitchen.

Paired with "builders' white" the bowl of lemons would be pleasant, but perhaps not exceptional. Layered in front of a well chosen background, the same bowl of lemons has the potential to become a stunning still life, as breathtaking as a valued piece of art. And the difference is only in the background. The color and finish of the backdrop has the power to elevate a piece to the status of art. In Color Flow we will call the transformation of an object from satisfying to stunning by doing no more than changing its backdrop, "*luminescing*." Hence, the name of our Color Bridge is *Luminesce*.

What you select then, is the known. You know that you are attracted to the color of your chosen object. Additionally, it is aesthetically pleasing to you in its style, form and texture. After tearing out the page, carefully cut out just the item you have chosen, cutting away all of the magazine background material. This can be a bit tedious.

Now it's time to find several backgrounds for your object. Remember to let your mind drift unfocused. Try to have no preconceived notions about what you believe will look best with your selection. Embrace all possibility. Think of finding the ideal background to enhance or set off your object as brainstorming.

There are a number of sources for solid background colors to pair with your magazine picture. If you are a seamstress or know one, you're in luck. People who sew are notorious for having fabric stashes. Ask if you can go through their piles looking for solid fabrics. The backgrounds I have collected are all 8 ½" by 11" to fit easily in my files, so usually a friend can spare this much cloth. Remember to relinquish judgement and take *any* solid colors you are offered. Cut a piece to size and glue or staple it to a piece of oat tag or half of a used manila folder that has been trimmed to 8 ½" by 11".

Another good source is craft store paper that is sold for scrapbooking. These come in fabulous hues. Each sheet sells for about twenty nine to ninety-nine cents. I watch for sales and stock up. When the sale is good, I purchase every solid color I don't have to be certain that I have a wide selection on hand. Once you begin collecting backgrounds, synchronicity will kick in and you'll begin finding them everywhere.

When you've gathered as many possible background colors as you can, it is time to begin the trial process. Mix up the backgrounds so that they are in random order. In other words, I'm trying to avoid having you begin with the one you're sure will be optimal, only to page quickly through the remaining possibilities giving them little consideration. This would be a prime example of relying heavily on your existing design repertoire. Once they are mixed, turn them face down and spread them out. Choose one background. Place it behind your selected item.

There can be no immediate decision regarding your attraction to the color marriage. If you have an instant reaction, it could be less than genuine. That's because initially you are reacting to the change itself *not* whether it is aesthetically pleasing to you. I tell this to people when they've just painted a room and are worried that they've made a huge mistake. In the first couple of days, our reactions are merely to the change itself. Later, as the novelty dissipates, our minds clear and we are better able to genuinely respond to the actual color.

If we were all able to make accurate, split second color and decorating decisions, wouldn't our homes be perfect? Wouldn't we be working as top designers in the field? In this Color Bridge and all of those to follow, it is important that you slow down and carefully consider each possibility.

Study the example that follows. The item selected is a simple lime given a botanical look by including the sliced view, leaf and blossom. The choice may seem unusual as a piece of fruit certainly doesn't seem like an object of décor! This ColorFlow student loves lime green and it actually works quite well. Remember we are considering color marriages. The lime can therefore represent a green chair, yellow-green drapes or whatever. Although possibilities are limitless, I've limited our discussion to three backgrounds against which the fruit design might be placed.

Just before placing backgrounds behind your trimmed picture, consider the color qualities of the picture you've clipped. The lime is green. Recall that green is a secondary hue made up of yellow and blue. Additionally, green is a "bridge" color meaning that it is roughly a balanced combination of warm and cool. The picture represents several values of green ranging from light through medium to dark. All of these qualities may affect your final background choice.

Below, a lilac background has been chosen. Whether or not it "speaks" to you should be a matter left to your viscera, that inner voice that says you either like or dislike something. Beyond that, it may be helpful to note that lilac or violet is also a bridge color. It is neither warm nor cool but balanced with regard to temperature.

Note also that any background you choose here is only a starting point. You may say, "I love the lilac, but in my room, I'll pair green with a lilac that's a bit deeper." This is your Studio, your workroom where freewheeling aesthetic exploration occurs.

A soft red combined with green is a hue many would not consider when purchasing paint. The beauty of working in your Studio first is that anything is possible. What does your authentic design voice tell you? This is actually an artistically logical marriage. Red adds warmth and contrast to the more balanced green. And if this combo is attractive to you, it doesn't mean that you must have red walls and green furniture. What about the palest green walls, a cream leather sofa, a soft red accent chair and brilliant green print pillows. Beautiful!

Perhaps you tend toward more neutral backdrops like this coffee brown. The brown, like the red, adds warmth because in reality brown is a dark value yellow to yellow-orange. Browns are many times a forgotten hue in our spaces. Look for them in hardwood furniture, floors and trim. They should be considered an integral part of the room's color composition.

Once you've placed your magazine picture against several backgrounds, select a few color marriages or partners that are pleasing. Paste the original picture along with small samples of each background color that you chose. Allow room for notes beneath each color background.

ANALYSIS
Color Bridge 2 Luminesce

With your magazine picture and most favored backgrounds affixed into your Studio, it's time to analyze what general qualities of color marriage make your spirit soar. Using the preceding illustrations and accompanying notes as your guide, comment on each of your favored combos. It is important to note that you are not choosing specific hues for your home just yet. Rather you are discovering families of color and more importantly general qualities of color pairings that are attractive to you.

Here the concepts of temperature and value begin to take on a more complex significance. Now, instead of considering these qualities in isolation, you'll need to look at each in relation to the color with which it has been paired. For instance, in our Color Study's discussion of temperature, you learned that yellow is warm, red is warm and blue is cool. That's temperature in a tidy package. But now, imagine that you've chosen a cranberry red chenille chair. Place it against a mustard yellow background and you've "warmed" or cozied up your room even further. On the other hand, pair the same red chair with a blue background and you've created a cooler, classic look.

It is a similar case with value. It is easy to look at a color and roughly identify it as a light, medium or dark value. Now, you are using that basic knowledge as a communicative tool to express a genuine and perhaps complex preference. Say that you have cut a picture of a pale, celery green vase. Certainly the vase is light in value. An affinity for a chocolate brown background shows your penchant for the drama of high contrast, light paired with dark. If, however, you preferred something closer to a medium value background, your artistic biases lean in the direction of gentler contrast. *Luminescing*, then, is about exploring these kinds of artistic preferences that you may have yet to discover about yourself. And these are discoveries that will profoundly change the aura of your home's décor.

There are few people willing to use dark backdrops, especially dark walls. Using medium to dark values especially on walls will be discussed in a later chapter. For me, rich coffee brown walls, for instance, are amazingly nurturing. They embrace like a cocoon. And darker walls are not as frightening as you may expect. For now, if you think you may have an interest in stronger value backgrounds, you may repeat the Bridge with a picture of a very light piece of furniture. Place it against backgrounds of varied values. Then analyze where your affinity for color *luminescing* leads.

To complete your analysis, simply jot notes below each color background. Comment on contrasts in temperature and value. Note how you might change one or both of the hues if you were to use them in a room today. Also, consider "gut reactions" that may seem to appear from nowhere. "These two colors together would never fit anywhere in my house, but they just energize me. They make me happy!" Remember this is your Studio. Exploration is encouraged. Finally, a written summary of this Color Bridge is unnecessary. *Luminescing* is more an activity of open ended exploration.

Before moving to another Cleanse, there are a couple of miscellaneous notes concerning this Color Bridge that are important. First, become mindful that now you are looking not only for emerging patterns and trends in your preferences within a *single* Color Bridge, but among *all* the Color Bridges you've experienced. Second, this particular Bridge is one that can be used anytime as a tool to find a specific decorating solution such as the paint color for walls. Use fabric swatches to represent the larger furniture pieces. Then prepare possible backgrounds for your furnishings by painting poster board. Remember to choose the items *within* the room first. When it comes to the background color, open your mind to all possibility and *luminesce*!

CLEANSE

"Order is the shape upon which beauty depends."
Pearl Buck

By now you have realized that one theme of ColorFlow is that life can be increasingly vibrant if we would only allow our miraculously unique nature to bubble to the surface. In many areas of our lives we've been less than fully conscious. It manifests in a lethargic, spiritless state in which we may be apt to use the same wall colors we've always used because they're safe. We may set our holiday table in a similar fashion year after year or avoid new furniture arrangements because our current one although not great, has served us for the last decade. Cleansing can take many forms, but they all help clear our connection to the perfect artistic spirit each of us possesses.

If you become willing to work in partnership with the Universe reducing excess and creating a more minimal environment than perhaps you had ever imagined yourself comfortable with, an aesthetically stunning phenomenon occurs. Luscious, deep, sensual beauty, heretofore obscured by all of the "stuff" we have been brainwashed into thinking we need, is unleashed into our surroundings.

To be surrounded by incredible beauty is as natural as breathing. The breathtaking beauty of nature teaches us that. It is as if we have sullied that which is already perfect by our excesses and consumptive nature.

But this is something that all of us already intuitively know. And that's why we now have people who are professional organizers, why TV is full of shows about how to clear out your stuff, why bookstores have shelves having to do with downsizing and why yard sales abound. I have noticed, though, an uncanny similarity to clearing out one's excess and dieting to shed a few extra pounds. All of it and more seems to creep right back!

In Western society, we have been taught since childhood that bigger is better. We strive to increase our salaries, buy homes with loads of square feet, install flat screen TV's that cover half a wall and have a garage for each car owned by the family. Fast food restaurants have made "super-sized" a household word. Naturally it follows that when most of us tackle the job of de-cluttering, we do just that. We *tackle* it with all the gusto that has been deeply ingrained.

There's clutter on the living room shelving, in the bedroom closets, in the bathroom linen closet, in bathroom drawers, in piles on the desk and on the coffee table. It is in our very nature to concern ourselves with all of it at once. In fact, we are proud if we get much of it organized in short order. But even if we could enlist the help of Aladdin and his Magic Lamp for instant clearing, it is my strong belief that a slower, carefully measured approach is far superior. I believe there's incredible value and untapped stores of energy locked deep within the *process* itself. I like to call this yet untapped energy reserve, the *Energy of the Process*. And this energy is a necessary component of the flow that becomes part of your life during the ColorFlow journey.

Be gentle with yourself working at a pace that is easy and comfortable You are in all likelihood fair to others, so why not be fair to yourself? No one can take on every issue of excess and disorder in one fell swoop. Becoming focused on only a few areas of excess allows you to think clearly, connect with your genuine inner aesthetic and harvest *The Energy of the Process*. Use *The*

Energy of the Process as you set out to concentrate your efforts on a few select areas needing attention.

Just before a recent move, I thought my house was in good order, relatively free of items I didn't need or want. Upon closer inspection, however, there was excess lurking in just about every room. It had become noticeable only now that the prospect of packing everything into boxes for a move to a new and smaller home had become a reality. I was forced to accurately evaluate what I did and didn't need, what did and didn't resonate with my design spirit. So I rolled up my sleeves and chose three items upon which to place all of my focus.

There was the set of silver flatware with an orchid design, a gift from my mother. When I was younger, I loved polishing each piece before a holiday meal. My priorities have changed and I've purchased stainless that looks just great for everyday meals as well as special occasions. Now I value the simplicity it has brought to my life. And there were the miscellaneous books, conference hand-outs and assorted papers in my office. Finally, in the shed was a glut of terra cotta pots accumulated over years. Although I adore their organic nature, my quest for convenience would win out. Plastic pots hold moisture so much longer. I'm able to soak my plants, slip away for a weekend and return to cheerful flowers still standing turgid with water. There were excess and clutter in other areas of my home, but at that moment I would focus on only these. I would put into motion *The Energy of the Process*.

Remember that the dynamic energy is in the process. Each day I extended my morning kitchen routine by just twenty minutes or so. I used this time to polish the orchid embellished silver. There were some mornings that my schedule didn't allow for this, so I simply rose a bit earlier. Bear in mind that whatever you choose, focus and commitment are important. But of equal importance is that the tasks remain gentle and include reflection. They should never become harsh and draining.

My act of polishing became nearly meditational as I reflected on heartfelt memories sparked by the pieces of silver. Christmas dinner with Aunt Sonia who is with me now only in spirit, Easter when Bobby was three … now he's a senior in college …   And when the morning came that the final piece, an ornate ladle, was polished, I felt a sense of sadness. There would be no more sunrise journeys to the past, no meditations on silver orchids. I had taken great pleasure in cleaning and placing the pieces in perfect order in their case. It had become precious time alone with my thoughts.

Now it was time to photograph the set and write a description for an eBay auction. Before taking the pictures I slipped the ladle out of the silver chest and stored it away with my stainless. This piece I would keep to remind me of those precious times with Sonia and Mom and Bobby. The silver was won by a young woman in Michigan who was recently married and setting up housekeeping. I imagined her as fresh and energetic as I was so many years ago. I couldn't have been more pleased for her to have it.

Only one item now was cleared from my home, but it was done in a deliberate and focused manner. It was executed with thoughtfulness and gratitude. And the quiet reflection on cherished memories and how I came to be who I am today allowed me to sink yet deeper into the knowledge of self. And it is only through an intimate connection with self that we can know our truest aesthetic needs.

Once you mindfully cleanse even just one item in your home, the Universal forces of synchronicity engage. I've found that the more focused I become at each task, the stronger the momentum to take on further challenge.

Recall that synchronicity means that we make an effort and the Universe furthers and expands our effort. *The Energy of the Process* gains you more momentum and increases synchronicity because you are cleansing in mindful, measured steps. Should you tackle large areas of your home in an aggressive manner, the Universe gets a very different kind of message. The quality of energy we send out is the quality we get back. And that energy will surround us in our daily living. Decide whether you wish the energy that returns to you to be aggressive and helter-skelter or gentle and focused.

On the days following, I kept myself busy with my new "morning twenty" sifting through the books and paper material in the office. Most of it frankly should have been tossed long ago. However, I was glad to have gone through it carefully as I came upon both a misplaced address that I had been searching for and a recipe for a faux paint finish that I wished to try in the new house. All of the terra-cotta pots have been given to an avid gardener who lives just down the street. She is 93 and doesn't drive. She takes great pleasure in watering her flowering pots each hot, summer's day!

By now you may be saying to yourself, "what does any of this cleansing and clearing have to do with knowing my colors?" Everything! Remain mindful that *everything*, every book, every knick-knack, every tool, all furnishings and objects that surround you are really nothing more than vibrating energy.

Each item, all of this vibrating energy together, affects the quality of energy that flows through your home and ultimately through *you*. Our environment changes our perspective on the outside world and *we* in turn change our lives. And this is precisely why each object's presence, or absence should we choose to remove it, has such a great effect for better or for worse on the manifestation of a more meaningful, increasingly joyous existence.

As we de-clutter our homes we feel lighter, brighter and more alive. With this newfound lightening of spirit, we are increasingly able to discover our genuine preferences for color and style in our homes. In short, reducing our clutter and excess helps us to create an atmosphere conducive to manifesting the dreams toward which we've aspired for so long.

Color Speak

Artist's Eyes: One who uses his or her *artist's eyes* observes the environment without judgement or bias, using the visual sense to its fullest in a joyful, child-like manner. When our eyes are freed to become *artist's eyes* the viewed object is actually seen for the first time. Hence, limitations are removed and possibility becomes boundless.

Energy of the Process: Hidden, untapped stores of energy locked deep within the process of gentle, mindful and reflective cleansing. This energy is a necessary component of the flow that becomes part of your life during the ColorFlow journey.

Luminesce: The color and finish of the backdrop has the power to elevate a pleasant piece to the status of art. In Color Flow we call the transformation of an object from satisfying to stunning by doing no more than changing its backdrop, *luminescing*.

Color Sophistication: The discrimination of colors based not simply on the color wheel hue, but additionally on its intensity, value, quantity and the environment in which it is used.

Color Study
The Quality of Intensity

"I found I could say things with color that I couldn't say in any other way – things I had no words for."
Georgia O"Keefe

Intensity measures the purity or brightness of a color. Although often confused with value, intensity is quite different. It is actually a measure of the proportion of pure color to gray in the mix of the color you see. Imagine a crisp, grass green. That's a high intensity green because it's rather bright and made up of almost all green with little or no gray added to subdue it. Now envision a gray-green, perhaps the color of a moss covered rock. That's a low intensity green because it's dull and muted. You see, then, that intensity does not measure the lightness or darkness of a hue. That's the job of value. Intensity, measures how bright or dull a color appears. Intensity is many times described as being low, medium or high.

Of the three qualities of color; value, intensity and temperature, intensity is believed to most affect the mood of a room. Therefore, understanding and using color intensity to your best design advantage is of major importance. Physical comfort, of course, is the key concern in interior design. Once our physical needs and comforts are addressed, then aesthetics takes over. At this point it becomes about emotional comfort, what we feel. And what we feel as we enter a room is mood.

High intensity colors are vivid, energetic and fresh. They are clear and bright. In design publications high intensity colors are often used in a child's playroom, a French Country kitchen or in a gardener's sunroom. Low intensity colors tend to be calm, soft and meditative. They are dusty and muted. Occasionally, the quality of low intensity is confused with being light in value. Recall that intensity and value are markedly different qualities. A low intensity green could be pale or it could be dark. The fact that it is low intensity means only that it contains a large portion of gray relative to its quantity of color. Low intensity hues might often be seen in a meditative space such as a library or a spa bathroom.

The intensity, or brightness, of a color cannot simply be divided into two categories of bright and dull. For instance, imagine the most vivid orange possible, a pure, saturated orange. This hue lies at the extreme high end of the orange intensity continuum. Now, envision the color of pumpkin pie filling. It, too, is orange, but a very dull version of orange. Pumpkin lies near the extreme low end of the scale.

If one were to move in small, successive increments from one end of the intensity continuum to the other, each orange hue would vary from its neighbor by only a minute degree. There are, then, not only bright and dull, but many degrees of intensity of the color orange and every other color on the wheel. Perhaps, what resonates best with your design tastes are neither exceptionally brilliant hues, nor heavily grayed, muted ones. You may be most attracted to an intensity of color that lies somewhere in the middle.

Additionally, if you think of intensity as a continuum or a sliding scale, the objective for your home is not to "pinpoint" a certain intensity or brightness factor. It is the ColorFlow philosophy not to be that precise with any area of color, be it intensity, value or position on the wheel. That would be taking away your unique, creative breath. Further, you would be creating a sterile environment of perfectly matched colors resulting in a cold, uninviting space. Look to nature with its rich depth of variation in color within a single blossom. Think instead of settling on a healthy chunk of the intensity continuum. For instance, I envision the intensities on my personal ColorPrint to be a thick slice somewhere beginning at the mid-point and moving up in the direction of the higher intensity, brighter hues.

At the beginning of my color journey a few of the puzzle pieces were roughly in place in my home's décor. With regard to intensity, however, I was way off base. Brighter hues had always intimidated me even though somewhere just below consciousness I knew my inner rhythms were ones of passionate vibrancy. I loved seeing brilliant shades in someone else's home, but when I attempted to incorporate intense colors into my own schemes I was never satisfied. In fact, I was usually horrified!

With further introspection, synchronistic help from the Universe and a piecing together of each clue about my aesthetic preferences into a meaningful whole, the clouds of color confusion began to clear. I could see the intensity of colors best suited to my unique aesthetic aura. More importantly I saw how, where and in what quantities to use the perfect intensity of colors in my home.

In the spirit of ColorFlow remember that your authentic color intensities are not a choice you'll make. The intensities that will best nurture you reside within. They will be a discovery, rather than a decision. A certain degree of color intensity has specific vibrational qualities that are innately restorative, calming and healing. In these early stages it suffices to understand the meaning of intensity, the profound importance it has on the mood you'll create in your home and the concept of the intensity continuum.

*"With color one obtains an energy that seems
to stem from witchcraft."*
Henri Matisse

Chapter 4

MIND, BODY AND COLOR
Exploring the Nuances of Color

I've always liked red-orange, but . . .
I am *exhilarated* by every aspect of a blazing fire on a wintry day. The ever changing brilliant colors as the flames swell and diminish warm me, though I watch them from a place too far to be touched by their actual physical heat.

I've always liked green, but . . .
I am *intoxicated* by the sharp yellow-green that is seen on the feathers of an exotic, tropical parrot.

I've always liked blue-violet, but . . .
I am *mesmerized* by a bank of blue bottles that blooms each Spring just beyond the meadow.

Color has the ability to stir emotion within us. Its power is subtle, but steady. Imagine, for instance, that a ColorFlow student who we'll call Desiree has surrounded herself in her unique, ColorPrint hues. One day while at work Desiree finds that at least for now she will not be considered for a promotion for which she had hoped. Certainly Desiree will not joyously return home with the sudden ability to clear her mind of all career concerns. She will, however, feel a gentle lifting of spirit upon entering. You see Desiree has mindfully designed her surroundings to act as a calming, restorative refuge from the world beyond. The colors within the walls that embrace her are so much more than hues that she merely likes. They are unique colors able to stimulate positive and revitalizing emotions.

The effects of color on our overall well-being are greater than we may initially believe because our colors are present every waking hour, minute and second that we spend in our homes. Even if we're not consciously aware of these effects, color continues to influence us at a sub-conscious level throughout the day. We see color in our home just before closing our eyes at night and upon awakening in the morning.

The persistent, steady nature of Desiree's ColorPrint hues in her environment may have contributed to her emotional balance on the morning the promotion list was released. Because her home had become a place to heal, restore and regain emotional equilibrium, Desiree arrived at work that day prepared with poise and clear presence of mind for the challenges of the day.

The Universe makes no distinction between how it echoes orderly, personally in-tune energy and confused, generic energy. It merely sends back the same sorts of energetic signals we emit. Had Desiree's house been one of disorder, furnished in a style that was not deeply congruent with her aesthetic core and drenched in colors of long since faded trends, her unfortunate, albeit temporary, set back may have stung just a bit more.

In this example, one may argue that the stress alleviated for Desiree by having her home and indeed her life in a state of flow was minimal. This viewpoint is valid. However, why the shift to a state of flow, specifically to ColorFlow, is so significant, so life enhancing is that although each single reduction in stress may appear less than earth shattering, the cumulative, mitigating effect makes a strong, tangible difference. Just consider how many stressors each of us has on any given day. And it is this tangible shift that turns our lives from lackluster to stimulating, from prosaic to poetic.

As a student of ColorFlow it's time that you begin to explore nuances of color to unearth not the hues that make you smile, rather those that make you sing. At the end of each chapter there has been a section entitled "Color Study." It differs from ColorFlow's typically subjective and innovative topics relating to color in that it is set aside for the presentation of traditional and widely accepted color theories and principles. The Color Study material is common to any art class or introductory text on interior design. Thus far, included in our Color Study has been the twelve color wheel and the qualities of temperature, value and intensity.

Although incredibly valuable, traditional color theory should be used with some caution. It is a neatly organized body of knowledge. Its information is highly logical, objective and its bounds appear finite. This simply means that it is quite easy to understand and memorize. Additionally, the breadth of information is not excessively large. For instance, there are twelve colors on the wheel. Their arrangement is orderly and readily committed to memory. The hues can be described according to their temperature, value and intensity. It's all very clear-cut. Because of this, the concepts are quickly grasped and many students erroneously believe that the theories once mastered will somehow magically culminate in the execution of an appropriate and aesthetically attractive design.

The magic of nourishing interior design will manifest with a far more pleasing outcome if you think of these color wheel concepts and theories as "tools" just as you would think of rakes, hoes and spades in your garden shed. The mere possession of the implements or even understanding their uses doesn't further in any way the creation of a healthy, well-designed flower bed. It is only through experience with the use of each tool in the garden that you become a skilled horticulturist and your lush beds the envy of all green thumbs in the neighborhood. And it is the same with all that can be learned with regard to the artist's color wheel. This is valuable information that must be analyzed and fully integrated into your existing design repertoire. Finally, it is applied to actual design.

Let's return to my personal color journey to explore an actual chain of events that ushered to my conscious mind a precise hue that is a part of my color fingerprint, my ColorPrint. It is the crisp, yellow-green I call Bamboo. The original green that I thought to be an authentic color was a low intensity hue. It was a soft, sage green, much grayer than the Bamboo I currently know to be mine. I'd lived with the color for years. It was neither extraordinarily appealing nor offensive, but attractively comfortable and so I had clung to it for reasons of safety. As the events of my discovery unfolded, it was as if my focus sharpened as the more authentic hue ascended through my consciousness. Finally, I saw with great visual acuity the precise Bamboo that is my balancing, nurturing green.

It wasn't that I hadn't noticed the brighter, fresher green before. The color had always been interesting. The particular hue had yellow tones and it was rather bright, a higher intensity color. Over the years, I had tried using the color always with the same result. It was just too much. The yellow-green that I thought I was attracted to was overly bright, nearly garish.

What I heard my design voice saying was, "too much color." So I continued to dilute and gray the yellow-green getting a lighter value, lower intensity hue until I settled on the very pale, sage green that I would eventually use on nearly every large surface in my home. And because it was pleasant and way less offensive than the brilliant yellow-green, I felt much better. At least temporarily, it seemed a solution had been found. There remained, however, a slight nagging dissatisfaction with the pale sage. It was a color that always made me smile, but could never make me sing.

I did not change the color just yet because I didn't have anything on which to base a new choice. Rather I decided to continue my color journey, to let my mind drift and float. I tried to expand my existing design repertoire by using my artist's eyes to see all color as perfect possibility, repeating Color Bridges and attempting to apply the concepts of each Color Study to my rooms in an unbiased way. I looked at magazine pictures in which higher intensity, brighter colors were used, separating them into those that were attractive to me and those that weren't.

What was the element that divided my attraction? My patience and curiosity were sending a strong message to the Universe. I wished to know the perfect green innately coded into my unique make up. Synchronicity was about to bring the answer.

As is many times the case, after a prolonged wait, the answer comes in a blink of an eye. One evening while paging through *House and Garden* magazine, I saw a photo spread of a living room that was decorated heavily in natural woods and neutral creams with splashes of brilliant color. I loved it. My design voice was absolutely right when it said, "too much color." It was only my interpretation that was flawed.

Instead of using diluted, low intensity color in large quantities on large surfaces, my authentic preferences are for higher intensity, brighter colors in smaller doses. I have an affinity for splashes of more brilliant colors coupled with a generous balancing proportion of neutrals. My design voice thirsted after a decreased quantity of vivid color in comparison to the colors around it rather than a decrease in the saturation of the color itself.

What had come into play here was my lack of color sophistication. On those occasions when I had both admired and considered the Bamboo green, I would innocently use the hue in rather large doses. It's a mistake common to inexperienced designers. A short time later I would absolutely detest the space and wonder why. It never occurred to me that the color was right, but the formula was out of balance with my spiritual essence. A friend would visit and wonder why I wanted to change such a beautiful space. It may have been gorgeous to others, but not to me. My dislike for the aura created was easily blamed on the color itself when in reality the quantity of color and balance in relation to both neutrals and contrasting hues was the culprit.

I am supposing that as a result of our "more is better society" we have adopted the notion that if there is a color we adore like my yellow-green, my Bamboo, we must cover half the room with it. With regard to color, that is definitely not the case. Color can be like concentrated medicine and does not have to appear in huge doses to have a significant effect on our lives. Think of it in the same way as you think of vitamins or medicine. Too much may actually have negative effects.

Ultimately, I chose a creamy white for the sofa and chairs and a neutral sisal rug. Some walls are brown while others are beige and there's lots of deep, rich wood in the room. My splashes of brilliant color are mostly in the violets and blues. There is, in reality, very little of my Bamboo color. I have used it as one would use jewelry to enhance an already stunning ensemble. Does this mean then, that I like the yellow-green hue less than the more predominately used colors in the space? Absolutely not! In the case of color, quantity is not an indicator of importance.

Various other of my unique and authentic design preferences had for various reasons been long ago become buried deep within. They remained, but now appeared confused and clouded. A number of predilections for style and color were ambiguous with regard to their actual expression in my home's décor. It's a feeling common to many of us. We believe to know our preferences, but have difficulty effectively translating them to actual decoration in our home.

Imagine for a moment that you are convinced, as I was, that a certain color is in perfect harmony with your aesthetic spirit. You continue to include it, however, with unsatisfying results. Certainly, then, there is something that is striking a discordant chord. You may be tempted to abandon the color altogether in favor of a completely different one perhaps from the opposite side of the color wheel. At the risk of using a cliché, don't throw out the baby with the bath water. It is my experience that in such cases there is inevitably what we call in ColorFlow a *seed of color truth* in the hue you have been trying to fit into your personally uplifting palette.

When a hue has a *seed of color truth* for any one of us, the color is made up of at least one quality that elevates our mood and balances our emotions. At the very same time, the hue has at least one quality or characteristic that doesn't align with our innate color desires. Because our intuitive design sense is both strong and reliable, we can relax and become more reliant on attractions that have no basis beyond the tinglings in the pit of our stomachs.

If a color continues to appear, but never quite works, perhaps there is a *seed of color truth* within the hue. Look for the quality or qualities that may be obscuring the precise color that belongs on your authentic ColorPrint. For me it was the quantity used. For someone else it may be value or intensity. It just as easily could be the context in which the color has been placed. Whatever the case, the exploration of the nuances of color is a vital part of your journey. Along the way, the concept of the *seed of color truth* will prove a powerful tool in the excavation of your ColorPrint palette.

Imprint
Colors Rising

Sit in an upright yet comfortable position such that the torso of your body is stretched vertically making you tall and straight. Focus on the mid-section of your body. Concentrate on a vertical path that a breath takes as it moves from the bottom of your diaphragm until it reaches your mouth and nasal passages. Imagine that this pathway has taken on a luminous, golden glow. It is radiant and you feel the soothing heat within. Take several deep, yet gentle breaths and notice both the passageway and the restorative glow that surrounds it. Continue to breathe with enhanced consciousness.

Now I'm going to ask that you change your breathing pattern slightly. Inhale deeply through your nose. As you exhale, release every last bit of air. When your belly feels deflated and all air is gone, keep on blowing out air. Recall that everything I ask you to do needs to be incredibly gentle. Push out all of the air without making yourself the least bit uncomfortable or agitated. When all of the air is pushed from your body you should feel your belly collapse. There is also a tightening of the muscles about two inches below your navel. Hold your breath for just a few seconds as this tightening occurs. Then take another breath and repeat the process. For the next couple of minutes practice breathing this way, in through your nose and out through your mouth.

Imagine that this luminous channel is a path not only for your life's breath, but additionally a corridor through which your spiritually healing colors are able to rise from the murky depths to the level of your consciousness for unambiguously clear recognition. As you continue to breathe, envision a variety of colors in this remarkable place where your muscles tense while

78

exhaling the last ounce of each breath. Although you know there are several colors, they appear nebulous, as if a heavy fog has settled within. It is impossible to discern their precise hue or intensity. It is as if you were viewing the colors through a windshield so covered in condensation that it would be impossible to continue travelling.

You are a person who embraces the open-mindedness and the free floating wanderings so vital to your personal color journey. You have become in essence a magnet for like energy. The Universe in its synchronous generosity now mirrors your desire to discover the colors that promote abundance, uplift, rejuvenate and restore. And so in this instant you see one cloudy color pull away from the hazy mass. Its fuzzy, amorphous form begins its ascent through the passageway that until now has been inhabited only by your breath. Observe the color no matter how blurry.

Notice now that with each breath the fuzzy colored form climbs a notch higher up the channel. With each movement closer to the surface, the color becomes increasingly clear. It is as if with every breath you were putting on a different pair of glasses each one closer to your true prescription. Finally, the color rises to the center of your consciousness with perfect clarity. Take a few moments to visualize a blurred color of your choice moving up your breathing corridor metamorphosing into a visually sharp color. Imagine that once the color is recognizable, you realize your strong, magnetic attraction for the hue.

Know that this is the way of your healing colors, the hues inherently encoded into your aesthetic essence. The colors of your ColorPrint are perfectly in place. They need not be chosen, but only discovered. Their natural tendency is to rise from the depths of your spirit to the clarity of consciousness. Obstacles taking many forms have restrained the colors causing them to remain below consciousness unable for you to see. Few of us are experiencing the joyous flow that manifests once one's perfect color palette is found. As the secrets of ColorFlow are revealed through the text, seek to free the luminous pathway allowing your authentic colors to come into focus.

With sincere gratitude for colors already moving into clearer focus, mentally count with me from one to ten. As you do, return from your Imprint rejuvenated and refreshed. You're ready now for the next Color Bridge. One two three four five six seven eight nine ten.

Color Bridge 3
Genuine Words

In keeping with the theme of mind, body and color, you will be asked in this Chapter's Color Bridge to mindfully consider how you wish your home to look. You'll do this by creating a list of words or multiple word descriptors that detail your thoughts. Notice that the words will represent the way your home *looks* even though the ultimate goal is to create a *feeling* in your space. This is a key ColorFlow concept. Everything that we see in our homes is a visual trigger to a feeling.

Imagine, for instance, that you enter the home of a friend and see a clean, organized kitchen with sparkling pots and pans hanging from a pot rack. On the counter are jars filled with beans, rice and pasta. A bowl of fresh fruit is on the wood farm table. All that you see triggers an emotional response that prompts a sense of nurturing and abundance. At the home of an acquaintance shelves are bursting with novels and ancient textbooks. Beside the crackling fire is an enormous reading chair. Someone has left a pair of glasses and the remains of a cup of tea on the table. Here, too an emotional response springs from what is seen. This time it is one of quiet academia.

In the examples above, the sentiment triggered by what is seen is both obvious and significant. However, even though rarely consciously noticed, there are smaller triggers that by virtue of their sheer numbers and repetitive nature represent an equally powerful, emotional response. The seemingly insignificant stack of bills on the desk emits a modicum of stress each time you pass. The living room chair fabric you settled for because of a great price slightly deflates your mood as you settle in to read the paper.

The fabulous news is that the Universe makes no distinction when transferring the quality of energy within an object in your surroundings to your spiritual energy. And that's the energy or vibe which expresses itself in your mood, motivation and general zest for life. And so the watercolor of brilliant yellow lilies in the upstairs hall lightens your step as you complete morning chores. The lustrous, Brazilian cherry hardwood floors bring just the slightest smile as you walk barefoot against their polished surfaces. All of us at one time or another has read about the good vibes we get as we caress a much loved pet. These are the same loving, uplifting vibes we can get from our homes. We need only to make a concerted effort to align that which we see each day in our homes with our true aesthetic essence.

A feeling or mood then is created in your home by what is seen; hence the list of visual descriptors. Try to avoid popular ideas such as, "I want my home to be welcoming and comfortable." A modern minimalist loft can be just as welcoming and comfortable as a country farmhouse. In most cases adjectives of feeling do not help design or add color.

Additionally, the more specific the words, the better mental picture you'll have of your dream space. A seldom used word tends to have very specific meaning. For instance, the words pretty and serene are both perfectly acceptable, six letter adjectives which could be used to describe a living space. However, "pretty" is quite general and so doesn't tell us much. Serene, on the other hand, is more specific.

If I were to decorate a room knowing only that the client wanted "serene," I'd actually know quite a bit. The colors could be of low intensity. If hues were more brilliant, certainly color would be used sparingly with generous portions of neutrals. Furnishings would have clean lines. And contrast would be kept to a minimum. At the very least, I'd have a starting point. Pretty, on the other hand could be expressed in a hundred different ways by an equal number of people. It delineates almost nothing.

Remember when making your initial list that these are exercises to get your existing design repertoire to not only expand, but to reshape into something that comes into closer harmony with your artistic essence. These are the scribblings that chip away at the blocked pathways of self-awareness. If you are erasing and rewriting, you're analyzing. If you are rereading and deciding that your words don't relate, you're judging. Just let your pen flow.

Recall that the "REAL" and colorful you will surely surface. Relax and let your mind wander. Embrace all possibility. Analyze, set aside, but don't decide. Let it go. Following is an example of my own Color Bridge, Genuine Words. Use it as a guide for the format in your Studio, although your words will be quite different from mine.

Color Bridge 3   Genuine Words
Current Date

My deeply genuine place looks ...

Meditative	Minimal	Rustic Modern	Forest Like
Avant-garde	Organic	Naturally Lit	Promethean
Bucolic	Botanical	Japanese	Writer's Retreat
Secluded	Sculptural	Atelier	Usonian
Bohemian	Pied-a-terre	Artisanal	Mid-Century
Painter's Hour	Aboriginal	African	Spiritual

ANALYSIS
Color Bridge 3 Genuine Words

It's time now to take a breather from the Genuine Words exercise. If you choose to continue reading, skip ahead and come back. You'll uncover most about your true preferences if you disconnect and engage in an entirely different activity.   Think of your time away as an "incubation" period. Several hours or perhaps a couple of days later, find a quiet time to reread your Genuine Words.   At the time of the exercise it was important not to judge.   Your mind needed to float freely unencumbered by criticism.   Now, remaining non-judgmental, add several specific descriptors to your list.

With few exceptions this second attempt at expanding the list of Genuine Words is surprisingly easy. This extra burst of creativity has been explained by Mihaly Csikszentmihalyi, Ph.D., psychology professor at California's Claremont Graduate University. When we leave a task and get involved in something totally unrelated, it allows your more creative sub-conscious free to continue working at the activity. "Although the problem you were working on is not at the forefront of your consciousness, the rest of your brain keeps thinking about it and makes new associations," [6] says Dr. Csikszentmihalyi. It sounds suspiciously similar to synchronicity. In any case, once you roll up your sleeves and begin this colorful journey, help is everywhere.

6.   Mihaly Csikszentmihalyi, "A Simple Way To Solve Problems," Ladies Home Journal, March 2006, pg. 20

Again read your completed list. Think about your house, apartment, loft, whatever your living space. Does your current décor reflect most, some or any of these descriptors? In my case, if you were to read my list of words and see my home, you would not only think the words were written by a person who didn't live there, but by a person who lived on a different planet! Your disparity may not be as great, but I've found that in most cases what a person wishes to see in their home and what they actually see are very much at odds.

There are a number of reasons for this disparity, but I believe the gap between what we truly love and what we in fact put in our homes is most often explained by timidity and fear in the cost of making a mistake. And by cost, I'm referring to both the expense in dollars and cents and the enormous effort we do-it-yourselfers put into our homes.

For instance, you may adore deep wood tones, but hardwood is expensive, so better to go for a mid-tone neutral. And you've had your eye on a cobalt blue sofa for months. It's got to last, so go with the beige one. A chocolate brown accent wall would dramatically set off the beige sofa, but you can never go wrong with antique white. So now you're left with a room with new flooring, sofa and paint, but nothing to brighten your spirit or soothe your soul. *That's* an expensive mistake.

The beauty of ColorFlow is that perhaps for the first time you are beginning to understand how to sort through colors, designs and styles to identify what exactly will transform your home into a haven rich in life-giving energies unique to you. You are engaging your artist's eyes to see the home you've truly never seen with such clarity. Positive energy builds with the discovery of which items in your space were obtained as a result of some sort of design chatter and which were perhaps acquired from a fear of fully embracing your personal authenticity in design.

Be prepared for the wonderful and inspiring realization that there are additionally those furnishings already in place that are perfectly congruent with your most basic inner needs. These pieces have simply been obscured by inauthentic colors or styles. Most of us are quite intuitive and know ourselves better than we might believe. Give yourself credit. Your home may be brimming with design seeds of truth.

Perhaps equally culpable may be that many of us have never taken the time to mentally or actually articulate a specific vision of the ambiance we wish to create as we did in Genuine Words. With no set game plan, we're easily infatuated with the latest trends. We incorporate into our homes one or two elements of a new trend. Not long after, a new look lures us in an incompatible direction. Our spaces end up looking like they were done by a designer suffering with multiple personalities. It has been my experience that even with a very specific design plan in place, I am sometimes tempted to veer off course when a new current strikes my fancy.

Or it may be that we decorated a number of years ago according to what was in vogue at the time. Soon after we became immersed in raising families and building careers and just haven't had time for renewal. Perhaps with growing families we have considered beautiful surroundings a luxury rather than something we deserve, an amenity that will nourish and sustain us. Or is it possible that until recently we just haven't thought about our surroundings at all. Oprah Winfrey, in her O at Home Magazine, reminds us, "When we fill our lives and our homes with things that uplift us, we become the product of that environment … Maintaining a gorgeous house or apartment is about respecting the very important person who lives in it. You." [7]

For now it will suffice to simply be aware that adjustments in your living space will be necessary to align it more closely to the genuine vision set forth in your list. Consider the words in your Genuine Words list as a preliminary directional guide rather than a mandate. Keep options open so that infinite selection remains yours as you shift in the direction of your authentic design voice. Once you begin making changes in your home you will find yourself refining and expanding your list of descriptors. At the same time, it will become increasingly apparent that what appears to be a simple helpful exercise will reveal itself as a profoundly valuable tool in the creation of both your ColorPrint and your deeply genuine place.

Color Bridge 3
Genuine Words Summary

Just as in Color Bridge 1, here it will be valuable to write a summary. Recall that the summary is a handwritten paragraph detailing your discoveries with regard to authentic colors and styles. Without concerning yourself with either spelling or grammar, concentrate only on content. Finally, include even the smallest discovery because focus on emerging patterns continues. Following is an example. Keep in mind that yours may be quite different.

7.   Oprah Winfrey, "Living Like You're Worth It," O at Home, Fall, 2005, pg. 21

This Color Bridge seemed so trite that I wasn't sure if it even would be of much value. I knew the words had to be what would be seen, not what was felt. That made it more challenging and so I became interested. I wrote a few thoughts like Artisanal and African. These were looks that had always mesmerized me. I was simply at a loss, however, at why I saw little to give a clue to my strong attraction for these genres in my home. I was suddenly charged with energy wanting to know what else I had been keeping inside unable to artistically express in my decor. The exercise in its simplicity was merely having me write a wish list for my home. I've naturally thought about what I needed in terms of practicality, stuff like a dining table that seats at least six, a recliner in the den for my husband and good lighting on either side of the bed for reading. But with each purchase or acquisition, I had only that individual piece in mind rather than how it would integrate into a whole, an eventual mood. With my list of Genuine Words, future acquisitions can eventuate into the mesmerizing atmosphere I desire.

The Genuine Words list you have at the moment should be viewed as your first blueprint for creating a mood rich in life force energies. Perhaps more than any other Color Bridge, this is one that will evolve and beg further refinement as your journey continues. What I have found to be most valuable is to rewrite the list in its entirety omitting words that you no longer wish to keep and adding new. In this way, you'll see your progress with each new version. In order to do this, you'll need to allow a couple of blank pages between the end of Bridge 3 and the beginning of Color Bridge 4.

As we leave this Color Bridge, consider now that the visual triggers to our emotional state that most commonly come to mind are our furniture, its shape and style. Then we tend to think of the quantity and size of items. Additionally, whether a room feels crowded and cluttered exudes quite a different feel than one that's sleek and minimal. Room arrangement whether we think of it or not, contributes significantly to the overall aura of a space. However, for as much as we profess to love color, we rarely regard it as a consequential visual cue for our emotions.

Color, as much as style, quantity and size of items, and room arrangement, sends us strong subconscious messages. I'm not referring here to the fun, yet mostly accurate articles we've all read that tell us red in the dining room enhances the appetite and that a soft blue is calming in the bedroom. Although resulting from scientific studies on vast numbers of the general population, these universal color signals cannot begin to influence our lives with nearly the same force as our unique ColorPrint palette.

In Chapter 2 there was a discussion concerning how a final ColorPrint looks. There are roughly five to seven colors on the palette. The majority are colors from the twelve color wheel and are named in that way (i.e. blue-green, violet, red-orange.) Black, white and gray which are the true neutrals or any of the popular neutrals make up the remaining colors on the ColorPrint.

Remember that a ColorPrint when viewed in its entirety is not meant to be a color scheme. For instance, suppose someone's ColorPrint is blue-violet, red-violet, red, green, creamy white and gray. The specific colors for each room in the home are chosen from this palette based on the kind of nurturing vibrations that ideally should emanate from the particular space.

The family room, for example, is a place for social gathering and high energy. There's lots of light for someone doing homework at the desk while others play a game on the generously sized coffee table. Vibrant, high energy colors here are appropriate. Perhaps a palette of red-violet and red with a splash of cool green for balance will be both stimulating and attractive. As with any color scheme, the addition of neutrals is a must. Crisp white woodwork and serviceable gray carpets with a fleck of red are excellent choices here to act as a foil for the reds and greens.

In the master bedroom of the same home, a different color scheme is called for to emit an ambiance of tranquility and disconnection from the cares of the day. Generous amounts of neutrals, cream and gray, paired with soft green is a dreamy combination. A touch of romance is added over the bed in the form of a watercolor depicting muted red-violet roses. The artwork serves as a focal point and adds just a hint of spice.

Move now to the kitchen/breakfast room. Vibrations of abundance and the nourishment of our physical bodies are fitting here. Recall the ColorPrint: blue-violet, red-violet, red, green, creamy white and gray. A scheme of nearly equal parts of blue-violet and green in floral patterns and checks with crisp, creamy white refreshes even on the dreariest of days. Gray can be incorporated with a brilliant twist when expressed as silver. The metallic tones are used in faucets, light fixtures, cabinet hardware and flatware.

Note in the lists on the following page the difference between a ColorPrint and a color scheme. Each room exudes a unique yet appropriately supportive atmosphere. At the same time, the common thread of color throughout the house provides the composition with a sense of calm and unity.

ColorPrint *Palette*	Family Room *Color Scheme*	Master Bedroom *Color Scheme*	Kitchen/Breakfast *Color Scheme*
blue-violet			blue-violet
red-violet	red-violet	red-violet	
red	red		
green	green	green	green
creamy white	creamy white	creamy white	creamy white
gray	gray	gray	gray

The merits of using the ColorFlow approach to drenching your home in healing colors are countless. However, in the example above, what is most obvious is that it is possible to have both a wide variation in color marriages while maintaining a common thread of color throughout, thus creating a balancing flow.

Yes, mathematicians, there is a finite number of possible color schemes or combinations that can be extracted from the original ColorPrint palette. However, designers are more than bean counters. Add to this mathematical formula our vast creative spirits, and the breadth of possibility from six colors is limitless.

For instance, consider the kitchen/breakfast room palette. Imagine if only the quantities of the colors were changed. Now the greater part of the room is done in blue-violet with only dashes of green in place of the nearly equal parts as before. Or vary the value of colors. Use several values of both the green and the blue-violet adding greater dimension to the entire look. Additionally, finishes and textures add interest. For instance, I love to express the creamy white on my palette in the pearlescence of the interior of large seashells placed on my desk or in a bookcase.

There are those who prefer a bit less variation from room to room. If, however, there were only one space in your home that might be distinguished from all others with regard to color, consider the bedroom. The activity polar opposite to the wakeful pursuits of working, eating, nurturing, playing and socializing is resting. Furthermore, all of the waking activities are dependent upon the restoration and rejuvenation gained from a deep, restful sleep. It is here in the bedroom that a visual color cue can serve as nature's gentle sleeping potion.

In my own home I have consciously designed the bedroom quite differently in both color and design when compared to the rest of the house. It serves many purposes, one of which is simply for variety. A more profound reason, though, is that I want this room to feel as if I'm entering another world from the one left behind in the living room where TV newscasters chatter away, the kitchen where pots boil over and my office where emails never cease.

Intuitively, I believe I knew that using a palette tending toward my cooler colors in more social spaces and warmer colors in private spaces was for me, emotionally balancing. In the evening, I move from the vibrant violets and saturated blues of the living room to the other side of the wheel where the red-violets and browns live. My bedroom is dressed in chocolate brown and creamy white paired with accents of deep fuschias and magentas. Along with the lavishly soft textures associated with comfort fabrics, the pervading ambiance elicits in me the same "ahhhhhhh" as removing a very pinchy pair of high heels after an endless day on my feet.

Although your ColorPrint is not a color scheme, each hue on your Print is harmonious with every other hue. In other words, there will be no combination of colors on your Print that clashes. This is a concept that goes against what most of us have always heard or believed about color. This is more true for those of us in the over fifty group who grew up learning deep truisms such as never to wear blue with green. They don't "go together." What is true is that not every blue works well next to every green, but there are myriad wonderful blue-green partnerships.

The concept also applies to color triads and tetrads. Imagine for instance, that I were given the task of decorating a family room for a couple with three teenage children. The eldest daughter loves violet, the middle son begs for red and the youngest wants yellow. A color scheme of violet, red and yellow sounds like a disparate trio if I ever heard one! It can be done, however with stunning results. The key is in the selection of the value, intensity and quantity of each of the colors used. It is also in the proportion of each color to the others. And perhaps most importantly, the success of this harmony lies in the generous addition of neutrals to balance the strong colors. The children feel a strong connection with room because the colors are theirs.

I raise this discussion concerning the specifics of your ColorPrint harmonies at this time for a particular purpose. You may be noticing a color or perhaps two colors that you know are certainly yours. The mystery, though, is that these hues don't seem to "go" with any other color on your palette or with any other hue you've ever used. In fact, at this point, your personal Print looks like a motley mix of unrelated hues. Be patient. This motley mix is yet to evolve, but remains what makes you so unique. Your home will be drenched in a melange of unusual color marriages not seen in every decorating magazine or show house. In fact, your Color Print will appear nowhere but your personally designed space.

If you have already discovered one of your authentic colors, then infinite selection, only with regard to this particular color is no longer yours. Let's say, for example, that you have discovered a red-orange that you feel strongly is on your innately encoded ColorPrint. We know that the name red-orange actually represents hundreds of color variations each of which are created by incrementally adjusting the amounts of red mixed together with orange. Your red-orange tends more heavily toward red with undertones of orange. You've named your hue Adobe Clay.

ColorFlow uses the term *Genuinely Limited Field* to describe the discovery you've made. A *Genuinely Limited Field* is, in essence, the opposite of infinite selection. The *field* in this case is all the colors represented by the term red-orange. Your field is now *limited* and *genuine* because you have followed a journey of self-discovery to unearth the precise red-orange that resonates with your spirit.

Although the word "limited" often times has an unfavorable connotation, in this case it is favorable, even liberating. As your journey continues, you will see that the concept of *Genuinely Limited Field* applies not only to each of your colors, but to your innate preferences with regard to intensity, value, quantity, venue and addition of neutrals. Even with a *Genuinely Limited Field* of only one hue, Adobe Clay, color selections for your home become based less on design chatter. Now, refreshingly, your choices are rooted in patient, self-discovery of the aesthetic spirit that is uniquely yours.

And what if you haven't yet brought into clear focus the first color on your ColorPrint? Don't worry. This is inconsequential to your journey. It wouldn't be worth mention except that it is our nature to become anxious to see the first signs of results. Remember that this is a journey of the spirit not a trip to Poughkeepsie that MapQuest calculates should take 3½ hours. Transcendent passages such as the quest for your Color Print do not unfold in uniformly measured increments such as average speed of 55 mph.

It is entirely possible for a student of ColorFlow to currently have discovered none of his or her authentic colors and further, feel as if there have been no clues signaling any recurring preferences. However, it may be that a couple of months from now it will be as if a blockage has broken free and two, three or even four colors come into focus virtually in unison. Those months when there were no visible results were a vital period of incubation. Each effort contributed to the final unearthing of the authentic colors. Whether your colors have already begun to surface or the veil of mystery remains intact really doesn't matter. What is important now is that each of us continues in our journey of artistic awareness. One wonderful way to do this is to cleanse.

CLEANSE

*"We are often inclined to think of art in terms of pure decoration
rather than as a vital part of our everyday lives."*
Eleanor McMillen Brown

It is the same for each of us. Whether we are young or old; male or female; whether we are of modest means or are incredibly wealthy, each of us needs the same basic elements to sustain a bountiful, healthy life. In the physical realm there is fresh air, water and nutrients from our foods. On the emotional and spiritual plane we thirst for safety, belongingness, order and beauty. In an increasingly hectic world, the element of beauty has become sorely neglected.

Poet, diarist and avid gardener May Sarton writes in her 1973 diary, Journal of Solitude, "I was stopped at the threshold of my study by a ray on a Korean chrysanthemum, lighting it up like a spotlight, deep red petals and Chinese yellow center, ...seeing it was like getting a transfusion of autumn light right into the vein."[8] Here Sarton beautifully expresses the undeniable bond that links what touches our soul with our physical well-being. The autumn light was so stunning that it acted as an actual transfusion into her pulsing artery.

Beauty ... in the strong, arching branches of a hundred year old sycamore tree, in the architectural genius of Frank Lloyd Wright's Fallingwater, the spirited cubism of African American painter Jacob Lawrence or the ten perfect fingers of a newborn baby ... each of these trysts with beauty are so profound that they transcend mundane experience and rise nearly to the level of meditation. And it is in this mental state that we manage to temporarily suspend from our minds the most mundane of cares to become relaxed, free floating and increasingly open to the flow of creative thought.

8. May Sarton, *A Journal of Solitude*, 35

We've all experienced these lovely rendezvous with beauty. We indulge ourselves in these moments of life so fully in the present. Letting all cares fall away from our core, we connect only with the beauty. These are experiences similar to that of May Sarton. They are transfusions of "autumn light" right into the vein. They are nourishing, uplifting, healing and joyful. Why then, do we continue to allow these trysts with beauty to appear in our lives so sporadically? Why don't we surround ourselves with sumptuous, genuine beauty in our homes to be enjoyed each and everyday?

Most of us will travel to a major metropolitan center to see an art exhibit. We'll take a summer vacation to enjoy the beauty at one of our many National Parks. Or we'll buy flowers for the table in the foyer for a very special occasion. But when it comes to what life is truly made of, the day-to-day rhythm of our lives, we tend to be not quite stingy with beauty, but perhaps lackadaisical. It's an odd phenomenon. Even those with the highest standards in all other areas of their lives, sometimes settle for mediocrity with regard to true beauty in their everyday existence.

Say, for instance, a friend shops for a pair of upholstered chairs for her living room. It wouldn't be astonishing to hear that she had come across a sale so fabulous that she had settled for both a color and pattern that were just a little off. She proudly remarks "For that price, I just couldn't pass them up. And now I don't have the hassle of choosing a fabric and waiting for delivery."

These are chairs that she will see and use over three hundred days a year for at least the next several years. Depending on her care in selection, each time she passes by, their color, pattern and shape could either be pleasing and stimulating or could further contribute to the unremarkable nature of her daily routine. Additionally, some may believe as I had in the past that in the grand scheme, only two chairs won't make a noticeable difference. On the contrary, consider the number of upholstered pieces normally used in a living room. The very largest of rooms with two conversation areas will perhaps have eight pieces. Each item of furniture, then, becomes quite significant.

In addition to choosing each piece with the greatest of care, there are myriad simple ways to bring genuine beauty into your space on a more regular basis. As you clear clutter and unearth your authentic colors and styles, living with beauty will become as natural as breathing. In the meantime, you may want to make a more conscious effort to begin incorporating beauty into your daily life. Following are just a few suggestions for living with beauty. Once you get started, you'll find the possibilities are endless.

- Use colored cloth napkins at dinner one night this week. You do many loads of laundry anyway. How much extra effort could several napkins require?
- Light a couple of fragrant candles on an evening when everyone's at home.
- Choose a few older, leather bound books from your shelves to display on the coffee table. Consider color, size and subject.
- Include a bouquet of fresh flowers on the grocery list or from the garden when seasonal. The extra effort takes only a few minutes.
- Skip sugary snacks this week and buy fruit. Display it in a bowl on the kitchen table. It may look appetizing enough to eat!
- Watch something grow. Try a couple of kitchen windowsill herbs or start an African violet from the leaf of a neighbor's plant.
- Change the position of a mirror you already own. Hang it in a spot where it will reflect something colorful, meaningful or abundant.
- Begin recycling those gorgeous gift bags we've all received. Use them around the house to store anything from notepaper to individually packaged snacks.

This chapter's Cleanse requires neither cleaning of closets nor eliminating of excess. Here you are asked only to effect a shift of the mind. Refer to the quote at the beginning of the section. Eleanor McMillen Brown believes as I do that art should be a vital part of our everyday lives. And what is art, but the beauty that we see in all things around us. This sentiment echoes one of the most important components of ColorFlow. Cleanse your surroundings by bringing only beauty, *your* beauty to the forefront. Give it a starring role and feel the flow.

Color Speak

Genuinely Limited Field: When a color or quality of color including intensity, value and quantity is discovered to be deeply genuine, this particular field becomes limited and can be placed on the ColorPrint.

Seed of Color Truth: A color can be made up of at least some qualities that elevate our mood and balance our emotions while it simultaneously possesses at least one quality or characteristic that doesn't align with our innate color desires. Whatever nourishing quality this color has that attracts us to it is the *seed of color truth*. It is this seed that needs to appear on our authentic ColorPrint.

Color Study
Highly Contrastive Relationships

*"All colors are the friends of their neighbors and
the lovers of their opposites."
Marc Chagall*

As I prepared for writing this portion of the chapter I returned repeatedly to the idea of titling it "A Little Bit of Knowledge is Dangerous." Although I have been interested in the topic for decades, until recently my training in color theory had come only from high school art classes and countless magazine articles that were never meant to be in-depth studies. In the case of color, lack of information can have the effect of misinformation.

A **complementary color scheme** is one comprised of two colors directly opposite each other on the color wheel. Complementary pairs made from the primary and secondary colors are red and green, blue and orange, and yellow and violet. Include tertiary or intermediate colors to add red-orange and blue-green, blue-violet and yellow-orange, and yellow-green and red-violet completing the list of complementary schemes.

It is generally accepted and commonly written that highly contrastive colors, i.e. colors that are located far apart on the wheel yield the most energetic, lively color schemes. Complementary pairs fall into this category because they are opposites. They are as contrasting as it gets and so, should be the most energetic schemes. However, this is not only an over simplification, but in many instances it is plainly untrue. It is possible and even recommended to create soft, subtle color schemes using complementary pairs. Once again a small widening in our breadth of knowledge generates a profound expansion in our expertise in the creation of interesting and unique color harmonies.

First, let's examine the origin of the misconception that says that all complementary pairs create strong, stimulating schemes. In all likelihood, it comes from a lack of understanding of a phenomenon called *after-image*. Say you were to stare at a red circle on a white background. Once you shift focus from the red to the white, a green after-image appears on the white background. You can try this with any color and the after-image will always be the complement of the first hue. In other words, the after-image will always be the color directly opposite the original color on the artist's wheel.

When red and green are placed side by side, each appears brighter. This occurs because the red creates an after-image of green that is projected onto the green thereby intensifying the green that is already there. The green creates an after-image of red projected onto the red intensifying the red that is already there.

The inexperienced colorist who opts for a complementary red and green color scheme will likely choose the red and the green *separately* not taking into account the phenomenon of after-image. Once the seemingly perfect red and green are combined in the space, after-image comes into play and everything appears brighter. It is as if the room were electrified. The originally sought after, more subtle effect could have been achieved if allowance had been made for after-image. This is done by choosing colors of lower intensity than you actually wish them to appear.

Also consider using lower intensity hues not specifically for the purpose of allowing for after-image, but to preserve an aura of serenity. Expressing these low intensity colors in light values will further enhance the quiet mood. Imagine a pale, dusty sea-glass blue set off by a delicate coral in a beach house bedroom. This is in fact a complementary pairing of blue-green and red-orange. Here the intensity is kept low and the value light, so the space will be anything but exciting and bold. But even here, be mindful that you are working with complements. No matter how low the intensity or light the value, after-image occurs. Make allowances. Select colors you love. Then purchase hues a few shades lighter and less intense.

With any color scheme, it is crucial to consider the quantity of color used. However, in complementary harmonies, this consideration becomes even more important. Generally speaking, the more color the more energy, the less color the less energy. A healthy addition of neutrals, then, is a must in a successful complementary harmony. Neutrals, literally "not decided in color, nearly achromatic," [9] give the eye a place to rest between colors and serve to break up after-image.

9. Ethel Rompilla, *Color for Interior Design*, 123

A second, equally important consideration, is the ratio of one color to its complement. Colorists generally agree that a complementary scheme expressed in unequal proportions is more pleasing than one in which the two hues are used in roughly equal proportions. Try to visualize a red and green room in which the two colors are equally distributed; about half of the surfaces and furnishings are expressed in various tonal and chromatic variations of red and the remaining half in green. There is, of course, some amount of black, white, or gray, to serve as the neutral. Most would agree that this color palette will result in a garish atmosphere and the composition will be difficult to live with for any length of time. A more comfortable harmony can be found, for instance, in a basically green and white room with accents of red for liveliness.

I can recall a time when I would dismiss complementary schemes based solely on their color wheel names. Who would want a blue and orange room? But remember color sophistication and realize that blue is simply the general name used to represent all the values and intensities of blue possible in any quantity in any environment. Imagine a French country kitchen with white painted cabinets. The fabrics and china are blue and white. The room is charming, but needs something for a little pizzazz.

This is where the color wheel is quite helpful. Look opposite the color already in place in your room. Orange! Now we have lots of options. Could we find an additional blue and white fabric with some orange in it? Could we hang some copper? In place of the expected floral arrangement on the breakfast table, a rustic bowl of painted wooden oranges would be wonderful. And remember, some browns are actually very dark value, low intensity oranges. Perhaps some rustic wood pieces would complement the blue nicely. So who would ever want a blue and orange room? Me!

Discussion of complementary pairs most often centers around the primary/secondary pairs of red/green, blue/orange and yellow/violet. However, it would be remiss to exclude from the discussion the tertiary colors forming three additional complementary pairs of red-orange/blue-green, blue-violet/yellow-orange, and yellow-green/red-violet. Considering these pairs adds three additional schemes to our selection of color harmonies. Perhaps more important, is that most artists and color theorists concur that tertiary colors are more complex in nature, therefore lend an unspoken refinement and sophistication to an interior design that is not possible with the exclusive use of primary and secondary hues.

We've reviewed six complementary pairs formed from the primary, secondary, and tertiary hues on the twelve color wheel. These twelve colors have proven sufficient for designers to communicate effectively. However, "as adults we have the capacity to perceive approximately seven million different shades." [10]   All of these fall somewhere on the color wheel. Theoretically, then, each of these shades has an opposite somewhere on the wheel that is its complement. My point here is that perhaps you'll discover, for instance, that one of your ColorPrint hues is a red that is not quite red-orange but leans in the direction of orange. Look at the color wheel "slice" to see where this red falls on the color wheel continuum.

If you wished to explore using a contrasting hue with your red, it would be helpful to know that "complementary colors are usually more harmonious if they incline towards each other on the color wheel." [11] Thus, in a red/green complementary scheme, a red that fringes on red-orange works best with a green that leans toward yellow. A green that leans a little toward its other neighbor, blue, will not feel quite as comforting.

Retain the liveliness of a complementary pair while adding sophistication and refinement by choosing a split complementary scheme. Choose a hue and complement it by using not its exact opposite, rather the two colors that lie on either side of its direct complement.

In place of violet and yellow, a split complementary scheme would use, violet and the two colors on either side of yellow, yellow-orange and yellow-green. In many cases a split complementary scheme is more appealing than a simple complementary one. This may be simply because it more closely mimics the complex color harmonies of nature which tend to be more interesting and keep our attention. Also in play, is the use of tertiary hues, which generally lead to the creation of richly sophisticated palettes. Add to the mix that a split complementary scheme is unexpected. For any or all of these reasons, a split complementary scheme is one worth consideration.

Complementary color pairs can be used for creating a high energy atmosphere. They are also capable of creating myriad other moods. Understanding their use is vital because their design versatility is phenomenal. When used with restraint, complementary hues bring us not the forceful energy for which their devilish reputation warns, rather the nourishing balance that both our eyes and our spirits crave.

10. Susan Sargent, *The Comfort of Color*, 23
11. Ethel Rompilla, *Color for Interior Design*, 169

In the spirit of the Asian yin and yang, each complementary pair has one warm color perfectly balanced by one cool color. Cool violet walks with warm yellow, cool blue with warm orange, and cool green with warm red. And each pair is, in fact, a perfect whole of all the primary colors. For instance, primary red is paired with secondary green made of blue and yellow. It is difficult to imagine an area of our lives where balance is not a wholesome, healthy concept. Maintaining balance in our diet, in our work and within our family is necessary to a happy and healthy life. Balance brings a flow. With regard to color, it manifests in ColorFlow.

"Happiness is a butterfly, which, when pursued, is always beyond your grasp, but which, if you will sit down quietly may alight upon you."
Nathaniel Hawthorne

Chapter 5
ADAGIO
A Graceful Slow Dance with the Universe

The title of the first chapter was "Letting Go," and the discussion was about slowing down. You took a break from any design or decorative activity in your home for the purpose of clearing your mind. A period for reevaluation and redirection was in order as you prepared to engage in a journey of self-discovery. Those of you who are familiar with the term "adagio," the title of this chapter, know that it refers to a slowing. In music, adagio is a slow, rhythmic tempo. It comes from the Italian *ad agio* "at ease."

The downtempo we'll discuss here is quite different from the clearing done previously. For ease in comprehension and sweetness of simile, I compare this deceleration in the decoration of our spaces to the adagio applied to dance. A slow, lyrical, love duet performed by a man and a woman, the adagio of ballet emphasizes technical maneuvers including well-controlled, graceful movements of balance, lifting and spinning. And this lovely adagio is one that you will want to permanently assimilate both into your expanding design repertoire and into your increasingly fluid flow of everyday existence.

You have removed from your home some of what doesn't resonate with your genuine design spirit. And at this time it still may be easier to know what colors and styles don't fit. These are the elements that sap precious energy due to their incongruity with your artistic soul. They block the passageway from your deepest breath upward to the center of your consciousness where perfect clarity of genuine colors is possible.

In his essay, "The Elimination of Color in Far Eastern Art and Philosophy," Toshihiko Izutsu discusses the lack of both color and sound in the minimal surroundings of the Japanese tea ceremony. He makes the point that it is this almost total elimination of distractions that allows for a heightening of the senses.[12] In the same way, any superfluous feature that is neither a source of comfort nor the inspiration for joy needs to be removed from your surroundings. The senses instantly sharpen and your authentic design voice becomes increasingly audible.

12. Ethel Rompilla, *Color for Interior Design,* 74

At this point some of you are feeling the efforts of your color journey languishing just a bit. Others have enjoyed smooth sailing with increased self-awareness at every turn. In either case, you may want to jump-start your journey by repeating the first chapter's cleanse. It will be easier and even more exhilarating this time around.

Recall that you'll choose an item that is simply beautiful, but not authentically genuine and eliminate this item from your decor. Clear a limited amount of clutter. Scrub and polish the area you've cleared. Rearrange just a few things to stimulate your senses. Vacuum and allow some fresh air into the space. Finally, bring some life into the room in the form of a single blossom or a graceful, flowering branch. Once again you have released blocked energy that now becomes yours. And once again, the synchronous Universe magnifies your efforts.

There has been much discussion about the paring down of possessions, the weeding out of items of particular styles and colors that don't support a nurturing environment. Even as that distillation of possessions continues, you'll begin again to acquire new objects and at appropriate times replace the old. It is in this phase of rebuilding that it is vital to understand that the discovery of your uniquely nourishing colors and styles is not the end of the story. The *manner* in which you rebuild plays an equally essential role. And it is in this rebuilding that you will learn life's dance of "adagio."

Adagio

In place of seeking, allow furnishings to make themselves known to you,
They come from unlikely places at unexpected times.

In place of planning, keep one's mind pliant and permeable,
Infinite selection allows for passionately creative solutions.

In place of striving for an end, value the beauty in processes.
Every incarnation is a love note from the stars,
And our gratitude, a genial nod to the cosmos.

Each movement, slow, controlled, graceful and balanced
A duet with the Universe . . .
Lift, spin, flow.

There is but one way to achieve an intensely personal aura in your space. It is to partner with the Universe and allow your home to evolve and blossom over time. As the game says, take one giant step back. Instead of acting as CEO of design and décor, think of yourself as a member of the design team. Rather than task master with a list of objectives and a planned completion date, consider yourself a master artist who revels in his painting at every stage of the process. Once you see how rewarding it is to feather your nest *adagio* style, the patience required is effortless. This "step back" relieves you of stress and becomes yet another channel for allowing your life to flow.

And so *adagio* becomes our newest Color Speak entry. It is the feathering of our nests in partnership with the Universe with emphasis on authentic desires and genuine preferences rather than tradition and expediency. It is what we notice perhaps synchronously rather than what we seek in a prescribed time frame. The *adagio* method of design employs a gently paced and well controlled layering over time. Colors are unusual and combine in breathtaking melanges. They are unique to the individual. Precise matches lose importance. Fabrics and furnishing need not be in perfect, showroom condition. Timeworn elegance is welcomed.

An experience I had several years ago exemplifies the genius of *adagio*. An acquaintance of mine had seen the extraordinary results in my décor and pressed for more information, my design secret. She said that her bedroom was just about perfect. She loved the upholstered headboard that coordinated so well with her drapes and the large dresser that was a cherished family heirloom. Her matching nightstands, however, had become the proverbial "thorn in her side." She had never cared for them and now they were showing wear. She had asked me on several occasions to accompany her in search of a new pair of night tables, but for one reason or another we had never made the trip.

In good conscience, I couldn't simply shop with her to purchase new tables. I had to introduce my friend to the concept of *adagio*. Instead of shopping, we met for a relaxing lunch followed by a pedicure. All the while we talked and exchanged thoughts about *adagio*, how it would relate to her bedroom and to design in general. There would be no nightstand purchase that day. What did occur, however, was far more than a lovely repast of grilled chicken Caesar and pretty feet.

My new colleague in design had stimulated within herself a mind *shift*. Her mindset had shifted from, "I want two matching nightstands to replace the ones I dislike so much. I can hardly wait to get rid of those awful, worn out things," to "I'm grateful to have something at each side of the bed for comfort at day's beginning and end. This gives me time to fully engage my artist's eyes in this direction to consider any possibility that will best nurture me for both comfort and beauty."

And so she went about life in a relaxed, graceful flow. There was neither stress nor negativity about the existing night tables. In fact, gratitude was her only sentiment. There were no mad dashes to blow-out furniture sales and no further combing magazines and catalogues for ideas of exactly what would look best in her bedroom.

One day when the needed furnishings were far from her mind, she stopped by a small consignment shop to drop off a bagful of outgrown clothing. There in the corner stood a petite, secretary desk. It had a drop slant front and was the shorter type of secretary with no glass door display on top. Realizing that it would be several minutes until her turn, she examined the piece more carefully for no reason other than to pass the time.

What a coincidence that the desk was the mahogany she loved. It seemed nearly synchronous that the lines of it looked so similar to her inherited chest of drawers. Opening the slant front revealed a generous desk area. Just above it were eight, small open-ended compartments. She couldn't imagine what anyone would find to put in all of those small spaces. Although, this kind of arrangement would be great to manage her husband's bedside "junk." There were his glasses, the remote, the TV guide, loose change, …

You know the end of the story! The secretary turned out to be the perfect piece in even more ways. The drawers below were used for pajamas and other small articles of clothing. And the higher shelf created by the eight drawers elevated his existing lamp to perfect reading height.

The "new" secretary was moved in and the single nightstand stored away until the perfect table was found for her side of the bed. At that time the two "new" pieces would not match perfectly, but would perfectly match the needs and aesthetic preferences of husband and wife who would use them. As if this were not reason enough to consider *adagio*, the room took on a lyrical, interesting atmosphere when the expected, mirror image nightstands were replaced. The two new pieces, the secretary and the yet to be found night stand, quite possibly would be forever finds instead of fashionable fixes.

Before moving on to further explore this creativity expanding concept, a note of clarity may be in order. There is potential confusion between a simply beautiful object in your home that is released during a cleanse and a piece of furniture such as the nightstand that is kept in the home with great gratitude. Every story in ColorFlow is meant only to illustrate or clarify an idea. You'll need to apply each concept with reason and good judgement to your unique circumstances. While cleansing, for instance, you wouldn't remove a bedside table that you depend on daily. You could as easily gain greater clarity by eliminating a so-so occasional table filled with only bric-a-brac.

Truthfully, *adagio* is an entirely new mindset, a novel approach to virtually every effected thought process that has until now occurred on auto-pilot. So the likelihood that you will easily change your modus operandi doesn't appear great. The first reason for this is because it is an old, deeply rooted habit. A second and even stronger deterrent to its adoption is that the new pattern of thinking I'm asking you to embrace requires that you dramatically loosen the tenacious control you may have on your life's path.

But here's the beauty of endeavoring to make the shift. I am 100% confident that I can guide you to think in this yet novel way *only* in the area of color and design. That's all you'll need to gain personal confidence and the synchronicity of the cosmos. Then gradually, bit by bit, your new thought patterns like gentle waves will permeate other areas of your life. This may even occur below your consciousness. One day, you'll hand someone this book and tell them how your life is flowing. The curious thing is you won't be quite sure how or when it happened.

This gently relaxed, slow dance with the Universe approach to design and ultimately to life is actually quite Taoist in nature. Zen and Taoism are both ancient philosophies rich with insightful tales of man's place in the Universe. One Taoist story tells of an old man who accidentally fell into the churning water at the top of a huge waterfall. Onlookers gathered and watched helplessly as his frail body swirled and toppled to the bottom. Rushing to the clearing at the base of the falls, they were astonished to watch the drenched, spidery figure pop out of the water and begin to dry off. Asked how he could possibly have survived such an ordeal, the old man said, "I adapted myself to the water, not the water to me. I did little thinking. I went up when the water went up and down when the water went down. It was really quite easy."

You may be able to recall a decorating experience in which you were forced to relinquish control over a decision and the results were more satisfying than your original and meticulously prepared plan. That's "accidental *adagio*," but it still exemplifies how the Universe works. It manifests even in spite of ourselves! One such occurrence happened to me more than 25 years ago, but it is only recently that I have understood the true nature of the events.

My first husband and I had decided to build, completely on our own, a dining room addition. Both teachers and on a tight budget, the entire summer was spent sawing, nailing, measuring. Close to the end and feeling rather proud of ourselves, we began pouring over wallpaper books for the interior. Remember it was the 80's. Design chatter was screaming mauve and I was going to have it. We found an elegant, understated mauve and cream pattern and placed the order. In the meantime, we got the news that the price for our large bay window had been misquoted and would be significantly more costly. It was too late for structural changes, so the window would stay in the plan. Now we were well over budget.

Finally, the mauve wallpaper came in. My excitement quickly turned to disappointment when the clerk handed me the clear plastic bag with the beautiful pattern I had remembered. But it was the wrong color! The paper was available in three colorways and apparently someone had copied the incorrect color code. The wallpaper in the bag was called brown sugar and resembled coffee with cream. The manager assured us that he could reorder the correct color, but also offered us the brown sugar paper at a ridiculous discount. I was tired after a summer of hard work and so wanted the mauve paper. My husband, on the other hand, was considering our budget blown project. In the end, we dined sweetly, in the embrace of brown sugar.

I had already painted the woodwork a cream color knowing how crisp it would look next to the mauve. Once the new toffee colored wallcovering was up, the space looked pretty, but certainly not extraordinary. The décor was austere and lacked depth. I decided to repaint all of the woodwork trim. It would really only need one coat since it was primed and base coated. Using a color very close to the brown sugar in the paper, the semi-gloss finish provided just enough variation in texture for interest. Now the ceiling was screaming bright white. With a coat of ceiling paint in the brown sugar hue lightened a few shades, mauve became the furthest color from my mind!

The resulting ambiance not only turned out more satisfying than I could have dreamed, it became my inspiration for other rooms. And the experience brought with it yet further self-discovery. The existing dining room furniture had belonged to my husband before we met. It was dark walnut and he knew that I gravitated toward lighter woods. We had agreed that first we would add the larger space. Then, in a couple of years we would search for my dream furniture. But now I was experiencing the rich, dark wood tones against a background that so perfectly resonated with my aesthetic spirit. I realized that I had been mistaken about lighter woods.

The deep walnut tones sharpened to perfect clarity in my artistic consciousness when placed against a backdrop harmonious to my spirit. This actual experience is similar to what I attempted to recreate for you in the Color Bridge, Luminesce. In it you were asked to place a picture of an object that was attractive to you in both color and design against various background hues. The purpose of the exercise was to demonstrate that although a certain hue may not attract your attention in isolation, when paired with a second hue, the marriage may capture your heart.

In ColorFlow we call this phenomenon, *design venue*. The simplicity of the concept belies the far reaching implications it has on the potential evolution of your décor. Your affinity for any design element whether it is color, style, pattern or texture may be obscured by the environment in which it is viewed. The element in question may lack any surroundings to enhance it. On the other side of the coin, the existing surroundings may heighten its beauty. *Design venue* is a key component to your ever increasing color sophistication.

What is apparent to me now is that the discovery of my affinity for mid-tone browns and dark woods with little grain and low luster was actually the beginning of my ColorFlow journey. Many years later these two preferences remain equally strong. It shows that once you find a color or style or any element of design that is genuinely yours, that is deeply coded into your very make-up, it is forever yours. It is then that you can relax and acquire ever so gradually and gracefully over time only those pieces that perfectly fit into your life and into your aesthetic. The resulting space will be one of luxurious comfort and incredible beauty. Relax. Don't fight the waves of life. Go up when the water goes up and go down when the water goes down.

This gradual layering of elements over time in partnership with the Universe eventuates in what ColorFlow calls *domestic patina*. A fine antique as a result of gentle wear, loss of moisture and exposure to light over many years has naturally formed a surface patina, subtler, richer and full of character. Perfection in color match has been lost to the years. In the same way, your décor will possess the luminous beauty of a personally expressive accumulation over time. Spaces with *domestic patina* are characterized by lyricism and a depth of artistic expressiveness that cannot be achieved in any other manner.

As your genuine ColorPrint hues come into focus and your authentic design voice becomes increasingly audible, assimilate *adagio*, this expressive and inspired approach to design. Become less impulsive when categorically dismissing a color or style as you work, making *design venue* a natural and regular consideration in all artistic thought. Patiently reflect on *domestic patina*. With components that are a bit nebulous, it is one of the stunningly beautiful yet mysterious qualities of décor that cannot be easily created with simple one, two, three directions.

This chapter's Imprint is a gentle, relaxed way to immerse yourself deep within the abstractions of that which you have learned regarding *adagio*, *design venue* and *domestic patina*.

Imprint
Domestic Patina

Once again find the sitting position most conducive to experience both total relaxation and keen awareness, the combination that best allows imprinting of fresh ideas into your personal realm. Become conscious of only your breath. Drop your head and notice that each muscle in your head and neck is perfectly relaxed. In your mind's eye lower your eyes. See wide, shallow steps winding downward. The stair surfaces are numbered from ten down to one. At the bottom of the staircase is an empty room that you can see into as if the ceiling were glass and you were able to peer in from above.

Beckoned by curiosity, lower yourself to the first step, the one with the numeral ten. Notice that as you gain firm footing on the step, your shoulders drop to their normal, relaxed stature. Stress in your upper back dissipates. Imagine placing a single piece of furniture in your room. Concern yourself only with color and comfort. Your piece is a color that you adore and it embraces you in healing comfort. Moving to the ninth step, a floor covering comes into view. You hadn't yet sought anything to cover the floor, but when the perfect choice comes into conscious view, the synchronicity of the Universe is easily recognizable.

On the eighth step take a moment to relax. You are deeply satisfied and do not want for more. Step number eight possesses thermal qualities and you welcome it as a time of rest. Feel a warm tranquility move through your arms, wrists and hands as you touch down onto the step.

In contrast, the seventh riser is charged with magnetism and signals a time for domestic movement. As you are pulled to riser seven, three objects come clearly into focus. Imagine each in your room. Each of these is deeply genuine and nourishes you with comfort or beauty. Increasingly, though, you acquire pieces for your authentic home that support you both in comfort and beauty simultaneously. Consider the colors you see now in your room. They don't match with precision, but each serves to magnify the qualities of the other to more deeply nurture your artistic soul. On the sixth stair, tension in your lower back and pelvic area melts.

Glide effortlessly to five. Imagine that in your room there has been a particular need for which you wished to find the appropriate piece of furniture or accessory. It is a need that in most cases would take little thought. For instance, a desk from an office outlet is the obvious solution to a work space for your computer. Now embrace the possibility of the unconventional. A studio table created from a salvaged Victorian door atop wood file cabinets cater to your office requirements. Additionally, it softens the aura to resonate more harmoniously with your sense of aesthetics.

Lose all tightness and fatigue in your legs, ankles and feet as you step to the fourth riser. Notice the luminous beauty of your space. It has been achieved by a gentle layering of elements. With renewed vitality move to the third step, the step of enlightenment. Your authentic design voice is clear. You know your ColorPrint. A day of explorative shopping is an adventure because your creative mind is free floating. Return with an impromptu treasure.

On the second step it occurs to you that although everything within the room is rich in life-giving energies, there is no boundary, no perimeter to render your space intimate and personal. An open air garden can be lovely, but a secret, walled garden is an enchanting, safe haven. Your walls will become those embracing boundaries. Only a color that is both from your ColorPrint family of hues and relates to the furnishings in the room will manifest this healthful aura. This color will create a common thread, a cohesion eventuating in rhythmic, balancing vibrations. The hue most luminescing to your possessions becomes apparent.

Take the final step now to the riser marked with the numeral one. Breathe deeply in gratitude. You are an artist, your room the canvas. It's your deeply personal work of art. Become immersed in its intense beauty and comfort.

Mentally count from one to ten as you climb up the steps renewed in spirit, anxious to continue your ColorFlow journey. One two three four five six seven eight nine ten.

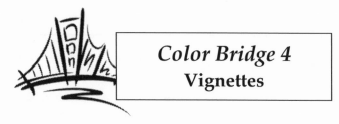

Color Bridge 4
Vignettes

More often than not the best ideas are the simplest. That's the case with an exercise I call "Vignettes." Developed through playful puttering, I found incredible insights into the essence of my ColorPrint an unexpected outcome. In the literary sense, vignettes are "short, descriptive, literary sketches." You'll translate this to design and create small scenes, like an artist's still life, to determine what strikes for you a rich chord of color notes.

The objects you'll use in your vignette may never end up in your home, but qualities of their style, color and characteristics of the composition guide you to align more closely with your personal authenticity. Vignettes are a design bridge in the real sense of the word. They help bridge the enormous leap so often made from that attractive room in a magazine to the actual redecoration of your own space. Vignettes provide a hands-on precursor to the real deal.

In the simple vignette at right a gathering of objects from around the house has been arranged just as an artist would prepare objects to paint a still life. Although it appears uncontrived, I actually "played" for quite awhile before feeling satisfied with my composition.

The depth of discovery possible is largely dependent on the first object you choose. Although the item does not have to be of great value, it must be extraordinarily beautiful in your eyes, something that brings you great joy. An item of beauty for beauty's sake seems to work best. I started with the pot of white narcissus with yellow centers. I tried placing the container on varied surfaces around the house. The creamy white vanity top seemed very stark. The golden tones of the teak dining table were not much better. Finally, I landed on a small espresso, black-brown chest. The combination of the cheery yellow and white paired with the espresso spoke to me instantly. This is *design venue* in action and it is key not only to this Color Bridge, but something you'll automatically consider in every design choice going forward.

Now I had the "bones" for my vignette, but wanted to add some depth and polish. I have always loved blue and white Asian pottery. As much as I am attracted to the combination, it's surprising how little is displayed in my home. I slipped a pretty blue and white Chinese bowl under the narcissus.

As you gain more experience staging vignettes and design in general, you will learn as I have that repetition and variation add a pleasing rhythm to compositions both small and room sized. With this in mind I searched for something else yellow to echo the centers of the flowers. I took into consideration the visual space the yellow represented in the composition thus far. It would be attractive to repeat the color, but vary other features such as size and shape. With this in mind, I was looking for an additional yellow element, something other than a flower.

In my china cabinet was a tiny chick just hatched from an egg. Not only did he meet my original requirements, but there was the additional repetition of the theme of rebirth in both the narcissus and the baby bird. And as I placed the chick at the bottom left of the potted plant I noticed yet another repetition, that of the Asian inspired chest and the Asian bowl.

Now I took a moment to quietly consider the vignette I had created. The still life truly delighted me. I absolutely loved the way it looked, the mood it created and how it made me feel. That's what you are aiming for. On an aesthetically pleasing scale of 1-10, you are shooting for a 10. If it's only a 9, but all of your friends say it's superb, keep on working. Remember, you are seeking *your* aesthetic essence.

A vignette should start off with at least three objects so that you can see the relationship among elements, most importantly color. Then you can add, subtract and rearrange.   Sleep on it and take a fresh look in the morning. It is like child's play, so you won't mind leaving it set up for several days.   The more you play, the more you will discover about your true aesthetic spirit.

You may borrow from friends or neighbors and even bring in treasures from the outdoors. The two limitations on your chosen objects are that you must be able to move them around yourself without help and that you must have strong, aesthetic attraction to each one.   Note that by "aesthetic" I mean artistic, so that your object should be chosen for its color, shape, line or texture.   It should not be selected for sentimentality.   For instance, photographs of your children or items of their baby clothing are wonderful keepsakes, but probably won't help to find your color or design personality.

ColorFlow student, Lisa, staged a Vignette that serves as an additional, valuable example.   Lisa already felt quite certain that the lustrous gold of brass was to appear on her authentic ColorPrint.   Although she had not yet named her golden hue, this yellow-orange was a genuinely limited field on her palette. For this reason, the brass tray that until now was enjoyed only on holidays became her starting point.

She cleared her dining table and placed the tray in the middle. Now Lisa had the most important element of ColorFlow, a clearing of both mental and physical space so that authentic design could evolve.   In front of her lay not only space into which infinite possibility could magnetically flow, but her nearly ceremonious placing of the gleaming tray was a clear signal to the Universe of her willingness to take the first step.   For this first courageous step forward, the ever synchronous Universe would compensate her many fold by stimulating a plethora of discoveries regarding her aesthetic spirit.

Allowing the tray to remain on the table for a little over a week, Lisa added, took away, arranged and rearranged. She knew that a vignette would be far easier than designing an actual room because here no element had to serve a specific purpose.   Nor would it be necessary for the items to actually exist together in a room. For instance, there wouldn't be functional needs of say a kitchen or bedroom.   Lisa would be looking only for what spoke to her genuine aesthetic with regard to color, texture, pattern, shape, style, mood and scale. In essence, this Color Bridge allowed her to isolate the aesthetics of design from the practicalities, using real objects that she could see, touch and move about at will.   Once Lisa was able to let go of these mundane concerns, she was able to bring into focus the colors, textures and patterns that would most lavishly nourish her artistic spirit.

Through the week, the brass tray was a busy thoroughfare of candles, statuary, spring branches, dishes on plate stands, rocks, pebbles, draped fabric remnants, potted plants, silk flowers, stacks of old books, china bowls, silk scarves, baskets, sea shells, fresh fruits and flowers. Lisa's ColorFlow training had taught her to try out an item even if her initial instinct was that it may not work. And when something had to be removed from the mix, Lisa didn't put it away altogether. She knew that it might work with tomorrow's incarnation of objects on what had become her brass palette of design.

At the outset of the Bridge we saw Lisa's freewheeling design playfulness evidenced by her golden hubbub of comings and goings. Had we been privy to each day's activity, we would have watched her hustle bustle experimentation give way to a slower, more deliberate metamorphosis as she began to fall rhythmically in sync with her authentic design self placing the perfect objects in the perfect colors into her still life vignette. Once it was complete, a friend commented that it looked like the window dressing for a chic, interior design establishment. But this was no ordinary window. It had become a window into Lisa's aesthetic spirit.

ANALYSIS
Color Bridge 4 Vignettes

Once your composition is your authentic art, a creation that lifts your spirit, nourishes your soul, calms your restlessness and welcomes you home, your vignette should remain undisturbed for consideration and analysis. If there is a camera available, take a photo to paste into your Studio. Label it allowing a blank page or two for analysis and notes regarding your experience.

Although it's unnecessary and in fact not preferable to specifically answer each of the following, the questions below are meant as a guide to stimulate your discoveries about your personal color preferences. Lisa's "Brass Tray Vignette" appears as an example in the following Color Bridge Summary.

- Which colors or color combinations in your vignette strongly attract you?
- What neutrals have you used? What quantities of neutrals in relation to saturated colors are pleasing to you?
- Did you use a wide range of value in colors?
- Did you use many colors or just a few?
- Do you tend toward the use of pattern? If so, what kind of pattern?
- Is there any design quality of your vignette that surprises you?

- What do you notice about the temperature of the colors you have chosen? Do you tend toward a complementary scheme with something from both the warm and cool sides of the wheel or do you stay mainly on either the warm or the cool side?
- Does your vignette exude a mood or an aura? If so, can you give it a name or title as an artist would give his or her piece of art?

Color Bridge 4
Vignettes Summary

"French Farmhouse"

When I started I really had no idea what I would put in my vignette. Then I found the fabric scrap with grapes, apples and some flowers on a black background. It was in my neighbor's fabric stash. The bright mix of colors against the black background are really appealing to me. I especially love the soft red that has hints of coral tones. Having had such a great start with fabric, I stopped by a fabric store to take a look at their remnants. Synchronicity must have been in play when I again noticed the soft red. This time the pattern was smaller, a good complement to my larger scale floral and fruit pattern. As I was about to check out, I saw the same fabric in a pale salmon. I took it along doubting that it would work. I was totally surprised to find that my first large-scale print had a similar salmon color and the coral tones in my red made this third piece of fabric an unexpected, yet attractive addition to my display.

Now everything was fabric and I wanted something else. Recalling that repetition of a color can add balance, I searched for something black to tie in my first fabric. The rooster cookbook stand is one of the few black items I own, so I gave it a try. Because the display had begun to take on a culinary feel, I borrowed a large stack of my mother-in-law's cookbooks. The recipes inside weren't important but the color and design of their jackets were. I placed each one on the stand and stood back. When I considered <u>Potager</u>, the cover's background appeared simply off white. However, when placed near the other colors, it was obvious that what I thought was a simple neutral was more complex. It had pinkish, salmon undertones in its creamy white that were just gorgeous with the colors already in place. I completed my design with "punches" of darker value complementary colors in smaller quantities.

I believe that red-orange expressed in the soft red shown here is on my ColorPrint. I have learned that when I use an off white, it will be much richer if I match its undertone to a color in the room. Although I like a healthy dose of neutral, my scale is tipped in favor of color. Pattern is more attractive to me than I thought it was. Perhaps that is because I have found patterns in colors that are authentically mine. Color against a deep background especially black is very appealing to me. Black is a good neutral for me and is uplifting when used as a background for my red-orange. My vignette is called "French Farmhouse."

The tremendous potential in this Color Bridge is that you are taking virtually everything else out of the decorating equation and allowing your aesthetic mind to play in a childlike manner. There is no fear of expensive errors that you'll have to live with for who knows how long. Additionally, issues like the size of an end table, the durability of a fabric and all the other practical gunk that has been clogging up the channels through which your true artist once flowed is not an issue. This Color Bridge in particular and ColorFlow in general seeks to isolate your authentic artistic spirit. Once you reacquaint yourself with the colorful, free-spirited child within, decorate to your heart's content. As you do, your left hand will be holding the measuring tape and the right will be the keeper of your palette of genuine colors.

CLEANSE

"Things that are loved, used and appreciated have strong, vibrant and joyous energies that allow the energy in the space to flow through and around them. (Further) you are connected to everything you own by fine strands of energy. When your home is filled with things you love or use well it becomes an incredible source of support and nourishment for you."
Karen Kingston, author, <u>Clearing Your Clutter with Feng Shui</u>

In previous chapters I have referred to the "energy" you feel at home and to the "energetic vibrations" given off by your surroundings. Each of you realizes that I'm not alluding simply to physical vigor, although this may be a part of one's personal energy. If perchance you are familiar with metaphysics or the ancient art of Feng Shui, you've guessed that the energy significant to ColorFlow more closely parallels that which for centuries in China has been called chi, in Japan, ki and in India, prana.

There has been much written about what exactly chi is and how it is important to our existence. Author Gill Hale captures the essence of chi energy this way; "Chi is the invisible essential life force present in every form of life in the universe. Where it flows freely and accumulates, there is health and abundance. Where it stagnates, there is sickness and decay."[13] Chi is not tangible. It cannot be captured for observation. Nevertheless, chi is undeniable. It is that wonderful life spark within us all.

How radiantly that life spark glows, how electrified its dance depends upon the ease with which chi is able to flow through your home and ultimately through you. It makes perfect sense that if your home is cluttered, the invisible river of chi will be impeded. The word "clutter" comes from the Middle English "cloteren" meaning "to clot." And coagulating or getting stuck is exactly what happens to the flow of chi in your home if you have areas of excess.

Minimizing the physical clutter you see day after day alleviates brain overload so that you can experience sharper mental clarity. Once you have pared down to life's necessities, comforts and that which is profoundly beautiful, the change in your home's energy will be amazing. But what's vitally important here is that revitalizing the energy flow in your home in turn transforms you. It is my belief that this energy shift doesn't cause you to become a different person; rather it causes you to step into the shoes of the person you were always meant to be.

When most of us imagine clutter, we think along the lines of unorganized stacks of paper in an office space or a spare bedroom stuffed to the gills with an odd assortment of junk. These types of clutter are the topic for a different book. More integral to the study of ColorFlow is specifically the overabundance of decorative objects or items of perceived beauty.

13. Gill Hale, *The Feng Shui Garden*, 32

Initially, accumulating beautiful objects makes our homes more attractive. However, there comes a saturation point when the scales tip away from further beauty. Now each new object, now matter how lovely renders itself and everything around it less of a treasure. Chi flows less freely and energy becomes stagnant. In this chapter's Cleanse I'll put forth a few thoughts about keeping a balance of both beauty for the nourishment of our artistic essence and open space for the healthy flow of energy in our homes.

Let's look at why we may have a surplus of decorative items in our living spaces. The first thought that comes to mind is the many gifts we've all received over the years. You may say that whether or not these items appeal to you, they are displayed in your home to avoid hurt feelings. But if you display each gift, the message is that you find the presents attractive, so much so that you want to see them daily. This approach only perpetuates the problem. The most honest and effective way to handle the situation is to find an opportune time to tactfully explain that you have plenty of housewares and decorative accessories. Suggest that spending time together would be the best gift. Make plans to get together for lunch on birthdays and other gift giving occasions.

The next culprit of surplus is that perhaps to some extent you still have in your home an aesthetically unrelated and unpleasing mixture of styles. These represent the various decorative "phases" you've dabbled in and bandwagons you've jumped on before finding the ColorFlow path to the discovery of your authentic design voice together with your genuine ColorPrint.

This is not to say that the mixing of styles is discouraged. On the contrary, it is very much encouraged. It simply means that each style in the final composition must resonate perfectly with your unique artist's spirit. You have considered this concept as you observed your home with sharp artist's eyes. You've thought about items in your surroundings deciding whether they were simply beautiful or deeply genuine. Recall the lovely tole-painted occasional table that resembled a stack of antique books. It was absolutely gorgeous, the hit of the Christmas house tour. It was simply beautiful, but did not speak to my aesthetic senses. Because it was not deeply genuine, it did not belong in my home. This, too must be part of your ongoing cleanse. Let go of anything that is no more than simply beautiful.

Now you are becoming intimate with your deeper artistic essence. You're able to identify and let go anything that is not deeply genuine. Clear, cleanse and move on. Just beneath what you have already cleared, there's another layer of energy. It is less viscous than the previous one, but still not the sparkling, fluid energy needed for the manifestation of your loftiest goals. Clearing and cleansing at this level will precipitate changes in you that seem more subtle, but in reality are considerably more profound. This deeper excavation guides you to nature's perfect ebb and flow of productivity, learning and transformation. Following the de-cluttering layer you felt lighter, brighter and more energized. Cleansing at this second, deeper level will quiet the mind, guide you to greater focus and free pathways to your innate creative spirit.

Here is where you cease being someone who simply has a flair for design and rise to the status of interior designer extraordinaire. However, your designs are so exclusive that your client list numbers only one, you. What sets you apart is your in-depth connection to your genuine, aesthetic essence. Integrated into this bond is your patient, artistic discrimination which has been set into motion by the assimilation of *adagio*. And at this more intense level of cleansing, you become distinctly cognizant of the difference between colors, patterns, shapes, styles and actual objects that are no more than pleasant or pretty and those that are genuine and supportive of an atmosphere rich in your spirit. Able to make this final level of sorting with ease, your surroundings are elevated to an extraordinarily beautiful cocoon of spiritual nourishment.

Malls, catalogs, flea markets, antique shops and online stores are brimming with attractive furnishings and accessories for your home. Those of us reading this book share a love of domesticity and a penchant for interior design. Buying something, anything to further enhance our space, feels like a treat. Be mindful, however, that deeply genuine furnishings and accessories are relatively rare. It makes sense when you consider that each element no matter how small, in some way supports your final composition. Objects you select must resonate deep within and seduce you with their beauty. Your enchantment does not wane as it does with "passing fancies."

It would be remiss of me to discuss the overabundance of beautiful objects in our homes without considering collections. An avid collector myself for many years, I now lean strongly toward minimalism. With these experiences, I can see the topic from many sides and have a few thoughts. The saturation point I referred to earlier when the scales begin to tip away from further beauty, I believe applies as well to collections of teddy bears, duck prints or whatever your passion. A few of the object of desire proves beautiful and many can be dramatic. But when collecting becomes an "extreme sport," the collectibles themselves actually become invisible and the space around them appears as distasteful spottiness. In short, your living space in relation to your collection spins out of balance.

Gretchen Schauffler, in her book, <u>When Color Sings</u>, tells of a woman who was obsessed with collecting blue and white china. In her dining room the china filled cabinets and covered walls. The blue and white was literally everywhere. Schauffler explained that everything else in the room such as floors and furniture was becoming spotty and distracting. Adding more blue and white would actually make what was already there disappear into a blur. Her advice was to keep the collection just as it was, adding no more. Paint the walls a rich, warm red. Schauffler's idea here was that the walls were a large enough expanse to balance the surface area taken up by the huge collection.

The warmth of the red would balance and contrast stunningly with the cool blue. Recall that blue is the *only* completely cool color on the wheel. It is icy. What a clever solution! Keep the collection, but add no further. Then balance it with an unexpected and warming twist. The woman in the example had the assistance of a skilled and creative colorist. You, too, can create at this same skill level of color alchemy. At work here was infinite selection and design venue. Without either, the warm red would have never been a consideration.

A second suggestion is to separate a large collection into smaller groups. Let's say you have 20 cup and saucer sets in the family room. Choose half of the collection to keep in the room. Taking away 10 sets brings greater importance to the collection and more balance to the room.

The remaining 10 cup and saucer sets will be separated into yet smaller groups around the house. You may notice groupings that naturally go together. For instance, floral tea cups might go in the guest room. Sets with gold rims are attractive on the deep windowsill in your office. These kinds of deeply personal, artistic sorting tasks should feel soothing. They are all part of puttering, self-discovery and the power of the enchanting process of transformation rather than a mad dash to the decorating finish line.

During my ColorFlow journey I have frequently found myself faced with "either or" quandaries. Either keep my collections and all the visual excess they bring or give up collecting. Either use sky blue when something about it doesn't feel quite right or don't use blue at all. Either way there would be some bitter medicine to swallow. A wonderful lesson for me has been to set aside such either or decisions and allow myself the luxury of an incubation period. This lovely, floating period is time for both subconscious and conscious evolution and expansion of the dichotomous thoughts.

At some point there would be a rendezvous with the cosmos and new thought patterns would emerge. I can *both* keep my collections *and* rid myself of the visual busyness. I can *both* let go of sky blue *and* discover another blue that heals me. My limiting world of "either or" has turned into a panorama of *"both and."* It heals me with no bitter pill and the eventual alchemy is sweeter than either ingredient on its own.

Consider cleansing your home something more magical than the cliche de-cluttering with which we are all so familiar. Deeper energy cleansing will nourish your soul and clarify your transcendent vision. The new quality of chi released will become your spiritual passport, not to distant lands in the physical realm, but to your infinite and magnificent potential within!

Color Speak

Adagio: The feathering of our nests in partnership with the Universe with emphasis on authentic desires and genuine preferences rather than tradition and expediency. It is what we notice perhaps synchronously rather than what we seek in a prescribed time frame. The adagio method of design emphasizes a gently paced and well controlled layering over time. Colors are unusual and combine in breathtaking melanges. They are unique to the individual, but do not precisely match. Fabrics and furnishings need not be in perfect, showroom condition. Timeworn elegance is welcomed.

Design Venue: Your affinity for any design element whether its color, style, pattern or texture may be obscured by the environment in which it is viewed. The element in question may lack any surroundings to enhance it. Conversely, the existing surroundings may heighten its beauty. *Design venue* is a key component to your ever increasing color sophistication.

Domestic Patina: The results of a gradual layering of elements over time in partnership with the Universe. A fine antique as a result of gentle wear, loss of moisture and exposure to light over time has naturally formed a surface patina, subtler, richer and full of character. Perfection in color match has been lost to the years. In the same way your décor will possess the luminous beauty of a personally expressive accumulation. Spaces with *domestic patina* are characterized by lyricism and a depth of artistic expressiveness that cannot be achieved by any other manner.

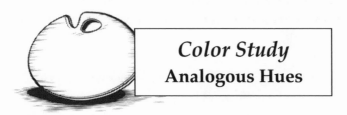

Color Study
Analogous Hues

"Why do two colors, put one next to the other, sing? Can one really explain this? No. Just as one can never learn to paint."
Pablo Picasso

In the last chapter, our color discussion centered around highly contrastive colors with the most contrasting being complementary pairs such as red with green and blue-violet with yellow-orange. These lie directly opposite one another on the color wheel. Now we'll examine hues that are closely related in coloration. These are harmonious combinations that lie side by side on the wheel and are referred to as analogous compositions. An example is violet, red-violet and red. Another is yellow-orange, yellow and yellow-green.

Simple analogous combinations are made up of three adjacent colors on the wheel. These three hued schemes will always have one color in common. For instance, blue-violet, violet and red-violet all share violet as a common link. Less apparent, but equally linked are blue, blue-green and green. This analogous trio has for its common color blue. Recall that green is a secondary color made from blue and yellow.

An analogous color theme usually has a similar visual temperature because of the hues' proximity on the color wheel and the common link of one color. The theme will tend to be mostly cool or mostly warm. Perhaps the colors themselves will balance in temperature. However, once they are distributed in the room, each color is not usually given an equal role, thus tipping the scale in favor of coolness or warmth.

Analogous schemes tend to be subtler and more serene than complementary ones. Often found in nature, they are harmonious and pleasing to the eye. Carefully examine a maple leaf in spring. In reality, it may be green, yellow-green and blue-green. That's nature's analogous palette. These subtle nuances of color add to the depth of beauty we enjoy in the colors out of doors. It would be wise for us to mimic nature's distribution of color. The ratios of

119

green to yellow-green to blue-green are random and natural. Further, analogous schemes inherently possess a depth of character and sophistication by their very nature.

There are twelve possible three hued analogous combinations. Each contains at least two hues that are secondary or tertiary colors. Recall that the secondary and tertiary hues are made by mixing two colors. This gives them more richness and complexity than simple, primary hues. And these colors more often than the primaries, red, yellow and blue, are those seen in nature.

Although analogous combinations are valued for their subtlety, a balance needs to be found for their soft quietness with a dash of vitality. This can be achieved by varying qualities of the colors. For instance, contrast can be created with regard to value. In a blue-green, blue and blue-violet composition, choose the palest blue to place against a midnight blue-violet. The colors are similar, but their values differ dramatically. And as with any color scheme, vary the proportions of color for additional interest. It is often said of analogous themes that one color dominates, a second supports and the third is an accent. Remember that one of the neutrals, white, black or gray, is always necessary to give the eye a place to rest.

With a true analogous color scheme, the clear definition of a focal point can become a challenge even when varying color values and proportions. In these cases further panache may be found in a vivid mix of fabric patterns. An ultimate energetic note is the addition of a dash of the complement to the analogous scheme. Violet, for instance, is the complement to a yellow-orange, yellow and yellow-green analogous harmony.

Color combinations that are analogous compared to those that are complementary are polar opposites. Analogous hues are similar, one color blending easily into the next. They tend to be subtle and understated. Complementary hues, on the other hand, are quite contrastive. They tend to be livelier, more energetic. Engage your artist's eyes to observe both complementary and analogous mixes in your environment. As you move on to the next chapter, begin to consider whether your innate tastes draw you closer to softly blending colors or to more sharply contrasting ones. This delineation is yet another clue to your clearly emerging ColorPrint.

"I wonder what it would be like
to live in a world where it was always June."
L. M. Montgomery

Chapter 6

COLORS RISING FROM THE MIST
Your Personal ColorPrint Takes Form as It Comes Into View

Since my earliest memory I have adored color. It has been an important consideration in every aspect of my life. In third grade I recall caring deeply about the color of my bedroom, the trim and the sheets. And on senior prom night my parents threw a small party before the dance. The color theme of that party more than thirty years ago is just as vivid in my mind as if it took place yesterday. And so a conversation I had with a furniture store clerk several years ago took me quite by surprise. It caused me to think about color in a way that until that time I had yet to consider.

It was just before Christmas and in the front of the store was an amazing, holiday red sectional sofa. Both the lines of the sectional and its fabric were stunning. The drama of the piece was further heightened by piles of white, shag throw pillows that looked like they were straight out of the 70's. A pair of mid-century style chairs upholstered in a large-scaled, red and green print completed the grouping. I simply paused, interested to take it all in.

The well meaning clerk hurried over to help, "Isn't this group fabulous?" she said, "I can have it delivered to you before the holiday." I told her that although I loved the lines of the sofa and the pieces were certainly unusual, I tended toward less contrastive colors and was more attracted to softly blending ones. Without skipping a beat she quipped, "Oh, that's where you and I differ. *I'm* not afraid of color."

Her implication, of course, was that because my aesthetic senses drew me to quieter, subtler harmonies that I was *afraid* of color. The converse, then would be that people like her who gravitate to brilliant colors and strong contrasts are not only fearless, but love color more than the rest of us.

Since then I've observed that hers is by far the popular opinion. The belief is so prevalent, in fact, that most times even those of us who prefer quieter, analogous schemes view ourselves as fearful of color. We believe that the color harmonies we create don't have the potential to be extraordinary because we are a little too meek about our choices. We must be missing some sort of innate color gusto that others have perhaps as part of their gene pool. I can say it no more clearly, but to say that this is sheer nonsense.

On my ColorPrint are two analogous pairs. Recall that an analogous color scheme includes three colors side by side on the wheel, but any two colors that are adjacent on the wheel are analogous in the broader sense of the word. One of my pairs is violet and red-violet. Imagine that I create a harmony with these analogous colors with an assortment of pillows in varying textures and subtle prints on a neutral cream sofa. Shades of the violet and red-violet are also seen in a painting over a bookcase and in the contemporary print of a small rug. Compare this to the highly contrastive red and green complementary scheme I noticed in that furniture store at Christmas.

My color harmony is analogous and blending while the furniture store harmony is complementary and highly contrastive. Is it reasonable now to say that I am fearful of color and those who prefer complementary schemes love color? Of course not. The preferences are merely different. I have noticed, however, that the greater a person's color sophistication, the more likely it seems that I will see an analogous pair rising from the depths onto his or her ColorPrint. A certain intimacy and finesse with regard to color is unearthed. The gentle nuances between hues like red-violet and violet gain greater significance. It is almost as if one becomes a connoisseur of the subtleties of color as if it were fine wine.

There is an additional piece to this general misconception. With regard to personal preferences, there are couple of qualities of color that generally "go together." Many if not most people who love strong contrast also prefer bright, intense colors. And the majority who love little contrast, in other words, more analogous blends, prefer softer, less intense colors. It most often aligns with personality. Contrastive schemes and bright colors are high energy, outgoing people, whereas the analogous schemes and subtle colors are the quieter, more introverted ones.

The problem comes when you assume that what is true for most, is true for all. Whenever blind assumptions are made, you are working from your existing design repertoire and not allowing your mind to embrace all possibility. My preference, for example, is for few if any strongly contrasting color marriages, but I do prefer rather bright colors. This is an atypical combination and so proved a stumbling block in the discovery of my authentic colors.

I've always used words like "soft" and "subtle" because I've remained confident that I don't want anything highly contrastive. Automatically, then I chose low intensity colors. In reality, I desired soft, subtle contrasts of rather *bright* colors. More often, subtle contrast goes with subtle colors. The dangerous word here is "automatic." Whatever you do automatically is coming from your existing design repertoire. That is the body of knowledge that has created what is currently in your home. Your new surroundings must be created at a pristine and completely conscious level.

At this point in your journey you have experienced a significant amount of conscious reflection regarding your authentic colors. Additionally, you've learned the following key concepts about the relationship between human nature and color that make surrounding yourself with nurturing, healing hues a profoundly gratifying experience.

1. Creativity is remarkably abundant in all of us.
2. Whether your preferences are for soft, analogous melanges or lively, contrastive themes, your love for color is no greater or less. Your choices do not make you fearful of color.
3. There is abundant and unending support for your creative design endeavors in the form of synchronicity from the Universe.
4. The changes in your surroundings don't need to be completed in a certain order according to a prescribed time frame. In actuality, it is better to design your space in a relaxed, layering process allowing time after each alteration to experience the new energy flow.
5. There is perfect color harmony within. In fact, pieces of your ColorPrint have risen from the depths of your artistic essence through the mists of your sub-conscious. You wonder why these nurturing colors weren't visible all along. They exude an amazingly strong familiarity and sense of rightness. You are poised now for your remaining hues to surface.

One excellent way to further shake loose a deeper knowledge of artistic self is to look at something you already profess to know and understand from a new perspective. For instance, you may consider the color wheel in a different configuration. This new vantage point has the potential to further loosen and even unblock long ingrained beliefs that have prevented you from becoming intimate with the hues that are key to a life of balance and abundance.

The color wheel has been created by artists and illustrators for paints and pigments. The rainbow, on the other hand, is the separation of colored light caused by refraction of the sun's rays as they pass through droplets of rain. But even though color in paint pigment and that found in light are different in many respects, they also share similarities. One of these is their order and placement.

If one could grasp each end of a rainbow and join them together creating a circle, the result would be an artist's color wheel. Now imagine cutting a color wheel on the line between violet and red-violet. Open up the wheel first so it looks like the arc of a rainbow. Now keep spreading it open further until the colors are in a straight line from red-violet to violet. You have created what is referred to in ColorFlow as a *Color Chain*. See the illustration below.

COLOR CHAIN

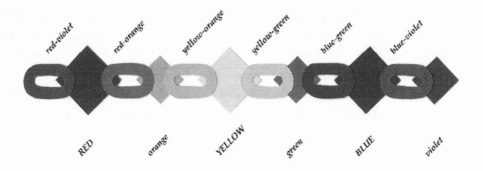

By way of review, the three larger diamonds in the *color chain*, red, yellow and blue are the primary colors. These are the only pure hues. They are not made from mixing any other colors. The three smaller diamonds, orange, green and violet are the secondary colors. These are each created by combining two primaries. The remaining six hues are the tertiary colors. Each is a combination of one primary and one secondary hue. Notice that the tertiary hues are represented by chain links that appear to "link" the primaries and secondaries together. In fact, these colors do act to visually link the primary and secondary members of their color families.

Whenever I present the concepts of ColorFlow, a frequently asked question has to do with the number of colors on one's ColorPrint. Many wonder how

124

with only 12 colors on the wheel, we have as many as five to seven colors on our Print. There are multiple justifications for the seemingly inordinate number of personal hues. First, recall the sample Print in Chapter 2. Not all hues are significantly saturated colors. Two of the seven in the example are neutrals. The job of neutrals is to separate the other colors giving the eye a place to rest. In other words, neutrals dilute the palette of a composition, so that the viewer is not overpowered by color. Each of us has genuine neutrals.

Second, recall that your ColorPrint is not a color scheme. Those of us with an interest in interior design have become quite accustomed to thinking in terms of a palette of three to four colors. Working with that size palette has become so habitual that considering of as many as five colors can be mystifying. All colors on your Print may never appear together in one space. All colors on your Print do, however, make up a harmonious palette. If you were to choose to put them together in a room, in the right proportions it would work. And because they complement one another, choosing various combinations of these hues for different rooms creates a rhythmic flow from room to room.

Finally, there quite possibly are colors on your Print that lie side by side on the wheel. These hues are closely related because they share a common hue. Blue and blue-violet share blue. Orange and yellow-orange share orange. Additionally, hues that lie next to or even close to each other on the wheel, share a similar temperature. Red and red-orange tend to be warmer, while blue and blue-violet are cooler. Because these hues have a "color connection," they don't appear as a distasteful jumble of too many colors.

Now as your unique ColorPrint comes further into conscious focus, it is important to refine your color sophistication even further. Remain mindful that the artist's wheel is a tool to facilitate clear discussion. If, for instance, your Print includes blue-green, we have a general idea of one of your nourishing hues. However, it would require a description with much greater detail for us to visualize *your* color because blue-green in and of itself is not one precise hue. Instead, it refers to a continuum of hues.

Imagine that you will mix your own blue-green by purchasing a can of blue paint and a can of green. Use measuring cups to create varying formulas. A combination of one part blue to one part green yields a balanced blue-green shade. Now mix one part green to four parts blue. Although this is still blue-green, it is quite different from the first mixture. This recipe is more heavily blue and hence cooler. Mix four parts green to one blue, and the formula warms considerably. Recall that a component of green is yellow. Once you are confident a general hue is on your Print, the precise formula that is most supportive to your unique make-up most times emerges without difficulty.

In the Color Study section of Chapter 1, there was a discussion of color temperature. It's a good point now to review and discuss in further depth the quality of temperature. At the simplest level we may have been taught that one half of the color wheel is made up of cool colors and the remaining half is warm. We have finessed our knowledge to realize that although this is generally true, certain hues are actually warmer than other warm colors. The same applies for the cool hues. Additionally, we discovered that green and violet are referred to as bridge colors. Because each is made by combining one cool and one warm, they are balanced with regard to temperature.

Keep in mind that while some colors are wholly warm or cool, others have a unique degree of temperature. Additionally, the wheel is weighted with warm hues. Five of the twelve hues including red, red-orange, orange, yellow-orange and yellow are completely warm. Of the remaining seven, all but blue have an element of warmth. Yellow-green, green and blue-green all contain varying levels of yellow. Hence each has the warming quality of yellow.

Red-violet, violet and blue-violet all contain varying levels of red. So these, too have a warming quality. As you explore your deepest color preferences, pay close attention to your unique affinity for relative color temperature. Do you gravitate toward mostly warm tones with accents of cooler hues? Perhaps you crave the cools with just a hint of spark. Some find themselves in spiritual equilibrium only when the temperatures are nearly balanced.

A final consideration as your genuine colors rise from your subconscious into the vibrant light of your consciousness, is the notion of *color restraint*. The use of color in design is readily noticed, frequently discussed, inexpensive and easy for even the novice designer to manipulate. As a result, a common way to stray from the most satisfying design, is to consider color as the *only* form of self-expression. However, in addition to color, we can create contrast and interest by bringing into play other elements, thus emphasizing the stunning subtleties of color. Spark visual interest by placing equal attention on texture, pattern, shape, style and proportion. With the support of these additional design elements, the pairing of violet and red-violet becomes a means of self-expression equally as potent as the juxtaposition of violet and yellow.

A good analogy for a clear understanding of *color restraint* is one of a choir in a large cathedral. If a single member of the choir sings, his or her voice must be quite loud to be heard. If six vocalists sing in unison, each voice can be softer. The unique qualities among their tones blend to create a pleasing harmony. Similarly, if color is the only voice expressed, bold hues and dramatic contrasts are necessary to be noticed. Even with your authentic colors in play, the risk is a space that appears harsh or even garish. It may lack finesse and life balancing support. In addition to color, consider the design voices of texture, pattern, shape, style and proportion. Now each element can be more subtle and your space will eventuate in a soothing harmony of design.

You see, everything we've been discussing is coming together, connecting. This layering over time, adagio decorating, has by its very nature effortlessly created contrast in the oft times forgotten qualities of texture, pattern and style. Against this rich, multi-faceted backdrop, a subtle contrast of yellow and yellow-green or deep violet and pale violet is sumptuous and adequately contrastive. When little thought is given to elements beyond color, the gentle nuances among analogous hues that make them so beautiful may fade.

An additional and equally important component to *color restraint*, is simply the amount of color used in a space. As children, if our favorite color was blue, we used shades of blue literally everywhere. Recall the concept of luminescing. You have seen that the color and finish of the backdrop has the power to elevate the visual significance of that which is in the foreground. No more than a splash of your genuine blue against a stimulating backdrop is potentially more gratifying than a roomful of blues.

This chapter's Imprint likens our spiritual need for color to our physical thirst for water. The following anecdote relates to the surprising, yet hidden power that color has in our lives. It comes from a design textbook that has been used by the New York School of Interior Design.

"In a New York Times article detailing the challenges faced by NASA in the design of the space station, color was cited as one of the many factors critical to the physical and emotional well-being of the crew. On a long space flight, energy conservation was a priority, and in order to provide maximum reflective surfaces, walls in the space station were white. The commander of the 1974 Skylab crew, who later became a consultant to the program, recalled that the "astronauts aboard (his) ship were so starved for color they would stare at the test color bars used to calibrate their cameras" and wanted "more texture to relieve the eye." [14]

14. Ethel Rompilla, *Color For Interior Design*, 65

Imprint
Color Sphere

Sit comfortably with your back erect. Stretch your feet out in front of you while pointing your toes. When they are outstretched as far as you can, let your feet drop gently to the floor. Drop your head as if to look down, but do not open your eyes. Stretch your neck and upper back muscles and release. Now lift your head and sit in a comfortable, upright position. Breathe so deeply that your belly rounds as it fills like a balloon. Continue breathing in this way as you bring all of your attention to your solar plexus. This is the intuitive area from where "gut instincts" and visceral feelings emerge.

Mentally count with me slowly and rhythmically from ten to one as you breathe in this calming manner. Ten nine eight seven six five four three two one. Imagine that in your solar plexus exists a perfect sphere containing all of the colors that appear on the color chain. But instead of being separated into twelve distinct colors as we saw them, they fade seamlessly one into another as if they were a misty, three-dimensional rainbow. This lovely hued globe suspended within your body is feather light. It both rotates and revolves, but you feel no movement, only a warm, radiant sensation.

The multicolored sphere within is similar to water in that we don't consciously think of it moment to moment although it is vital to our existence. And like water we utilize color both consciously and unconsciously. Many of us are in the habit of carrying around a bottle of cold Evian because we are consciously aware of our need for water. However, with little sentient thought we enjoy and indeed, need, fruits and vegetables having a high water content. It is the same with color. Sometimes we seek it. For instance, when we are designing a room, we'll search for the perfect hue. Unconsciously, though, color is always around us. And some hues are spiritually uplifting to us, while others drain precious life energies. In some cases, perhaps, it is the lack of color, that preys on our vibrant spirit.

Color is a gift from the Universe. It has the power to bring joy, to heal, to warm, to refresh, to calm, to embrace and uplift. As you consider the sphere within, become aware that all color has value. Because life is full of paradoxes, make room for the possibility that any hue in your nurturing sphere may have a vital place in your life. As you breathe deeply give equal space to all colors in the luminous, rotating globe. For this is your healing gift of color.

Imagine now that you crave your spiritually nourishing colors in the same way you thirst for water on a sweltering hot day. Because your judgmental mind now has virtually disappeared, it is natural that your authentic colors rise effortlessly through the mist to the sparkling clarity of your conscious mind. As they ascend through your body, savor the sense of peace and contentment that floats on the vaporous droplets of your genuine colors. You have an innate right to become the peaceful being you are at this moment.

Mentally count with me slowly and rhythmically from one to ten. One two three four five six seven eight nine ten. Return from your Imprint mentally refreshed and eager to continue your journey.

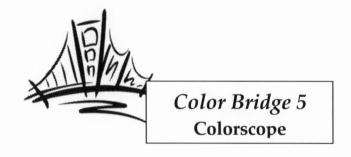

Color Bridge 5
Colorscope

"With color one obtains an energy
that seems to stem from witchcraft."
Henri Matisse

The idea for this Color Bridge, Colorscope, occurred to me after careful thought regarding the Henri Matisse quote above. When Matisse used the word "witchcraft," he appeared to refer to a kind of sorcery or magic. The spell that color casts on us is real, but how this wizardry works is beyond simple explanation. And finding the precise recipe for each of our unique healing "brews" of color, is, in fact, the very essence of ColorFlow.

The image of a "color microscope" began to take shape in my mind. What if one were able to identify rooms having color harmonies that resonate deeply with his or her aesthetic essence. It's what each of us has done when we cut and file magazine photos of spaces decorated in colors that speak to our deepest artistic attraction. No more than a casual look at the picture as we make a mental note of the colors represented in the design is usually what follows. It seemed to me that finding an example of a composition that strikes a resonant color chord is a veritable treasure and warrants a kind of "due diligence" beyond the simple naming of hues.

After scrutinizing pictures under my color microscope, what I now called my "colorscope," I was able to more precisely discern what drew me so magnetically to a particular color combination. Now, instead of making a simple mental list of the hues, I was considering qualities of composition such as quantity, proportion, temperature, value, intensity, use of neutrals, texture, line, pattern, shape and style. By using the colorscope, the information gleaned from my photo was not only vast, but defined with amazing clarity. I knew more specifically how I would apply the colors to my own space. It's an easy and enjoyable exercise. And you will be amazed at the broadening of your color sophistication since embarking on your design journey.

Look through magazines or decorating idea books to find a photograph of a color composition that genuinely speaks to your authentic design voice. Preferably, the picture you choose should not be one that has been stored away for months or years. You have been discovering bits and pieces of information regarding your genuine ColorPrint daily. Even during those times when your conscious thought has not focused on your study of ColorFlow, the relaxed subconscious mind is perpetually engaged. A currently found photograph may be the truest representation of your ColorPrint hues.

Bear in mind that your ColorPrint colors along with the exact way you choose to execute them in your design is unique to no one but you. Your selected photograph, then, will not represent your *perfect* space. You are looking only for a color combination in a design layout that is similar enough to your preferences as to warrant careful examination. Remember also, that there is potentially equal value in becoming adept at recognizing what isn't genuine to your aesthetic spirit as what is.

Refer to the magazine picture I've chosen to serve as an example for this Bridge. Directly following the photograph is a list of twelve observations. Recording your observations will cause deep examination of all aspects of color in the room. As you analyze each topic, you'll become increasingly aware of not only the color combinations that are yours, but the personally unique context in which these hues need to be combined to manifest the most supportive and nurturing environment. The list represents your "Colorscope." Your written impressions are your personal passport to yet greater intimacy with your genuine color essence.

In your Studio write a heading that includes Color Bridge 5, Colorscope and the current date. Once you choose a picture, paste it below the heading. You may need to copy it decreasing the size to make it fit. Beneath the picture allow plenty of room for the 12 Colorscope questions along with your responses. There will also be a Bridge Summary.

This is a Bridge that I do again and again. At this point, I have almost an "internal colorscope" for examining color themes for interior design compositions that attract me. However, I reached this level by repeating the exercise in the way I have described here. At the end of the final Bridge in our ColorFlow study you should have plenty of room in your Studio for repeating any Bridge you feel will help refine you color palette.

Color Bridge 5 Colorscope
Current Date

1. List the main colors in the room. Create a second list for the neutrals.

Colors	Neutrals
red-orange	*cream*
orange	*brown*
yellow	
green	

2. Comment on the ratio of colors to neutrals.
    The room is heavily neutral. Even the neutrals, cream and brown, are unevenly distributed. There is lots of cream with only a bit of dark brown in the woods to give the room some weight.

3. Comment on the value of each hue and the overall contrast among values.
    There is a nice connection linking the cream and brown with a mid-tone neutral beige or tan in the background of the Jacobean print of the sheets. Repetition and variation are seen in the darker value, solid red-orange pillows and the inherently lighter value orange in the print sheets.

4. Note the background that acts to luminesce the furniture and accessories. Consider the value of the backdrop as compared to the objects appearing in the foreground.
    The background, a cream, really wouldn't work as well in this room if the solid, red-orange pillows and dark framed artwork were taken away. Both set up some interesting contrast. Because this is a bedroom, the absence of high energy contrast keeps the room calm and restful.

5. Describe the intensity of the hues.
    In ColorFlow I learned that intensity, more than any other quality of color, sets the mood for the room. In this space, the intensity of colors in the print fabric are all just about equal, that is soft and tending toward but not quite muted. The persimmon pillows echo that intensity level.

6. Describe the temperature of the hues.
    The room is warm. The colors, red-orange, orange and yellow, are all warm. Even the neutrals, cream and brown, are warm neutrals. Although almost everything in the space is warm, the room seems warmly cozy but not extreme. I think this is because of color restraint. There's simply a sophisticated restraint in the quantity of color used.

7. Describe textures and variety among textures.

   Textures of warmth echo the warm colors in the three oatmeal toss pillows and the nubby, linen lampshade. The persimmon pillows and cream duvet look to be a soft, brushed cotton.

8. Describe shape and line.

   There is a strong repetition of rectangles here seen in the bed itself, most of the pillows, the artwork, the door and the nightstand. Straight lines are further repeated in the subtle stripe of the oatmeal pillows and the border on the bed shams.

9. Describe the patterns in the room.

   The bed linen choice, a curved line, Jacobean print, is an excellent foil to all of the straight lines.

10. What sense do you get about the overall style of the room?

    This space has the rare distinction of being beautifully appointed while at the same time appearing uncontrived and totally livable.

11. If this were your room, what is one element you would change?

    I probably wouldn't change anything about the portion of the room that can be seen from this photo. However, with all of the wholly warm colors, I do like the addition of the green in the houseplant. I might consider adding another touch of that same hue somewhere else in the room. A jade green, porcelain garden seat might be pleasant.

12. What do you love most about the space?

    I love the cozy livability of it. So many of the magazine picture I see are gorgeous, but could anyone really live there? This one is simply beautiful, but could also be deeply genuine.

Color Bridge Summary
Colorscope

Colorscope guided me to use what I've learned to better understand how colors are chosen and combined to make a spirit soothing composition. Because the photograph shows a space that I feel deeply attracted to, it has helped me study a specific scenario that sparks my inner artist. And I'm surprised at how much I know about color!

It occurs to me that this room is all about simplicity and restraint. Because the room is uncluttered with both a minimal number of objects and colors, one would think that this design was easy to "throw together." In reality, I think that just the opposite is true. It must be a design paradox! Because there is only one pattern and not three, the pattern choice becomes more important. Even though we can't fully see the artwork, we know that it is simple, repetitive and graphic. It is not part of a gallery wall of art and so the decorator's choice is vital. Quantity of color is restrained and so each color choice is more critical. A mantra of the 21st century is less is more, but less is only more if the less is genuine and of high quality.

I realized the value of looking at an attractive composition with my color microscope. It gives me "hands on" information that I can put to work in my own home. Had I not examined this room with such "intensity," I would never have realized that the equalized intensities had contributed so heavily to the deliciously restful mood. It isn't simply about the colors used, but how the colors are expressed. If the identical colors were chosen, but expressed in varying intensities, the room would have had a much different mood or aura. Everything about this room is serene perfection.

As evidenced in this example, Colorscope is a great way to "pull together" the concepts you've learned and meld them with your authentic preferences. Here, the ColorFlow student has a solid grasp of color theory. In addition, she chose a room in which both the colors and the way in which they were executed closely mimicked her authentic design voice. Simply knowing that red-orange, orange and yellow was a favorite palette had until this point not been enough to ensure a pleasing design. By looking at the photograph through her "color microscope," she learned a few ways to combine and distribute these authentic hues to her optimum, soul supporting advantage.

Neutrals that played key roles in this Colorscope were brown and cream. Recall, however, that there are really only three true neutrals, black, white and pure gray. Brown along with cream, beige, taupe, gray-blue and even some greens fall into a category that some designers refer to as "popular neutrals." These hues differ from true neutrals in that they are not totally devoid of color. The popular neutrals have at their core, a *color essence*.

The colors on the wheel add emotion and spirit to a space. The neutrals give the eye a place to rest among color saturated hues. The popular neutrals are something of a hybrid. Having the best of both worlds, they combine a true neutral with a *color essence*. Their *color essence* helps tie the scheme together because it relates to a color in the room and it is restful to the eye. For this reason, popular neutrals are extremely useful in many schemes.

Color essences must be taken into consideration when creating a color harmony in any space. In our Colorscope bedroom, the cream on the walls had a warm essence and therefore related beautifully to the more saturated warm colors throughout the room.

This Color Bridge can and should be repeated as you notice pictures that strike a resonant chord with your color aesthetics. Soon you will be able to look at the work of another designer and identify the manner in which the colors, style, textures and patterns have been combined. You'll notice variation and repetition, color intensity and value, proportion and distribution of hues. It is only then that you can apply the artistry of trained and experienced interior designers to your own spaces.

With this in mind, it may be wise to insert into your Studio a clean copy of the 12 observations of Colorscope followed by a generous number of blank pages. When you discover a design that speaks to you, paste it into this section. Then at your leisure, use the techniques developed in Colorscope to glean viable and constructive information from each photograph.

CLEANSE

"For whatever we lose, it's always ourself we find in the sea."
E.E. Cummings

Much of what E. E. Cummings has written is so achingly beautiful because his message has the ability to fluidly metamorphose into the perfect answer befitting each of our questioning souls. Might we always find ourselves in the sea because we are in fact so like the sea? Who and what we are at the moment of birth can move and rush, come in and go out, remain calm or become turbulent, swirl or rest, but *nothing*, no part of our being, is ever lost.

Our innate character appears first as the tiniest of seeds. Its size, however, belies its significance for within is held both perfect and meticulous instructions for the care and nurturing of our unique soul. As children, our innocence allows us to blithely follow the blueprints of our hearts. Especially in the aesthetic realm, the young have a strong connection to the authentic self. Sadly, though, for many of us as years pass, this lovely bond weakens. Sometimes the link to our true artistic souls all but disappears.

By now you have realized that ColorFlow is filled with paradox. In an attempt to connect even more deeply with our true artistic selves, in this

Cleanse we won't be clearing anything away. Instead, we'll look with fresh vision and gratitude at particular items we wish to keep.

You have accumulated much during your years of "keeping house." Now, in all of the stuff that inhabits your space there must be something with an essence, a spark or possibly even the full fledged aura of your genuine aesthetic spirit within. In other words, if you believe that your authentic artistic self has been ever present, then at some point, it was strong enough to rise above any design chatter from the world around you. Your authentic design voice spoke clearly and you acquired *something* that was genuine.

Okay, fine. Then why on earth don't you see that item or those items now? The answer is simple. They are hidden among all the busyness of everything that doesn't resonate with your true self. That stuff crowds out the clarity of your authentic design voice.

Several years ago I heard Christopher Lowell, interior designer and author of <u>Seven Layers of Design,</u> speak about this very phenomenon. He had been asked to redesign a woman's very cluttered space. His first task was to consider what she already had. He sorted out her genuine preferences and visualized how the space might best serve her needs. Losing count after seeing twenty some elephants, Lowell said, "how did you come to be interested in collecting elephants?" The woman replied, "What elephants?"

As Lowell began to point them out, she explained away each one still insisting that she didn't collect elephants. In reality, though, he knew that she had an affinity for the lovely pachyderms and somewhere deep down, so did she. Weeks later as the project progressed, Lowell collected every last elephant and placed them on a table. He asked his client to choose seven that were most attractive to her and store away the rest.

A carpenter on the job crafted seven simple boxes that were painted with a subtle, antiqued gold finish. These were hung on a chocolate wall in the foyer. On each was placed one of the cherished elephants. The "collection" had gone from invisible to incredible, from unnoticed to soul nourishing. As a seasoned, intuitive designer, Christopher Lowell knew that traces of his clients authentic design voice lay hidden within her existing possessions. In the same way, the essence of your authentic design voice lay hidden among possessions in the space where you live.

In this Cleanse, you won't need to tear the house apart in search of hidden treasure. You'll simply need to accept that the possibility exists. Once you do this, you'll gain fresh vision for your space. Then eventually without warning, an object, a color, a pattern or style of furniture you've been unconsciously living with will capture your attention. You'll be experiencing a resonance in vibrational quality that is so rhythmically similar to your own that, if only for a moment, there will be a palpable tremor in the atmosphere.

For me, the once obscured object that so resonated with my inner artist was a hand thrown, pottery mug that a student had given me. It had lived high in a kitchen cabinet with other mismatched china. Once rediscovered, I loved its artisanal quality. The vessel's no-nonsense utilitarianism along with the unique drips of blues and violets made possible only by firing in a kiln spoke to my deepest aesthetic. Worried that this couldn't be it because it was not chosen by me, I recalled the many mugs, vases and whatnots given to me by well-wishing students over many years of teaching. I had kept almost none of them. But this mug, I had moved from house to house. Now I knew why.

And as if a synchronous wink from the Universe, several days later I came across a small pottery vase among my floral design supplies. It had the same hand made qualities and even more brilliant cobalt blues and violets. Since that time I have on occasion treated myself to a few pottery pieces in the same hues. I look for serving pieces to brighten the cream colored dishes that I use for both everyday and holidays. Now, instead of making my apple crisp specialty in a clear baking dish, it becomes even less labor and more love as I prepare and serve it in my vibrantly colored, lidded pottery baker.

Your discovery, like mine, may not make a dramatic story like Christopher Lowell and the elephants, but the joy, the nourishment and the flow that can be reaped from this small journey within will be equally rewarding.

Color Speak

Color Chain: Imagine cutting a color wheel on the line between violet and red-violet. Open up the wheel first so it looks like the arc of a rainbow. Open it further until the colors are in a straight line from red-violet to violet. You have created what is referred to in ColorFlow as a *Color Chain*.

Color Essence: Any color that is actually a blended hue containing a greater amount of neutral than pure color is a popular neutral. The color within the popular neutral is its *color essence*.

Color Restraint: The use of color in interior design is readily noticed, frequently discussed, inexpensive and easy for even the novice designer to manipulate. However, in addition to color, we all need to create contrast and interest by bringing into play other design elements thus emphasizing the stunning subtleties of color. Spark visual interest by placing equal attention on texture, pattern, shape, style and proportion. Self-expression through design becomes more personally meaningful by restraining the use of color while supporting your design with these additional elements.

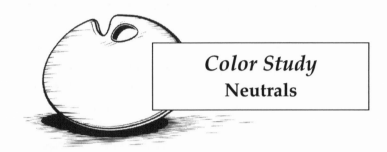

Color Study
Neutrals

"The notes I handle no better than many pianists. But the pauses between the notes – ah, that's where the art resides."
Arthur Schnabel

Imagine your interior as if musical notes were color and pauses between the notes were neutrals. If this were so, the character of the art you create may well lie in your use of neutrals or *pauses* just as in the Arthur Schnabel quote above. Actually, neutrals are color pauses. Color is energetic while neutrals are restful. In design, it is the creative and artful balance of energy and rest, color and neutral, that makes your palette a lyrical masterpiece.

On your final ColorPrint there will be at least one and more likely two neutrals. In the same way that we have a strong, natural affinity to certain colors, so do we have specific neutrals that perfectly support us. Because colors and neutrals have a synergistic relationship in artistic design, it would be impossible to discover your personal neutrals by simply viewing them in isolation. For this reason people most often unearth some color before beginning to get a sense for the neutral tones that complement their palette.

I have found it quite valuable to think of the energy inherent in color contrasted with the restful nature of neutrals not as an "either or" situation, but rather as a fluid continuum. In other words, when choosing a specific palette from your ColorPrint for any given space, you will not choose *either*

138

saturated color for energy *or* true neutrals for rest. In reality there are literally infinite gradations in between.

Imagine pure, brilliant blue paint. This is a high energy color. It is unadulterated, saturated with only blue. Nothing has been added to tone down its vibrancy. Now add just a touch of gray. Recall that gray is one of the three true neutrals, black, white and gray. With only a small addition of gray, the blue paint becomes a bit less intense. And with each subsequent addition of gray, the energy level, or intensity, drops in proportion to the amount of neutral added. Finally, the scales tip in favor of gray. Now there is more of the neutral gray than the color blue.

Any "color" that is actually a blend containing more neutral than pure color is a popular neutral. Popular neutrals have a bit of color in them, a color essence. However, they are considerably more subdued and restful to the eye than a more saturated color. Popular neutrals, then, have the best of both worlds. They are restful and calming while retaining a "kick" of color. This is undoubtedly why popular neutrals have become so popular!

Study the sample continuum of pure color gradually lowering in intensity, or brightness, until it becomes no more than a color essence. Finally, the neutral replaces all of the blue and there is only pure gray. Between each of the paint cans illustrated, there are many more gradations of blue to gray.

COLOR TO NEUTRAL CONTINUUM

Let's consider the proportions of color vs. neutral in a particular space. A novice designer may think in terms of each item in a room as being *either* a color *or* a neutral. Your color sophistication has now made it possible for you to realize that the majority of furnishings in your room should be *both* a color *and* a neutral in varying proportions. Further, you can look at a fabric, a carpet or a vase and quite easily determine where on the color to neutral continuum it falls. There are, in fact, few examples in any given space of pure color or pure neutral.

Knowing this, you have a greater ability to balance colors and neutrals creating subtle links between areas of visual energy and rest. Without it, you could unwittingly end up with jolting switches from high energy to near complete rest. There are occasions, of course, when the juxtaposition of a very saturated color against a nearly pure neutral is dramatic. However, an entire roomful of drama is overpowering.

In the Color to Neutral Continuum illustration, the neutral represented is gray. Because of the enormous popularity of off whites, creams and ivories, we'll discuss a second neutral, white. You need only go to your local paint store to pick up a "white chart" to realize that there are hundreds of whites from which to choose. Each has its own character because there is a unique color essence within. In other words, only pure white is void of any color. Every other popular neutral on the "white" paint chart has a color essence.

Identification of the color essence embedded in any popular white is vitally important to the success of your color harmony. A color essence is really just a small splash of color largely concealed within the white. Its seeming insignificance belies its considerable power to affect the appearance of your design. Using the most appropriate white can subtlety finesse a color melange from mundane to mesmerizing while an unharmonious white can throw off the entire harmony. The optimal white for your scheme is the one possessing a color essence that either closely mimics or strongly relates to the saturated colors in the room.

Study white paint charts and you'll notice that some have a yellowish cast. Many whites are cooler and have blue undertones. Still others possess essences of gray, green, peach or pink. If you experience difficulty in identifying the color essence, it may be helpful to place two quite different whites side by side. Scrutinize them carefully to determine if either appears significantly cooler or warmer than the other. Determining the temperature helps to narrow down the actual essence by placing it to one side of the color wheel. It is only with practice, however, that you'll become proficient at recognizing the color essences of popular neutrals.

Suppose that your color scheme is largely blue-violets, blues and greens and you've chosen to paint the trim molding or ceiling an off white. The walls are another option for painting a neutral white, but will be discussed on the following pages. Selecting a white with a blue or green essence is the best choice to coordinate, or blend with the already existing hues. You may wonder why a white with yellow undertones couldn't be used to enliven and warm the cool scheme. Yellow is a near complement to blue-violet and blue which lie on the opposite side of the wheel. But recall that the best white is the one that is similar to the already existing hues in the space. And if there is no other yellow in view, it simply doesn't relate.

Now imagine that this same room of blue-violets, blues and greens has rich oak floors and golden bamboo shades. In this scenario the scheme would be equally beautiful with either a warm, yellow white or a cool, blue white. Here it becomes of question of whether you wish your cool furnishings to stand out against warmer whites or blend with cooler ones. The white with an essence of yellow will work because it relates to or repeats the yellow in the floors and shades. In other words, the yellow doesn't look "like it came out of left field." It's all about repetition and variation. Variation is effective *only* if there is an element of repetition within to tie it back to the room.

Before leaving the topic of popular whites, I feel compelled to share what I believe is an amazing color wisdom. It comes from Gretchen Schauffler, author of <u>Devine Color</u>. It has to do with our existing design repertoire and bag of color truisms to which we've tenaciously held. These quasi design "rules" have become so deeply ingrained that we've ceased to question or consider their merit.

Imagine a room in your home that has insufficient natural light. Most of us have at least one and many have several such rooms. When choosing a wall color for a dimly lit space, the majority will opt for some shade of white. And those who don't are likely to select a pale hue. "This space needs some light," you'll hear us say. But according to Schauffler, a light deprived room is really very gray. Place white on the walls and you have created a perfect screen onto which will be projected the dim, gray light of the space. Conversely, paint it a bright, rich color and the gray won't have a fighting chance to make its appearance on your color saturated screen. What you'll see is not dingy gray, but the vibrant color you love. That's how to brighten the room!

In addition to a rich favorite color for the walls, Schauffler points out that light deprived spaces need lots of contrast. This means that special attention must be given to light and dark values. If each color is the same value, you won't be able to distinguish anything. Mix values of light and dark and, in essence, you've created light through the use of color. "You can make a room clean up its dirty cast with good contrast, bright rich color and the right color partners. If you just want more light, call the electrician." [15]

15. Gretchen Schauffler, *Devine Color, When Color Sings,* 124

141

We also choose white walls because it goes with everything. Fearful of commitment, a creamy white or very pale background allows for furnishings and accessories to be changed at whim. But saying that "it goes with everything" is a bit strong. In reality, white just doesn't clash with anything. Additionally, it isolates and separates the colors you have specifically chosen for their pleasing interplay. Remember that colors sing in harmonious marriages, not in isolation. Try picturing a print fabric that you love. Now imagine cutting apart each motif in the design and spreading them out on a large white tabletop. The once loved design will lose much of its character and your eye will be drawn to the stark contrast and brightness of the white instead of the beauty of the hues that once magically played off one another.

Those who choose a white background for the sole purpose of having the ability to replace furnishings, often do redecorate. They grow tired of the brown sofa and buy a blue and green plaid. There is no need to repaint because the white isn't offensive with either couch. Let's imagine that the original brown is an authentic ColorPrint hue. Placed against creamy coffee colored walls, the effect may provide such lasting satisfaction and nourishment that thoughts of purchasing new furniture soon fade.

Those who select rich and *related* wall colors most often enjoy greater contentment and longevity with regard to their design. Now free to accept from the creative Universe ideas for uplifting accessories, comforting arrangements and all-embracing ambience, a remarkable depth of both color and design sophistication becomes possible. An easy flow to design is established and eventually permeates other aspects of life. It is the flow we know as ColorFlow.

"An interior is the natural projection of the soul."
Coco Chanel

Chapter 7

INTEGRITY BEGINS AT HOME
Creating an Atmosphere Rich in Your Deeply Genuine Spirit

Imagine standing in the entryway of the home of a woman who "has it all together." She exudes a degree of self-assurance that comes only with truly knowing oneself. An aura of composure and effortless independence hangs in the air. Surrounded with genuinely nourishing colors and styles, she emerges from her sunroom office and moves closer to greet you. You are struck by an all encompassing sense of authenticity. Floating blithely about the room, she appears almost non-human, rather as if part of the magical animal kingdom.

Consider now the savannah leopard in his natural African habitat. Here he enjoys a perfect, life supporting environment. It is where he flourishes. Move him to a Louisiana marsh where it is the alligator who prospers and the leopard displays anxious discontent. Here the leopard will weaken and decline. So it is with the woman who has surrounded herself with deeply authentic colors, styles and motifs. She emanates a glow of natural grace and vibrancy for life. It is this integrity of habitat that you have already begun to create. And your ideal habitat is the only one that will wholly support each of your goals and dreams.

If your surroundings don't balance and support your life, you simply cannot expect to manifest the abundance you deserve. And if you try to attain your dreams in a non-supportive space, your life is in danger of taking on the frenetic, helter skelter pace to which many of us have become accustomed. Even your movements become sharper and more angular. Run from the refrigerator to the microwave in a race to get dinner before rushing out to an evening meeting. There is no time to simply be. Perhaps more unfortunate is that there is not a spare moment to even consider whether our hectic lives are the journey or have they become the destination, our normal way of living.

Like a toddler who struggles to learn to walk, the first steps of our color journey were a bit unsteady. If your experience was similar to mine, it began amidst confusion. Even so, each Color Flow exercise seemed rather easy and in fact, fun. The Color Bridges were enjoyable. The Cleanses cleared your space as well as your mind. The ColorFlow text brought fresh originality to a much loved topic. But somewhere along the way you wondered if all of your efforts could possibly come together in a spirit reawakening composition. You had removed several design elements that did not speak to your artistic essence and added others that did. Cautiously, you moved forward not totally convinced you were on the right path. Instead of lifting your spirits, had your redesign become yet another stressor in your life?

It is just at this moment, when your decor plans seem to falter, that an entirely different but quite attractive look attracts your attention. No wonder! It doesn't take much to lure you away from the feelings of uncertainty and the less than satisfying space you've created thus far. So you purchase a few pieces to support your most recently discovered style. At this point simply shopping for anything new and different is uplifting. Once at home your buoyed spirits are short-lived as you begin mixing your latest acquisitions with what's already in place. Nothing relates. There is no integrity of design.

The solution is to stay the original course. Remain patient during your journey of self-discovery. There will be periods when your space looks as if it has one foot in the confusing past and the other in your growing, aesthetic self-awareness. The very nature of reworking your environment adagio style requires that your surroundings experience numerous metamorphoses. With each small shift you have, in essence, a new canvas ready for the next incarnation. The beauty of redesign with genuine, measured steps is that each emerging canvas gives direction for the next modification. Instead of planning every design detail at the outset followed by the execution of the décor in its entirety, you allow for "the way to show the way."

Remain mindful that you are working in cooperation with the Universe. In our fast paced lives we have become accustomed to perpetual action. At the office, one report is complete so immediately we move on to the next. At home we begin thinking of the weeding outside before finishing the vacuuming inside. We rarely allow ourselves to be wholly in the present. Universal time, on the other hand, is quite different. It is a healthy, yet irregular pendulum of motion and rest. It is paramount to accept that periods of *apparent* rest are necessary and crucial to effective periods of motion.

Consider the following example of Universal time and how each alteration can lead to the next. Your living room, although clean and orderly, had become a hodgepodge of colors, styles and design trends. In the very first Cleanse you were asked to choose and permanently remove one item that was *simply beautiful*, but not *deeply genuine*. Your choice proved a bit difficult because there were both items that did not resonate with your authentic design voice and very worn pieces that desperately needed to be replaced. Imagine that in the end you selected a Queen Anne style coffee table that you were never crazy about.

A neighbor was pleased to acquire the piece, but now you were left with a glaring hole in the middle of your seating arrangement. To make matters worse, the newly created space further emphasized the poor condition of the carpet. Deciding to adhere to the concepts set forth in the ColorFlow course, you didn't simply rush out to find a replacement coffee table that would work. Instead, you lived with the altered canvas remaining open to the endless possibilities of design. The reward for your patience and non-judgmental mind proved remarkable.

As the days and weeks passed, your focus shifted from the need to find a coffee table to the carpet. It truly wasn't in as bad shape as previously perceived. Really there was only one stain just next to where the table had been. Further, as your authentic ColorPrint began to reveal itself, it had become apparent that the carpet color was one of the few hues in the room that was genuinely yours. Although definitely a clue, the solution in its entirety was not yet obvious.

This precise point in the execution of your design is both critical and thrilling. Drench your home with your innate ColorPrint palette. Be attentive to your authentic design voice. And surrender to the creative Universe with the gentle layering of adagio. With these three principles in place, the experience of remaining patient and open minded followed by a revelation of a yet unconsidered and surprising clue will materialize for any decorating perplexity. When it does, you can be certain that the most uplifting and life balancing solution for your unique personal scenario is on the horizon.

This "clue," however, is valuable only if you are perceptive enough to detect its appearance. I have given this phenomenon a name so that you will remember its importance. This creative signal from the Universe is a *clarity marker* because genuine, aesthetic clarity is precisely what it portends.

Returning to our example, the *clarity marker* appeared giving your focus a gentle nudge away from the coffee table and toward the carpet. Still patient, you became poised for complete clarity. As is many times the case, the design solution proved quite different than any initially obvious fix. Additionally, it surfaced when least expected. Here is what happened.

A friend had invited you to a tag sale. Not looking for anything in particular, it was fun to simply browse. However, several colorful area rugs stacked in a corner caught your eye. Flipping through them revealed a faux zebra throw rug. It was love at first sight! In this instant, the *clarity marker* turned to a clear solution. Keep the toast colored carpet. Define and brighten the conversation area *and* cover the stain with the brown and cream print rug. And remember my expectation that one design element often guides the way toward the next? Now a specific direction with regard to the table style had come into focus. It would need to be one without a solid, bulky base. You would choose a table with spare, unadorned legs so as not to obscure your new treasure.

Had you not been prepared to notice the *clarity marker*, you may never have perused the tag sale rugs. In fact, your focus would not have been on floor coverings of any kind. Instead, you most likely would have been searching for a vintage table with no distinct idea about shape or style. And worse, had you leapt ahead skipping any journey for the discovery of your inner artist, you may have simply replaced the carpet and table. Fresh new furnishing and accessories can certainly elevate your mood temporarily. However, such a solution is usually simply beautiful, but not deeply genuine. In the ColorFlow course, we have learned that it's more satisfying to remain determined to settle for nothing short of deeply genuine.

And so the feathering of your nest will go. There will be extended time spans when it is vital that you simply step back and experience the atmosphere of the space. Then without warning, inspiration surfaces. And this inspiration will not emerge solely from your existing design repertoire. Instead, the new ideas spring from your repertoire of knowledge in cooperation with the vastly creative Universe. Creativity, in essence, is just that, a new perception of what already exists manifested in a novel form. What exists, then is your design repertoire. The innovative twist comes from having an unrestricted mind inclined to accept enlightenment from the creative cosmos.

A comfortable rhythm of energetic innovation followed by tranquil inactivity settles in. Initially, your space reflects a proportionally greater number of elements that do not resonate with the unique vibrations of your spirit. This is the stage we likened to a toddler learning to walk. Design chatter, fads, trends and even the neighbors' décor, can easily entice you to abandon your course during this unsettled phase. However, the pay off is great and comes when you reach a "tipping point." This occurs when the greater portion of your room reflects your authentic colors and styles. In other words, a minority of design elements remain in the confused past. Reaching this "design critical mass" tremendously diminishes the temptation to jump ship in favor of every attractive new look you discover. Your genuine course is one to which you effortlessly remain true as a depth of peace and warm contentment washes over you.

Reflect once again on the self-assured woman in her genuinely nourishing space. She is not blind to new fads in décor. She, too, enjoys the wonderful diversity in the decorating venues we love to explore, but doesn't waver from her personal design integrity. Rather she interprets the new wave in trends through the lenses of her authentic design voice. Perhaps the next time she is inspired to rearrange her book shelves, the composition will be colored by what she's observed. Proficient at sorting through design chatter garnering bits and pieces that speak to her or spark yet another idea, the girth of her design repertoire is widened, the patina deepened.

Seek your true north. Design chatter must not replace your authentic design voice even when what is heard from within is barely a whisper. Instead, allow new ideas to gently color your interior while remaining authentic in every detail. This perfect integrity created at home effortlessly permeates all other realms. We are at our best when all is natural and true.

Imprint
Getting Back to What's Natural

Sit comfortably with your feet flat on the floor, your back upright, and your palms resting upward in your lap. Close your eyes, draining your mind of everything but your breath. Recalling the energizing, belly breathing of the last Imprint, focus on the area in the center of your body that is level with a point about two inches below your navel. This is an acupressure point called The Sea of Energy. Although most of us have become accustomed to breathing from our chests, life-giving energy flows most naturally and abundantly when we breathe from this internal center of gravity deep in the belly. Feel your belly rise as you inhale and collapse as you exhale.

As I count slowly and quietly from ten to one, practice taking deep breaths that originate from your Sea of Energy. This incredibly potent spot where vital life forces reside is also called the Hara. And so we will call this deep belly breathing, Hara breathing. Let's begin. Ten nine eight seven six five four three two one. You are incredibly relaxed and a wave of contentment settles over you.

This is the way we used to breathe as babies, so Hara breathing is a way to revert to a more natural way of being. And although on the surface we may think of our color journey as searching for something new, in actuality it too, is a reverting back to what is our most natural way of being.

It is vital that you learn to recognize how nature meant you to feel every day. It is only then that you can accurately gauge your response to colors, shapes, styles and textures. In other words, if you are not feeling "yourself," it is difficult to accurately perceive what the inner self craves. It is akin to knowing true hunger and then eating what your body lacks for optimal health and vigor. You must discover your natural, emotional state in order to recognize your true, aesthetic essence.

And so finding this place in the viscera, this Sea of Energy, calls us back to our roots. It is an emotional place where perfect clarity is normal. In the beginning, in the natural state of youth we were free to know ourselves. Further, we had not yet learned to harshly judge and weigh and question. In that most simple state, we lived according to what felt right.

Begin again to breathe from your Sea of Energy. As you do, imagine that this place deep in your gut produces a pearlescent liquid. Continue to breathe. Envision now that the liquid turns to one of the precise hues of your personal ColorPrint. Visualize the mystical elixir spreading to each extremity of your body. Breathe, as the liquid warms ever so slightly.

Turn your attention now to a color or a specific furnishing or accessory that is far from your favorite. The pearlescent fluid has dissolved and you begin to breathe from your chest. If this proves awkward after experiencing the comfort of Hara breathing, exaggerate the raising and lowering of your shoulders just a bit. This will help your chest do the work as you breathe. The design element now in your mind's eye does not speak to you. It is not congruent with your nature just as breathing from your chest is unnatural. You feel anxious and ready to turn away from this image. Relax your shoulders as the vision disappears.

As I count once again this time from one to ten, take deep Hara breaths. As you do, envision each color that you believe to be uniquely yours. One Two Three Four Five Six Seven Eight Nine Ten. Open your eyes now and remain in your most natural state of contentment.

According to one a my favorite authors and spiritual teachers, Shakti Gawain, "Every time you don't follow your inner guidance, you feel a loss of energy, loss of power, a sense of spiritual deadness."[16] This advice has been invaluable and can be implemented in virtually every area of life. Applied to ColorFlow it means that we must be guided in design by that which lies within, our authentic essence. Most if not all of us truly believe in the significance of listening to our instincts. However, the precise way to find and follow this guidance remains a bit nebulous.

I am confident that Color Bridges, Cleanses, Color Studies and the highlighting of my own personal color journey have facilitated your discovery of self and your core aesthetic essence. However, even with these in place, I have had an underlying, nagging sense that there was yet another technique that would more specifically and concretely define one's innate design tastes. And without realizing, each of you has already begun to use this technique. It is a concept that I have dubbed *"Word Stylings."*

Word Stylings requires only one tool and that is *words*. The key is that they're your words and come directly from your heart. They should not express what you decide might look best or reflect current design chatter. With childlike innocence, you simply say the words that divulge your heartfelt loves. *"Word Stylings"* are your own collection of words that guide you in the creation of a unique environment manifesting in marvelous, free flowing energy.

Our own words are a very natural choice for a design tool. In our everyday lives words are the embryo of that which we manifest. And our thoughts are merely words. On a busy evening you think, "I'm hungry and I feel like something filling, but quick." After dialing the local take-out restaurant, a hot, thick crusted pizza appears at your door. The pizza is the physical manifestation of your thoughts or your words. According to featured co-author, Michael Bernard Beckwith, of Rhonda Byrne's life changing, best seller, <u>The Secret</u>, "Creation is always happening. Every time an individual has a thought, or a prolonged chronic way of thinking, they're in the creation process. Something is going to manifest out of those thoughts." [17]

16. Shakti Gawain, *Creative Visualization*, 16
17. Rhonda Bynre with Michael Bernard Beckwith, *The Secret*, 16

This sounds suspiciously easy. The hitch here is that monitoring our thoughts so that they remain both positive and genuine is something we must first do on a conscious level. At some point then, these life supporting thoughts become our "chronic way of thinking." When this occurs, we can relax and life begins to change for the better.

The first time you experienced *Word Stylings* was in the Color Bridge, *Genuine Words*. Recall your list of terms that genuinely and specifically described the way you wish your surroundings to look. In this Color Bridge you will again use deeply personal words to further define your design direction.

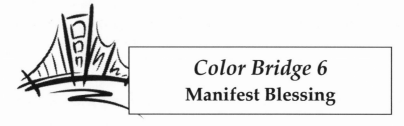

Color Bridge 6
Manifest Blessing

Note: This Color Bridge is actually twofold. It is important that the tandem activities be done in the order which comes most naturally to you. No one sequence is more correct. When I use the term "first," I mean only that it is the first activity explained.

First, you'll give your home a name! Although this sounds unconventional and peculiar, I believe you'll be amazed at the aesthetic path it will illuminate. Examples of homes with names are "Tara" in <u>Gone with the Wind</u>, "Thornfield" in <u>Jane Eyre</u> and interior designer Elsie de Wolfe's "Villa Trianon." Naming your home doesn't mean that you're trying to make it grander than it may be or that you are trying to be pretentious. Your home's name is for you only and doesn't need to be shared with others.

Giving the most important space in your world a title simply defines its personality to which you can more easily stay true. It is the most concise statement of your goals. Your thoughtfully chosen name helps you to view your home as a living entity with a lyrical character of its own.

To others, your home's name will have little meaning. However, for you, it will express a myriad of qualities that you've found to be uniquely nourishing, healing and spirit strengthening. My home's name is "Midori," the Japanese word for "green." I imagine it as the fresh yellow-green on my palette. The color itself conjures up the idea of Spring's rebirth, an ever-cycling rejuvenation and most importantly growth. "Midori" reminds me that my most basic desire is to create a space where like a flexible young shoot I relentlessly reach for the light in order to grow and evolve. The Japanese reminds me of my strong desire to replace Western materialism and worldliness for a more Eastern approach to life that emphasizes simplicity, contemplation and retreat.

The name "Midori" did not reveal itself to me instantly nor was it the first name I considered. You, too, may have to "try on" several names for your home until you find the one that most suitably expresses your essence.

Next, you'll write a detailed description of what you see and how you feel in your home once your design goals have been manifested. This portion of *Word Stylings* is called the Manifest Blessing and is, in fact, a mantra or positive visualization of your ideal space. It is vital that you write it in the present tense as if it already exists. Acting as if your goal has already been realized is powerful. Be, feel and become immersed in your vision.

Word Stylings, which includes your list of Genuine Words, the name of your home and your Manifest Blessing help you stay on track maintaining a vital integrity to your truest personal style. *Word Stylings* more than any other design experience have helped to transform my style from a haphazard melange drifting in disparate directions to a deeply contemplated, authentic style. And staying the course required increasingly less effort as it became clearly apparent that I was on the path to ever expanding abundance in every area of my life.

Your Manifest Blessing is a written portrait of your most intimate thoughts concerning the way you choose to live. For that reason, it's best to keep your Blessing confidential. However, the creation of a fictitious Blessing that adequately conveys the essence of the Color Bridge proved impossible. Hence, the example below is word for word my Manifest Blessing for Midori. Any disadvantage in revealing my innermost thoughts is far outweighed by sharing this gratifying design tool with my readers.

Manifest Blessing for Midori

A still retreat where my creativity flourishes, an artistic interpretation of the yin and the yang, a minimalist simplicity and the nourishing beauty found in the rich authenticity of nature. These four ideals are the essence of Midori.

A Zen-like peace radiates from my surroundings creating a channel through which enlightenment and growth flow. At Midori the custom of diminishing distractions to heighten the senses is borrowed from the minimalist surroundings of the Japanese tea ceremony. Furnishings are pared down to only that which is necessary for comfort and utility. This allows for ease of movement, visual quietness and free flow of energy. Objects of beauty are carefully chosen, each one having a specific, aesthetic purpose. Many surfaces throughout remain bare, poised palettes for the next creative spark. In this way, I become effortlessly immersed in an endeavor wherever the light and warmth and energy draw me.

My minimalism has now reached new levels of restraint, allowing Midori to effortlessly breathe with a sparkling zephyr of life enhancing chi. This sparsity serves to heighten the splendor of each piece. And in this restraint, I am reminded that simplicity and the avoidance of excess in each area of life is my natural and most auspicious path. A single, meticulously executed endeavor begets profound gratification as deep in its process as in its completion. My former path marked by a desire to attain quantity in accomplishment rather than quality and joy in the process has faded. Midori's simplicity of design allows me to fully experience gratitude for what I have and remain poised to expand and accept fresh perspective and innovative thought from the Universe.

Areas of contrast are few, but where each exists, they are bold conveying the beliefs that heal me . . . a pair of black cranes, sculptures against the water color green of my Japanese garden, a brilliant magenta kimono of delicate silk juxtaposed against a rugged, gray stone wall and a bowl of vivid limes, a luminous still life atop a craggy, live edge wood table. These stunning contrasts embody true beauty. They speak of the yin and the yang. When darkness of night descends, can dawn be far behind.

My love for natural materials and artisan made objects is evident throughout Midori. A cherished piece of hand thrown pottery brings the elements of earth, wind, fire and water to my home. Fabrics are hand woven and colored with natural dyes. A tribal carved, African fetish personifies the innate fertile nature within each of us. Beyond its beauty and vibrations of fertility, the carving serves as a reminder of peoples who live even now in natural step with the rhythms of the earth.

My colors of blue, violet, red-violet, green, yellow-green, brown and cream gently embrace but do not suffocate me. Scattered among my belongings are multi-hued objects of art, a hand woven pashmina on an ultra contemporary chair, a modern oil painting perched above an antique English chest. Here in these small color kaleidoscopes are many colors that are not on my personal print. Even so, the hues live in delicious harmony with each other and with my palette; a soft red with the perfect warm violet; a creamy yellow with a powdery blue.

Midori is in every detail harmonious with my life essence. Simplicity and order sustain my clarity and focus. My innately nourishing colors, lines, shapes and textures draw me to a clearer meditative state. Beauty is my life sustaining elixir and so it abounds both in objects of art and objects of utility. Each treasured element rests effortlessly into the room where its energy resides, and each room into the home because my personal integrity has been meticulously maintained. Midori emanates an honesty of atmosphere that infuses the space with profound comfort and a sense of being truly at home in the Universe.

This is a wonderful time to pull out your Studio and simply page through the first five Color Bridges. In addition to making discoveries about your aesthetic self in each individual exercise, the sum total of experiences may show strong artistic currents that have until now remained unnoticed. When you reach the end, write a heading for this Bridge. Even if at this moment you have no idea where to begin, the simple act of writing "Manifest Blessing for My Home" sets the wheels of your unconscious mind in motion. Add patience and confidence to the synchronous Universe and pen will soon be scrolling across the paper with amazing ease.

In all likelihood you will write several drafts of your Blessing until it perfectly expresses your desires. What you compose is a formal endorsement of that which you wish to manifest. Hence the term "blessing." You are, in fact, putting your blessing on this plan. And the more honest and complete your ideas, the more fluidly your deeply genuine space unfolds.

Once you've given your home a name and composed your Manifest Blessing, the Color Bridge is complete. Unlike previous exercises, it won't be necessary to write a personal analysis. Your Blessing is, in and of itself, a comprehensive evaluation of your authentic, artistic spirit. The generic analysis below is a general discussion regarding the most effective application of Word Stylings.

Color Bridge Analysis
Manifest Blessing

Your Genuine Words, your home's name and your Manifest Blessing serve now as the only criteria for what comes into your home as well as what is removed. The following thoughts may no longer influence your decisions regarding your deeply genuine place.

1. It's free.
2. It's on sale.
3. I need something by the date of a particular life event, so I'll have to settle.
4. I can't stand to look at that bare space anymore.
5. It wouldn't be my first choice, but it's a family heirloom.
6. It wouldn't be my first choice, but it's the best I can afford.
7. It'll do until I find something better.
8. I wouldn't want to live with it forever, but it's a nice change.
9. It comes in fabulous colors. To be safe, though, I'll go with the beige.
10. It's only available in these 4 colors, so I'll just need to choose the best one.

The *only* criteria is, "Does this piece *honestly* reflect my unique, aesthetic needs?" With further scrutiny of the ten justifications listed above, it becomes clear that each has something in common. In each you are *settling* for something less than genuine. The only variable is the reason you've chosen a less than ideal option. When you settle, there's no opportunity for consideration of the unexpected, no option for that lovely dance with the creative Universe. Consciously learn to recognize the moment when you're about to settle. The "settling moment" is the time to back off. Once you retreat and regain a cleared mind, the excitement begins. What you originally had considered the best of all solutions is most times not as exceptional as a yet unimagined alternative poised to reveal itself.

Let's pick up now where we left off in the story of *clarity markers*. In our scenario your focus had shifted from the purchase of a coffee table to the realization that the rug wouldn't be replaced as first thought. Instead, the stain would be covered by a stunning area rug that provided direction for the best table style. It would be one with spare, unadorned legs to show off your new treasure.

After carefully measuring, you found that if it weren't for the one substantial side chair, you could use one of the larger square tables. You had been noticing such tables lately and they were quite attractive. Just that one corner of a square table would make it a little tight. In a passing silly thought, you wondered why no one's come up with an "L" shaped cocktail table.

Again, you remained patient, living with your current canvas. Now your wall to wall was shampooed and topped with zebra stripes. You continued to window shop and pay particular attention to the types of tables friends and relatives had in their homes. So far nothing had resonated with your *Word Stylings*. Then one day a home décor catalog arrived in the mail. Paging through with no intention to buy, there was "your coffee table."

Your table was better than any you could have imagined (i.e. existing design repertoire). It had spare legs that would best feature the throw carpet. Additionally, it was a nesting table. Although familiar with nesting tables, you'd never seen one meant to be placed in front of a sofa. The taller piece was a large rectangle and a matching smaller table nested beneath. Measuring exactly half the size of the rectangle, this one was square. When pulled out, the configuration was an "L"!

Instead of settling for either a smaller table *or* a larger table, you had found a table that provided the best of both. Your patient confidence had created a magnetically charged vibrational field. This potential rich field caused you to attract what you most needed both practically and aesthetically.

For me the simple act of naming my home, creating a list of genuine words and frequently reading my manifest blessing has averted impulse buying and decorating disasters. The home interior marketplace is designed to offer ever more unusual and stunning merchandise season after season. If you purchase your dream contemporary sofa this fall, by next spring there will be a more titillating one in the window. In most cases, however, it's the novelty that is enticing. Steadily build an interior with genuine pieces and the hunger to keep up with the latest and greatest begins to fade and eventually disappears.

When something grabs your attention, mindfully evaluate whether or not it is congruent with the authentic style you've set down in Word Stylings. Then, if you believe the item both resonates with your spirit and is a piece you need, you may wish to purchase it. I've found, however, that even when I feel certain about a particular object of desire, simply waiting a day or two, is valuable. This acts to remove the emotional element, that thrill of the find, from the prospective purchase. Restraint and what you "don't do" is as important as what you do. Recall that Chapter 1 was about letting go. Now we might want to let go of the desire to acquire.

When you decide not to purchase an item, the reward is twofold. First, a piece that isn't perfectly harmonious with your style doesn't clutter your space. Second, and perhaps more importantly, your decision in favor of restraint frees space physically, spiritually and financially for something that will truly nourish. If you are familiar with clearing clutter for optimal Feng Shui, you know that the best way to find the perfect pair of shoes is to clean out your shoe closet. Good things flow from the Universe when we have created space to receive them. With this in mind, I have come to be equally satisfied when I pass something up as when I purchase it.

Although there is no analysis to be done after writing your Manifest Blessing, there is something that can make it even more powerful. Essentially what you have done by writing a manifesto for your home's décor is the first step in "creative visualization." The idea is to create a clear mental picture of what you desire. Once you are able to envision your specific objectives and are certain that they honestly portray your dreams, then you must drench the images in positive energy that includes a belief in their possibility. Now you have created clear intention. This tremendously increases the likelihood that your desires will come to fruition.

This idea of creative visualization was first widely popularized in the late seventies by Shakti Gawain in her book, Creative Visualization. Gawain introduced us to the idea that abundance rather than limitation and lack is our natural path. Additionally, she revealed that for these concepts to work, it is not necessary to have a belief in any power outside of yourself. What is crucially necessary, however, is an unwavering belief in the possibility of your visualization. Gawain coaches us to "bring your mental picture to mind often both in quiet meditation and casually throughout the day." She continues, "Our mental commentary influences and colors our feelings and perceptions about what's going on in our lives, and it is these thought forms that ultimately attract and create everything that happens to us." [18]

Making your Manifest Blessing part of your daily mental commentary in order to enrich the energy that swirls about your ideas is easy. My suggestion is that you read your composition once or twice daily. Try not to make it a chore. If you are very busy, simply skip a day. What is more crucial than how frequently the Blessing is read is that you give your full attention to the words and ideas while creating a clear, mental image of your deepest desires. In subsequent chapters we will expand our creative visualization techniques even further in a fun and thought provoking Color Bridge.

18. Shakti Gawain, *Creative Visualization*, 28

There is a word of caution regarding the manifestation of our dreams by creating images in fields of positive energy. Recall that cosmic energy attracts that which is like itself. Remain mindful then, that fear of *not* reaching your aspirations can potentially energize the idea of *not* realizing your desired outcome. In other words, your repetitive thoughts of failure attract failure. It is best to not hold on too tightly and try to keep fear at bay. As with anything, this new way of thinking will become easier with each endeavor.

Word Stylings are complete. Your list of Genuine Words, your home's name and your Manifest Blessing are designed to work together to help you maintain integrity with regard to your personal style. With each carefully considered addition, elimination and rearrangement, you move closer to that tipping point when the greater portion of your room's design reflects the quintessence of your soul. At this signpost in your journey, remaining authentic becomes your natural path because your surroundings are nourishing, uplifting and ever so satisfying. Impatience dwindles. Confusion subsides while a profound contentment settles in. *Word Stylings* costs you nothing but your time and thought. Results, however, are dramatic!

CLEANSE

"Things that are loved, used and appreciated have strong, vibrant and joyous energies that allow the energy in the space to flow through and around them. (Further) you are connected to everything you own by fine strands of energy. When your home is filled with things you love or use well it becomes an incredible source of support and nourishment for you."
    Karen Kingston, Clearing Your Clutter with Feng Shui

In this month's cleanse you will take a breather from the physical removal and rearrangement of furnishings. Instead, you will become still and consider the phenomenal, magnetic qualities of both the objects in your home and your thoughts connected to them. Even before the publication of Rhonda Byrne's blockbuster bestseller, The Secret, it was generally accepted by those who study metaphysics that there is an "unfathomable magnetic power emitted through your thoughts."[19] Byrne's book stirred controversy and became the object of much satire because the concept simply sounds too easy and therefore unbelievable. Are we being asked to accept that if we only direct our thoughts toward wealth, health and happiness, then we will attract such riches to our lives? The answer is a "qualified" yes.

19. Rhonda Bynre, *The Secret*, 19

Our thoughts are like magnets. Good fortune gravitates toward positive thinkers. And conversely, those who look for the worst in every situation are likely to find it. The rub so to speak is that not only conscious thought, but also that which is subconscious is equally magnetic. An enormous portion of our thoughts are below the threshold of consciousness. And these are the deeply buried thoughts over which we have little control.

Learning to slow down and focus our attention is one effective way to become aware of the nature of our thoughts. Some who see the glass half empty don't realize the depth of negativity festering in their subconscious. This pessimism serves to attract further misfortune. The resulting misfortune stirs yet more gloomy thought. And so the spiral continues. However, a spiral in the opposite direction is also attainable. Calming the frenetic pace of our lives to provide opportunity for focused, reflective thought helps us censure some of that negativity. Each of us is to some degree innately optimistic. Dig deeply to uncover it. Then, like the song says, "accentuate the positive."

There is a second, less explored path to sweeten the thought patterns that swirl beneath consciousness. It is to bring our physical environment into closer alignment with our core aesthetic essence. This is the sum and substance of ColorFlow. Once you deeply internalize this premise and experience first hand the incredible rewards inherent in remaining honest to your inner self, what belongs and doesn't belong in your space becomes increasingly clear. As a growing proportion of furnishings reflect your artistic essence, the incredible source of support and nourishment to which author Karen Kingston refers, becomes palpable.

The quotation above from the book <u>Clearing Your Clutter with Feng Shui</u> by Karen Kingston is perhaps the most valuable in ColorFlow. The invisible fine strands of energy to which she refers are the magnetic field of attraction we discussed. Consider unfavorable attractions by imagining a block on your street where most of the houses are pristinely kept. Each is freshly painted and the yards are well manicured. There is one house, however, that is the neighborhood eyesore. The children who live there, from toddler to teens are unsupervised. They toss candy wrappers, soda cans and the like wherever convenient. Unfinished projects are piled in the side yard. The grass is infrequently mowed and trimming around the clutter is almost impossible.

No matter where we live, all of us at one time or another has had to pick up some form of litter in our yards. Why is it, though, that the "neighborhood eyesore family" we imagined attracts other people's litter more than the rest of us? It is the like attracts like magnetism. Theirs is already a messy yard. What's another gum wrapper? The person waiting to toss the used wrapper unconsciously perceives those fine strands of negative energy that emanate from the unkempt space. In the same way, if our own homes are "littered" with furnishings and accessories that are incongruent with our genuine self, other such items can take over before we realize.

I have noticed this most obviously in my family room/office. In the upstairs living room we had the hardwood refinished with a carefully chosen stain color. But in the family room, the distastefully colored linoleum tiles were left. The thought was, "they're in good shape and it's just a rec room." I love original artwork and so my most cherished pieces hang in the living room. Downstairs I hung a very traditional painting that someone was getting rid of. Certainly it didn't speak to me, but it was okay just to give a little color. I soon began to realize that all of my "decorating orphans" ended up in the family room where I write. At the same time I found myself bringing my laptop upstairs where I could think more clearly and creatively.

Many of these decorating orphans that appeared to collect on their own were simply beautiful but certainly not deeply genuine. Others were plainly not appealing no matter who the beholder. However, all were sapping my creative energy. I was subconsciously connected to them via an unseen magnetism. These furnishings did not genuinely uplift my spirits and so attracted disingenuous feelings deep within.

I am not proposing that you rush out to spend all of your efforts and a veritable fortune to bring each room in your home perfectly in line with your inner essence. What I do enthusiastically propose is that you become diligently attentive to each object in your surroundings. Equally scrutinize spaces where you might entertain guests as well as private areas of work and rest. Changes you decide upon should begin in the form of gentle shifts rather than abrupt, room wide transformations.

In my office, for instance, I removed the painting that hadn't stimulated me in subject matter, color or style. My intention had been to keep my artist eyes poised for something truly inspiring. I finally realized that amidst all of my busy bulletin boards and bookshelves, I craved the peacefulness of the absence of further wall décor. As for the flooring, it was impractical to replace the cold linoleum tiles. That could wait. But in the meantime, I found a luxuriously plush rug to fit under my desk. I love its warmth and texture under my feet as I write.

Now that I had become more cognizant of the décor in my workspace, I was less likely to allow the addition of new items that didn't belong. Those that were already in place, I saw with sharp artist eyes. I acquiesced to my husband's request to have a small TV in the room. However, a year earlier I would have thoughtlessly placed it on a rather homely table that had been stored in the attic. But at this point in my journey I took the time to sand and paint the little TV stand. I lovingly distressed the new green paint and chose a quirky knob for its single drawer. Previously, my mismatched jumble of furnishings only drew more of the same. Now, I had rotated my magnet in a new and favorable direction. I was furnishing the room with objects that stirred in me vibrant and joyous energies.

What all of this boils down to is that once you begin experiencing the rewards of a soul nourishing space, it becomes a joy to be discriminating about all that surrounds you. It is, in fact, the nest that keeps you safe from the world and joyously stimulated with the life you're creating.

Your living space will continue to draw the decorating clutter that clogs the flow of lively, nurturing energy unless the source of the attraction is addressed. Once you begin to use authentically nourishing colors, patterns and shapes, you will lose your desire to buy simply beautiful "stuff." These are the objects we tend to purchase for the temporary lift in spirits they provide. Instead, you will experience profound contentment in your deeply genuine space. Recall the concept of like attracting like. Your genuine space will attract only that which is authentic. The source for extraneous clutter will be gone and so it will no longer manifest.

Color Speak

Clarity Marker: Your home is drenched with your ColorPrint palette. You are attentive to your authentic design voice and have surrendered to the creative Universe with the gentle layering of adagio. With these principles in place, a subtle clue to a yet unconsidered design direction or solution materializes for any decorating perplexity. The idea promises to be the most uplifting and life balancing solution for your environment. This creative signal from the Universe, a *clarity marker*, portends genuine, aesthetic clarity.

Word Stylings: Your own collection of words that gently guides you in the creation of a unique environment manifesting in marvelous, free flowing energy. A list of Genuine Words, a name for your home and a Manifest Blessing are the key components of *Word Stylings*.

Color Study
The White Chart

"Never use pure white; it doesn't exist in nature."

Aldro T. Hibbard, American Painter 1886 - 1972

In a previous Color Study we discussed the color to neutral continuum and the role of neutrals in the décor. There was a bit of thought provoking information about white that until now you may not have considered. The use of both pure white and the popular neutral whites is so extensive, however, that further discussion is warranted.

Recall that choosing a backdrop of white walls is not optimal if your purpose in doing so is to leave the options open for palette changes down the road. It is also not ideal for brightening a dimly lit room. But by far the worst reason for choosing white is because you have been unable to come up with any other selection. The environments we create for ourselves are much too important to leave such a vast expanse of color to default. So you may wonder if there are any instances when pure white or creamy white walls are the optimal selection. Most definitely, yes.

The answer goes directly back to our discussion of repetition and variation, two techniques that can give a coherent flow to design. The eye is naturally drawn to white. And the closer to pure white, the stronger the magnetism becomes. The phenomenon is similar to our natural impulse to glance over at oncoming bright, white headlights on a dark night. Imagine then, that you have chosen furnishings and accessories with a tranquil analogous scheme. Envision each piece belonging to the yellow, yellow-green, green slice of the color wheel. And because your furnishings have been collected over time, there are no prosaically perfect color matches. Instead, there is watercolor imperfection in their relatedness.

Recall that ColorFlow suggests creating a nourishing environment *before* painting the walls. This provides a graphic opportunity to consider the ideal color to enhance your space. Now picture your rich, yellow-green analogous design against stark, white walls. Rather than luxuriating in a background that further enriches your carefully chosen decor, the severity of the walls only competes with the composition. The sharp contrast and lack of relatedness between the background and the foreground weakens the overall aesthetic impact.

Your color sophistication has become so profound that at this moment many of you are correctly speculating a far more satisfying solution. Add a color essence to the pure white rendering it a popular neutral. In other words, the walls will become an "off white." Choose a creamy white with undertones of yellow, yellow-green or green so that the walls relate to your sumptuous color palette. Now, rather that separating the elements in the space, your creamy walls tie each element one to the next. If you had your heart set on very light walls, you can still have them. This popular neutral will provide both the light value and the relatedness that make for a satisfying space.

It's important to note here that the popular white with a color essence extracted from your palette may make only the subtlest difference. A color skeptic may even say that the distinction is so barely noticeable that it isn't worth the trouble. There is a modicum of truth in that observation. The difference between the stark white and the white with undertones to mimic your furnishings is minimal on its face. However, the change in atmosphere as you take in the entire space is enormous. Your new white with a color essence to match the décor connects each element, whereas a pure white separates causing them to be dissociated. The pleasing interplay of related colors is something that is more felt on a visceral level rather than seen on a physical level. And how a space makes you feel is everything!

There is a second set of circumstances when white walls can be quite pleasing. Again, we go back to repetition and variation. If there are a number of pure white pieces among your furnishings and accessories, then white may prove a delightful background. And this time, there is no need to add even an essence of color. Once again, my color sophisticated readers know why. In the same way that terra cotta colored walls support a décor rich in red-oranges, so do white walls strengthen a design that includes elements of white. The color, no matter if it is terra cotta or white, appears to belong when it is repeated. In other words, it looks planned and deliberate. The eye is not drawn to a single element that looks out of place. Instead, the eye is rhythmically pulled around and through the composition by similar elements of color.

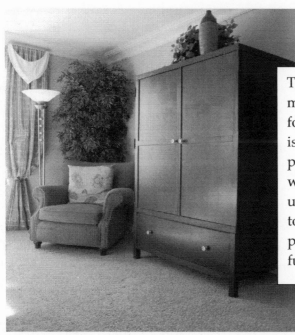

The color on these walls may very well have been found on a white chart. It is not a pure white, but a popular, neutral white. The wall color has warm yellow undertones that relate well to the browns, golds and pumpkin oranges of the furnishings.

The walls in this bedroom, by contrast, have been painted a stark white. The pure neutral works in this setting because the same white had been chosen for the bedding and accessories such as the picture frames and lampshades. The white of the walls relates to the items in the space.

Another consideration is the pairing of a single color and white. A black and white tiled floor, green and white gingham curtains, red and white toile de Jouy fabric and blue and white porcelain are all classics. They are fresh. They are no fail. And we never seem to tire of these "and white" combinations.

Let's refresh our knowledge of the artist's color wheel. The primary colors are those that are purely one hue. They are not a mixture of other colors and are in their most saturated form. They are bright and bold. The primaries are red, yellow and blue. Be cautious of using any of these paired *only* with white. Because both the primary and the white are pure, these pairings can sometimes appear shallow, two-dimensional and at worst juvenile.

This by no means says that you shouldn't use any of the three primaries with white. But red, yellow or blue when paired with white usually needs something to provide depth and character. This can be accomplished with one or any combination of three techniques. First, add an additional deep value, popular neutral to ground the composition. Second, instead of using pure white, opt for a creamy off-white. And third, adjust the ratio of the colors used in the room to add interest and sophistication.

Secondary and tertiary hues also pair beautifully with white. Remember that these lie between the primaries and are made up of more than one color. The secondaries, green, violet and orange are each equal mixtures of two primaries. Each tertiary hue is also a mixture of two colors. However, now the two hues appear in *unequal* portions. The components of red-violet are red and violet. But because violet, itself is made from red and blue, then red-violet is actually roughly two parts red and one part blue. This uneven ratio of colors adds further complexity to the tertiary colors. And complexity of color is one element that adds depth and refinement to a scheme.

We've discussed several techniques for finessing a palette of a color and white to create more sophisticated harmonies. Now you may be wondering if there are specific circumstances when a combination of exclusively a single hue plus white can be pleasing. In other words, is there a setting when we wouldn't consider changing the white to cream, grounding the room with a deeper value popular neutral or manipulating the ratios of hues? Yes!

There are rooms that I think of as "specialty spaces." These are rooms where you wish to create an atmosphere that is significantly different from the balance of the home. When walking into a specialty space the change should be palpable. Your mood is transformed as you leave the mundane behind.

Two great examples of these kinds of spaces are a baby's nursery and a Florida or sunroom. Think of the purpose in creating these unique places. A baby has a dramatically different lifestyle than any of the teen, young adults or adults in the household. Therefore, the mood of this room can and should be softer, gentler, dreamier. An airy, lemon yellow and white, for instance, that may not be appropriate for any other room conveys a gentle, playful atmosphere just right for baby.

Similarly, a Florida room or sunroom exudes an atmosphere of relaxation and mimics the outdoors. This is a space for plants and trees. People are visitors to this lush, botanical space. Here, too, any color and white can serve as a wonderful background to the vivid greens of the foliage. You may have a specialty space unique to your family. Consider whether one of the "and white" schemes could work for you.

A final consideration when deciding to use a palette of a single color and white is the hue of any permanent element in your space. There are myriad items in our homes that have color even if we've never thought of them in this way. And if any possesses even a subtle color essence, then this undertone must be considered in your overall harmony.

These kinds of permanent items often have to do with wood, whether it be hardwood floors, trim or furniture items that will not be replaced. Beyond wood, there are brass and chrome furnishings, stone and brick fireplaces, kitchen appliances, bathroom fixtures, rugs and tile floors that may appear to be neutral. Upon closer inspection many neutrals in your space have an essence of color. Engage your artist's eyes to consider all existing hues before creating a color palette for a particular room.

The "and white" palette never loses popularity. This is testament to its crisp, timeless allure. So go ahead. If you love the look, choose a color from your authentic ColorPrint, pair it with white and enjoy the flow.

"What I dream of is an art of balance."
Henri Matisse

Chapter 8

THE BALANCING ACT
Your Personal Color Recipe

When it comes to design and specifically to color in design, balance is key in the attainment of one's aesthetic ideal. But paradoxically, we give the concept of balance little attention. For many of us, the consideration afforded balance of color in our décor is so minimal that an in-depth discussion is in order.

First let's look at exactly where you are in the journey to discover your authentic ColorPrint. I would venture to guess that the initial colors, perhaps the first two or three, surfaced rather easily. Whether you have unearthed the next hue, have only a clue perhaps with regard to its temperature or remain at a complete standstill, each one of us experiences some level of plateau. In all likelihood there will be a phase during which you'll feel a marked slowing in your rate of discovery.

I believe that this plateau occurs after discovering hues that are already rather familiar. Additionally, the most easily discovered colors are those that will eventually occupy the larger surface areas of our spaces. Perhaps a green has always appeared in our designs, but we were just never certain of the precise green. Or maybe, we had consistently gravitated toward the shades of autumn. The reds, golds and oranges were safe and so we never ventured further in search of additional hues that would support and deepen their nurturing powers. We became lulled into believing that the best décor we were capable of creating was an anemic caricature that mimicked the richly genuine palette that remained yet partially obscured.

So why then, are the remaining colors on our Prints so difficult to shake from the depths of our psyches? One reason is because our color creativity has been slowly yet systematically squelched beginning in childhood. And we've come to believe that if we accept a color onto our palette, it will be utilized in the same way as every other color. In other words, we assume that each hue will occur in approximately equal amounts and in the same kinds of places.

To illustrate the point, ask anyone the color of their living room. Almost everyone will answer with the color they've painted the walls. That's *only* the background. What about the sofa and the chairs and the pillows and the artwork? Two hues on my ColorPrint are a red-violet which is actually magenta and a medium to light value coffee brown. I would be much more likely to paint the walls with the coffee brown and save the red-violet for a small accent pillow. It is no surprise that I discovered the brown to be one of my authentic colors before the red-violet. *However, the red-violet plays an equally important role in the palette of my room.* Remove the magenta, and the coffee brown loses its smooth flavor.

It is interesting to note here that there are a few tertiary colors that for reasons unknown are simply unconsidered by most people. They are yellow-orange, yellow-green, red-orange and red-violet. Because red-violet is on my ColorPrint I enjoy including it as a dramatic accent in my almost exclusively neutral living room. Recently I had enlisted the help of a clerk in a needlework shop to choose yarn colors for a needlepoint canvas I was about to begin. It was a botanical design with three orchid blooms on a pale green background. I began to pull strands of yarn that were a red-violet instead of the more expected pure violet. The clerk looked very dismayed and warned, "Do you realize that's magenta?" When I said that I did, she gave up on me and busied herself in another part of the store.

As is often the case, the ColorFlow analogy that comes to mind is one related to food. Some foods are more potent than others and so are normally consumed in smaller amounts. Garlic is a good example. If you love garlic, it is as necessary to your spaghetti sauce as the tomatoes, although you use much less due to its powerful flavor. And in the color harmony of my living room the neutral brown and the red-violet also share equal importance. However, the red-violet, or magenta, is more potent and therefore like the garlic considerably less is needed for equal aesthetic nourishment. We tend in most areas to consider starring roles rather than those that support.

It's a good time to begin thinking about the balance of color. There are main colors and supporting colors. Each is as vital as the other and in many cases are not interchangeable. A color that might be used as an accent may never be attractive to us on a large surface. The plateau in our color journey usually occurs just after the discovery of our main colors. We may decorate a room with only these, feel pretty good and call it a day. But a rich flow in our lives can only be achieved if we are willing to dig deeper, unearthing our supporting colors. Although these hues may appear only in small doses, they have the potential to elevate our surroundings from satisfying to sumptuous.

Each of us has heard some version of a rule of thumb concerning proportion in the use of color. The most popular is that a successful design has a main color, a supporting color and an accent color. I recently heard a television diva tout the formula 60, 30, 10. Almost any proportion advice having to do with color in design is similar. And it will all work beautifully provided that you know how to implement it. But for a pleasing balance of hues, it's a bit more complicated than dressing 60 percent of your room in one color, 30 percent in another and rounding out the final 10 in an accent hue.

The value of color, its intensity and how each hue is distributed around the room serves to either enhance or detract from that which it colors. These three qualities share equal or perhaps more significance than simply the quantity of each color in a room.

Let's begin with value and intensity. The lightness or darkness of a color is its value. Intensity is the measure of its purity or brightness. When dealing with the balance of color within a space, value and intensity are actually far more important than the colors themselves. It is these qualities in combination that lend either pleasing balance to the composition or skew the room into lopsided disproportion. A few simple examples will illustrate the point.

We've all heard an amateur decorator or a TV designer say something to the effect, "To balance the large entertainment center on this side of the room, we'll place the tall Chinese screen across from it on the opposite side." It makes sense. However, this is balance as it refers to size. And we're all pretty good at that. Our discussion focuses on balance as it refers to colors and particularly to the value and intensity of those colors.

The illustration at left is a literal depiction of the outcome were an elephant to jump on one side of a seesaw and a mouse on the other. The elephant, of course, weighing far more than the mouse will cause the seesaw to tip completely in favor of his side. Notice that both the mouse and the elephant appear in their natural, light value, low intensity gray coloration.

Now banish all thoughts of actual physical weight. Instead, this picture represents "visual weight." The elephant has remained pale gray which is light in value and low in intensity. A color with these characteristics has very little visual weight. In other words, even though the elephant is large in size, the qualities of his coloration make him a featherweight.

The mouse now has become a rosy pink which is a bit darker and higher in intensity than the pale gray. The increased potency in both value and intensity gives the mouse more visual weight. Hence, the mouse weighs down his side of the seesaw. The small mouse is able to more significantly balance the elephant by virtue of his coloration, not by his size.

Finally, the mouse has become a brilliant magenta. The value of this saturated hue is even darker; the intensity yet brighter. Without any increase in size, the mouse's potency with regard to value and intensity has given him enough visual weight to be in perfect balance with the elephant. Now, although the elephant physically weighs many more pounds than the tiny mouse, visually they are perfectly balanced.

In the previous illustrations the mouse's color increased in both value and intensity. As he did, he became visually more weighty. However, a mouse, a pillow, a piece of furniture or in fact anything gains visual weight if its color becomes a darker value or its intensity heightens. In other words, both value and intensity both do not have to change to add visual weight.

For instance, imagine in the seesaw example that value were the only variable. In the second illustration, the mouse would have become a darker gray, but intensity would remain low. He wouldn't be brighter, but his value would be darker. Still he would gain visual weight. In the third illustration, the mouse would become charcoal gray or almost black. Again, simply by increasing his value, he would gain more visual weight.

But how does visual weight apply to your décor? Recall the scenario of the large TV armoire on one side of the room balanced in size by a tall Chinese screen on the other side. On TV design shows, exactly what's needed is often serendipitously stored away in the homeowners' garage. If you aren't quite as lucky, such obstacles can sometimes be worked out with color.

To balance décor with color I find it valuable to make a sketch plugging in key pieces of furniture. Then I briefly describe those pieces with regard to value and intensity. Armed with this information, I know unequivocally to which side of the room my imaginary scale of visual weight is tipping. It is really like sketching an illustration similar to those on the previous page substituting articles of furniture for the elephant and the mouse. This simple exercise has proven so worthwhile that I have named it the *ColorFlow Scale of Visual Weight* and have chosen to include it in Color Speak.

Imagine the TV armoire. Most are sizable. However, the thrust of our discussion is that visual weight as well as actual weight must be considered in the creation of a pleasing, aesthetic balance within a space. To say that it must be counterbalanced with a large Chinese screen is assuming that the armoire is visually weighty. However, the entertainment center/armoire which houses all of the media equipment in my home is a luminous, white lacquer fitted with glass shelving. All of the elements in this type of cabinet are visually lightweight; the white, the sheen and the glass. This is a good opportunity to note that luminous or shiny finishes tend to be lighter in visual weight than heavier, matte surfaces.

On the wall opposite the TV is the sofa. Before purchasing our new couch we lived for a couple of years with a bulky, medium to darker green one.

Although the sofa was actually smaller in size than the entertainment center, its value and intensity caused it to be visually weightier. Eventually we purchased a new sofa. The lines were sleeker and the color was lighter in value. In the meantime, there were ways to visually lift the old, heavier sofa that needed to remain for reasons both financial and practical.

The first and most obvious way to lighten the bulkier side was to decrease the surface area of the visually heavy green couch. It was, indeed, the green hue that was disproportionately weighty. The sofa had come with four pillows in fabric identical to the body. I covered two of them in a highly textured, nubby cream fabric and the remaining two in an equally textured, celery green.

These first steps, the sketch and simply lightening the pillows, released sparkling, positive energy of transformation into the Universe. And so in my knowing, I relaxed. With the path toward further artistic equilibrium yet obscured, I delighted in other aspects of domesticity assured that the synchronous cosmos would in perfect time signal the next step.

And not surprisingly, synchronicity materialized. Searching eBay for something totally unrelated to my living room, I had typed in a couple of key words. As frequently happens, a few unrelated items popped up. The category was Home and Garden > Furniture. I quickly scrolled through the list, but luckily stopped at a set of four unfinished, wood bun feet suitable for a sofa or chair. My old green couch was worn mostly on the bottom skirt from the claws of a cat we once had. The bun feet would take only minutes to stain and install. The skirt could easily be removed and I would be left with a sofa not only visually, but physically lifted!

Needless to say, I purchased the bun feet and proceeded with the plan. The room was instantly more balanced and I felt a greater sense of emotional equilibrium when spending time there. It was all part of the flow that had become significantly noticeable in my life. At this point in my metamorphosis there was a pleasing balance of visual weight between the entertainment center and the sofa. However, my symmetry of visual weight had been achieved only with regard to value. I had not addressed a balanced distribution of color between the sides of the room.

The white of the lacquered finish was mirrored in the pillows on the opposite side. Recall that the eye is comforted by repetition. A soothing balance of color could have been further enhanced by placing a lush, green plant next to the armoire. The green would echo the green couch while the soft curves of the leaves would serve as a foil to the straight, sleek lines of the cabinet. Perhaps a decorative green box could be placed on one of the glass shelves.

Balance in both color and visual weight needs to be considered not only laterally as in the example, but vertically. As a floral designer, I like to think of the entire room as a mixed bouquet. If the palette is yellow, pink and blue, you wouldn't want all of the pinks on one side of the arrangement and the yellows and blues on the other. Nor would you want all of the pink blossoms near the bottom, the yellows in the middle and the blues near the top. Most of us do a far better job at side to side than bottom to top balance. This could be because addressing balance of color and visual weight as it appears vertically is not as clear-cut as side to side equilibrium.

An aesthetically pleasing balance of visual weight and color from floor to ceiling is truly more a matter of a pleasing dispersal than equal distribution. For instance, if you have a visually heavy, brown leather sofa at floor level, you do not need an equally heavy piece of artwork above. On the other hand, placing a miniature mirror above it won't work either.

Think of this pleasing dispersal as the leafy branches of a plant. The largest and most abundant leaves are near the base. The number of leaves *gradually* decreases until there are none at the very tip. Further, as you move up the branch, each side shoot becomes more slender, the leaves more delicate. The whole package is a lesson in grace. And this is the grace in design we need to mimic in order to achieve an aesthetically seductive balance of vertical, visual weight. Repetition of color, mass and visual weight in gradually decreasing increments as you move toward the ceiling is a good way to achieve pleasing vertical balance. It will add amazing finesse to your final design.

Here, just before leaving our discussion of balance is an instructively valuable time to caution you of a common design hazard. It has to do with both balance and with the best place to start in the seemingly enormous endeavor of redecoration. We often begin by choosing the smaller items; lamps, occasional tables, ottomans, pillows, gorgeous cashmere throws, and then work outward to the larger pieces. We do this because it's easy and the gratification is instant. You can come home with something wonderful this afternoon and your bank account isn't completely drained. Ethel Rompilla, author of Color for Interior Design, calls this the "pillow or footstool syndrome." She continues, "It is best to consider the largest areas first; floors, walls, major pieces of furniture." [20]

20. Ethel Rompilla, *Color For Interior Design*, 194

173

This pillow syndrome can get you into trouble. Start with a couple of pillows and now you have specific limitations with regard to the larger pieces. They are the more expensive items, ones you'll want to live with long term. It is better to choose the substantial elements first and then create balance and interest with the smaller pieces.

| *Imprint* |
| **The Ascent to Balance** |

Close your eyes and sit comfortably in an upright position. Imagine yourself alone under an ancient sycamore tree. Autumn nears and the summer's warmth begins its retreat to the earth's core. In spring the soil was cool and the air warm. Now as the air chills, it is the soil that retains the heat of the passing season. The atmosphere is exhilarating and brings us a resurgence of energy just before winter's slumber. And as the world experiences transformation, our perceptivity sharpens.

Sit comfortably with your feet flat on the floor, your back upright and your palms resting upward in your lap. Close your eyes and begin to inhale and exhale slowly from your belly practicing the comforting and now familiar Hara breathing. Recall that life-giving energy flows most naturally and abundantly when we breathe from this center of gravity deep in the belly.

As I count from ten to one, take deep breaths that originate in the Hara, your vast Sea of Energy. At the same time, imagine rays of energy that originate within your body and radiate from your feet downward. These rays parallel the fluid, winding pathways created by the roots of the aged tree under which you sit. Just as the sycamore draws nourishment from the earth below, so too, do you extract power and enlightenment from the earth's primordial core.

Let's begin. Ten nine eight seven six. Recall that Hara breathing is a way to revert to a more natural way of being. And rediscovering your innately authentic colors in perfect balance will help you live in the natural life flow you deserve. Five four three two one. You are incredibly relaxed and grounded in the earth below. The rays of energy emitted earthward from the soles of your feet both help you remain steady in life's journey and serve to connect you to the family of ancient artistic souls from which you've sprung.

Imagine now that you are able to maintain your connectedness to the core while ascending effortlessly into the leafiness of the tree. A single, massive limb reaches eastward as if waiting to welcome each recurring sunrise. On the opposite side of the sycamore, a pair of limbs, smaller in size, balance the enormous, solitary eastern arm. The two limbs in tandem are charged with gently placing the sun back on the horizon at day's end, their strength together equaling the tree's opposing side.

Continue your ascent. As you look from side to side, there is equal balance. But look below and you will see a broader mass of limb and leaf. It is nature's perfect plan. Supporting you from below is a solid foundation. No matter how far you move skyward, there will always be a firm underpinning keeping you afloat. This gives both the composition of your design and the fabric of your existence the nourishing balance each of us desperately craves.

Until now the missing link in achieving balance has been the clear, strong connection to our authentic selves. It is necessary to re-enter the natural flow of life. Only then is it possible to rebuild the complex root system that connects us to our authenticity. Perfect clarity and balance is normal once this vital connection is rediscovered. Life becomes simpler as you lose the need to judge and weigh and question. You know yourself and live according to what feels right for you.

When a storm appears, life may change. However, your life is in perfect balance, in a state of perfect flow. Changes, then will be more gentle because you are in a natural state of flexible preparedness for transformation.

Storms will come and storms will pass. And when they do the ancient tree will sway and it will bend and it may shake. But ah ... perfect balance is its protector. The tree will not fall and neither will you.

> *"The old tree shook. White blossoms slowly float down,*
> *Dancers in the wind."*
> *(Alexandra Kim)*

Mentally count with me slowly and rhythmically from one to ten. As I say each number, visualize a perfect white blossom floating downward from the tree. One two three four five. Look down and see five pristine blossoms strewn about the massive roots of the sycamore tree where you sit. Six seven eight nine ten. Return from your Imprint mentally refreshed and eager to continue your journey.

This chapter's Color Bridge is designed with two intentions. The first is to guide you to unearth the final hues on your ColorPrint. Recall that the initial colors to reveal themselves were easier because they were the ones hovering closer to the surface of your conscious mind. In many cases these are the colors that you may actually have used before. They are what I have come to refer to as *comfortable large surface colors*. You can comfortably imagine using them on large surfaces such as walls, floors and sofas. You are familiar with these hues simply because you've had trial and error practice in using them. We've all *had* to cover large surfaces.

It is the accent colors, those edgy, offbeat, anything but neutral hues that remain tenaciously concealed from our conscious. Used in much smaller doses as accents, many of us have been too timid to experiment with these supporting hues. Once the larger surface colors are chosen, we believe our palette to be complete when in reality the excitement hasn't yet begun. It is the *edgy limited surface colors* when added to our yet thin color harmony that cause the large surface hues to literally sing!

The second intention here is to explore the precise balance of these two types of colors that most appeals to you. We'll do this in a way that allows for creative, artistic experimentation while removing the fear of costly decorating mistakes. In fact, it won't feel like decorating at all. We're about to play.

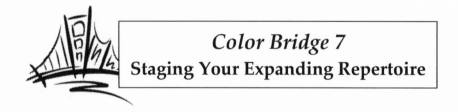

Color Bridge 7
Staging Your Expanding Repertoire

"The ability to simplify means to eliminate the unnecessary
so that the necessary may speak."
Hans Hoffmann, Introduction to the Bootstrap, 1993

When Hans Hoffman wrote this thought provoking sentiment, he did not have the design of our domestic spaces in mind. However, the essence of the thought is universal and can be applied to any number of areas in our lives. It has to do with sweeping away the extraneous so that focus on the elements of greatest importance is both possible and encouraged.

If, for instance, you receive an urgent phone call, you may turn off the TV and ask the children to quiet down. Or say you decide to pay bills and realize that your desk is full of correspondence, homework papers to be signed and recipes that haven't been filed. In order to fully focus on the bills, first you clear the desk of everything but the bills. It's time now to apply this same principle that we use on a regular basis to the haven we are creating.

In this Bridge you will sweep away the extraneous, the hues you know *not* to be on your ColorPrint leaving only those that are an innate part of your deepest, artistic essence. Enveloped only by your genuine colors, you will for the first time, experience total connectedness with your palette. The effect will be as if you were infused with both profound support for your dreams and incredible, life balancing energy. These qualities are not inherent in the colors themselves, but in your idiosyncratic relationship with their vibrational qualities. Your perfect combination of hues produces an aura that effortlessly aligns you with the flow of a gentle, balanced life rhythm.

The Bridge is actually sort of a hybrid. It is a Bridge that is a Cleanse. As we become more sophisticated students of ColorFlow we see that each portion of our study, the Cleanses, the Imprints, the Color Bridges and the Color Studies are all irrevocably and beautifully interrelated. Begin by choosing either a room or an area of a room that will undergo a "color cleanse." Once it is clear how this works, it will be easier to choose the specific area of your home that can manageably be transformed.

Make a list of the hues that you know to be on your ColorPrint. Write them in your Studio. Refer to Chapter 2 for a detailed review of how they are written. Basically, each color is given two names, the color wheel name and a personal moniker you have chosen reflecting the theme or aura of your perfect space.

Now observe the space you've chosen to recolor. Remove items that have as their main color, hues that are not on your Print. Take away only what you can temporarily live without. For example, although you may detest the color of your husband's recliner, it must stay for reasons of comfort and practicality.

Additionally, there will be furniture and accessories that are multi-hued. It is appropriate and in fact beneficial to have small splashes of colors that do not appear on your personal palette. Remember that colors are like vitamins. You need a little bit of everything. Your ColorPrint hues are simply the ones most vital to your inner essence. If you love blue and tend toward cooler colors, your seascape painting will stay even though there are touches of green, gray, yellow and the warm red of a fisherman's boat. Any space would appear stark and void of character if your ColorPrint hues were used to the *total* exclusion of any other color.

Next, it's time to attend to those items that are not on your palette, but can't feasibly be removed. Let's say that so far blue-violet, green, blue-green and a creamy, off white neutral are on your ColorPrint. Imagine that the fabric on your recliner is a muted green and red plaid. Until engaging your artist's eyes for this Bridge, you may not have noticed that the recliner's green is actually quite close to the green on your personal Print. The red, on the other hand, truly doesn't work for you.

Search other areas of your home for an item that could be used to disguise the piece bringing it more closely in line with your desired palette. Bear in mind that this is your first rough draft, a tentative sketch of your final, genuine color palette and design. Your "disguise" will not be a permanent solution. You are simply trying to "flesh out" the new harmony you believe to be yours. Think of it as a dress rehearsal before making long term and many times expensive changes to your décor.

In your bedroom is a cream colored throw. It is a popular neutral that appears on your Print. Opening the throw blanket to its largest dimensions, toss it over the chair. I have discovered thin U-shaped pins at the sewing store that are great for tucking in your disguise around the arms and cushions for a neater look. Even though all of the red is not gone, the proportion of red to the other, more desirable colors in the space has decreased. And that's the object of this exercise. You are tipping the balance in favor of your true colors.

Now, scour the house for an accessory that will further shift attention away from the remaining plaid fabric. Perhaps there's a small, blue-violet pillow in the family room that could be placed on the chair. This "staging" of an area shares similarities with the Vignette created in Color Bridge 4. In that exercise, you borrowed from family or friends and even looked outdoors for color inspiration. Use these resources once again. It's possible that blue-violet is a color you've never used in your décor, but perhaps your neighbor has something in just the right hue for you to try.

Consider swapping accessories and even furniture from other rooms. It is often the case that a color you've discovered to be on your unique palette currently appears somewhere in your home. You may have never given the color much consideration until recently. But at the time of purchase, somewhere deep in your subconscious you recognized a genuine affinity for the hue. Several years before my ColorFlow journey began, I bought a solid, violet colored bedspread. It was summer and I wanted something different, something lighter and brighter to revitalize my bedroom. It was a hue that back then I would never have considered for say, my living room. On sale at an unbelievable price, I purchased it for a quick pick me up.

Years later I recognized violet as an authentic ColorPrint hue. I recall folding the purple spread into a lengthwise panel to cover all three cushions of my gray green sofa. If colors could sing, the green sofa that I had once thought of as just okay, transformed into a sweet melody. But this was simply the stepping stone to the more permanent, sophisticated furnishings I have today. When the green couch finally succumbed to snacks, kids and animals, I chose one covered in a cream microfiber. On it are pillows in violets and blues.

Finally, fill in the space where appropriate with additional items in your Print hues. Think beyond interior design into other realms. Silk scarves and pashmina are wonderful to either add a ColorPrint hue or to camouflage one that you believe to be out of sync with your Print. As a part-time florist, I am always thinking of flowers as a means to introduce elements of color. If you have unearthed orange as an authentic hue, a generous vase of persimmon mums can help to fill out your "work in progress."

The effort exerted during this Bridge stirs and enhances life energy. Expect the appearance of synchronicity. Once when experimenting with this sort of activity, I ran out to a local nursery for an unrelated project. For years the nursery had a giftware section. Dispensing with that part of the business, the items were on sale at incredible reductions. I spotted a contemporary glass vase in the yellow-green on my ColorPrint. Back at home I remembered that my white lilies were in full bloom. They were perfect for the new vase. The arrangement added both color and sparkling ch'i energy to the room.

Now you've removed all possible extraneous color from the room and camouflaged the unfavorable hues where necessary. Colors from your ColorPrint have been added. Whatever your initial reaction, postpone final judgement until you've lived with the space for a couple of weeks. In the meantime keep a "Staging for Expanded Repertoire Diary" in your Studio. Simply jot down thoughts and feelings about the space as they occur to you. You may even become inspired to make further alterations to your staged space. It is important that you write about these ongoing inspirational bursts. Following is an abbreviated example of what your diary may look like.

Color Bridge 7 Staging Your Expanding Repertoire

Friday, June 8

My first reaction isn't great. The space I staged looks unpolished and less sophisticated than the rest of my home. I'm trying to observe with my artist's eyes. I think I can see that what I'm focusing on is the temporary look of things . . . the coverlet thrown over the chair and the pillows that are the right color, but way too elegant a fabric for the room. I'm hoping I just need a few days to get used to the lack of perfection I have always strived for.

Friday, June 15

The most significant, positive impression I'm noticing as the week goes by is how I feel when coming from other parts of the house into my color cleansed, staged space. The only way I can describe it is, "Ahhhhhhh." The most amazing experience is that twice, I started a small task in another area of the house only to pick up and move to my authentic, color enriched room. It's where I really choose to be. Could this be that nebulous "flow" that's been discussed again and again?

Thursday, June 21

Today I began to make some changes to my space. The blue-green appears just here and there in very small quantities. Even though it's just meant to be an accent color, it looks "spotty." What I did was group together a couple of items that share the blue-green making fewer, but larger statements. I especially like the large turquoise and brown urn on the table beneath my seascape. Love that brown! Until I saw these two items together, I wouldn't have imagined how pleasantly the brown of the pottery relates to the brown in the frame above it.

Tuesday, June 26

Brown must be another popular neutral for me along with cream. By itself, I've always been pretty ambivalent about it. But along with my blue-violet, green and blue-green, it really speaks to me. I'm wondering if its warmth is what I needed to balance the coolness of my other hues. I'm thinking of getting the chair reupholstered. It'll be a great start to the space that has become my favorite retreat.

Saturday, June 30

I chose this space to color stage because my family seems to use it less frequently than other rooms in the house. Thought I wouldn't disrupt too much by experimenting in here. But now my husband and kids use this room more often. I think the nourishing energies here are making me calmer and more upbeat, nicer to be with. It's beginning to be a space we can all enjoy.

Wow! If your color cleanse yields half as many discoveries as the one above, you will have certainly leaped forward on your journey. A couple of key points brought to light by the sample diary are vital. First, notice that there was no "love at first sight." No matter what significant alteration you make to your décor, whether it be a new paint color or a new piece of furniture, your first reaction is not solely to the new item, but to the concept of change itself. It is wise to reserve judgement until the jolt of the transformation settles in. Then you can be completely objective about the new look.

Also bear in mind that what you see is not your final interior design. You have isolated color to the exclusion of style, pattern, texture and proportion. We all have had many opportunities to think only of color. That's what we do when placing two paint chips side by side to decide if we are attracted to the marriage. We drape a fabric next to the wood of the floor, again isolating the element of color. However, the color staging exercise thrusts us deeper. Paint chips and draped fabrics provide no more than a fleeting brush with our innate color chemistry.

This Bridge is longer term and occurs in your own home with your own belongings. Thus it allows a more genuine evaluation of your attraction to the harmony. Surrounded by your unique color palette, you go about your daily routine enveloped in the hues. You get a sense for the pervading aura created by the color melange. Beyond this sense, take into account that eventually you will attend to those remaining elements of design and enhance your already nourishing color composition.

The greatest gain during this exercise may be that you will live with your colors at times when your conscious mind engages in matters having nothing to do with color or design. While in your color cleansed space, perhaps you'll read a novel, balance your checkbook or play with the dog. In these moments, your conscious mind with respect to your décor, is completely at ease and therefore non-judgmental.

Your relaxed subconscious continues to accurately measure your deepest feelings toward the color aura. At the same time, it effortlessly generates additional information to fill the voids in your discoveries thus far. Your subconscious could, for instance, note a distasteful imbalance among saturated hues and neutrals. It could even sense an intrinsic need for an additional color.

Contrast this to the occasions when you are focusing your attention only on color. At these times, you bring a great deal of emotional baggage to your observations. "Will that green be too muted?" "I've always heard that blues and greens don't combine well." " These hues are so brilliant. I've never thought of myself as this colorful. Better just choose off white, *again.*" Remember design chatter? All of this wondering, questioning and fear can all but silence your authentic design voice.

The lesson here is to relax, let go of perfection and feel the flow of your authentic palette. This is nothing more than a dress rehearsal of your nourishing ColorPrint.

CLEANSE

"Go confidently in the direction of your dreams!
Live the life you've imagined. As you simplify your life,
the laws of the universe will be simpler."
Henry David Thoreau

There is a nearly magical catalyst for moving forward in the direction of your genuine dreams. It is the elimination from your surroundings all things relating to past dreams that were less than genuine. In brutally simple terms, get rid of unfinished projects. Don't beat yourself up over a seeming lack of focus. We've all experienced this and in many cases these "false starts" were a necessary part of the discovery of our authentic aspirations, those ambitions most closely in sync with our inner essence.

Recall that everything, all that we physically see and the entirety of what we think and feel, is nothing more than energy in motion. And the characteristic of energy most vital to attaining life's sweet flow is that energy attracts like energy. Therefore, if your home is filled with unfinished tasks and projects that represent unfulfilled dreams, you are simply attracting additional detours along the path to your truest dreams.

Examples of such mired energy might be all of those Moroccan spices that have languished in the kitchen cabinet four years after taking an evening class in Near Eastern Cuisine. The notion of a hobby in international cooking has faded as the kids' schedules got busier.   And recall the resumes you had worked on so diligently when thoughts of a new career path were at the top of your list. It was just then that an unexpected opportunity beckoned you in an entirely different direction. It is one that you are happy with and don't wish to change. The freshly copied resumes, now out of date, remain abandoned somewhere in the bottom desk drawer.

An additional, less slow moving energy, lies in items associated with goals already realized. I have a mantra for these kinds of accomplishments. "Keep the kudos; ditch the clutter." A common example here is college textbooks. You may want to hang on to a few that are very specific to your field, but let go of the others. It frees the flow to continually deepening knowledge. In other words, you are not stuck at your previous educational level. Open yourself both physically and emotionally to the infinite wisdom of the Universe. A diploma hung on the wall is a great reminder of your enormous accomplishment. Those are the kudos. However, the text, _Intro. to Basket Weaving_, most likely should move on. That's the clutter.

Each of these items is a form of stuck energy from your past. They are not only impertinent to your present, but have no relevance to the sparkling future you so deserve. This type of clogged energy emits vibrations consistent with the absence of progress. In fact, it signals the Universe of your desire to remain stagnant. Clear away the stuck energy if you feel any sort of "block" in the movement and rhythm of your artistic journey.

You may be experiencing something akin to the dieter who after several months of effort ceases to shed pounds as rapidly as when the diet began. Nutritionists call this a weight loss "plateau." A new strategy can many times jump-start the process. The same is true for your aesthetic journey. Cleansing your living space of both abandoned and already fulfilled dreams can be precisely what is necessary to jump-start your color journey.

Become mindful that yet another characteristic of the energy flowing through your home is that it is literal, non-judgmental and all encompassing. That which surrounds you leaves a detailed imprint on your psyche. You may believe that you haven't noticed the half completed sweater sitting in a basket near your desk. You began knitting it two winters ago, but simply got too busy to continue. _Everything_ in your environment speaks to your unconscious in the most literal manner. The sight of the knitting and any long overdue, unfinished project negatively affect you each time you enter the room.

Still not convinced of the power of color and form and literally everything we see in our environments? Consider that millions of dollars are spent annually by advertisers on logos and other visuals. They know the enormous potential that lies in what we see. I once worked in the publications department of a financial services company. At that time the appearance of a dollar sign ($) on the cover of a mutual funds investor report was strictly prohibited by the Federal Trade Commission. The reasoning was the strong visual connotation of a promise of profit with the purchase of a particular fund.

That which surrounds you at home is equally if not more potent. Unlike the cover of the mutual fund report that gets a quick glance before filing away, the decor in your home is experienced over long periods of time. You may take it for granted, but its effect is profound. Clear and cleanse as many of these items as possible. You will be transforming the paralyzing energy of the past into the sparkling, flowing energy of your future.

Color Speak

ColorFlow Scale of Visual Weight: A sketch of key pieces of furniture made with the intention of balancing the décor with regard to color and visual weight. Briefly describe each piece considering value and intensity. This information will reveal to which side of the room the imaginary scale of visual weight is tipping. Appropriate adjustments to achieve a more pleasing balance can then be made.

Comfortable Large Surface Colors: Colors that can be comfortably envisioned on large surfaces such as walls, floors and sofas. These hues have become familiar simply because each of us has had to cover large surfaces. Therefore, practice in choosing colors for these spaces has been frequent.

Edgy Limited Surface Colors: Colors used in relatively small doses as accents. These hues tend to be edgy, offbeat, anything but neutral hues. They are many times unfamiliar to us because we have been too timid to experiment with supporting hues. Once the larger surface colors are chosen, we believe our palette to be complete. It is the *edgy limited surface colors* that when added to our yet thin color harmony will cause the *comfortable large surface hues* to literally sing.

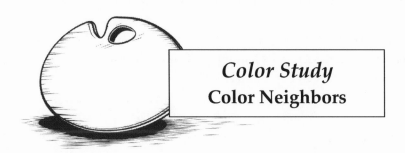

Color Study
Color Neighbors

"The meeting of two personalities is like the contact of two chemical substances; if there is any reaction, both are transformed."
C.J. Jung

Colors, like people, don't exist in isolation. In the quotation above, Jung makes two points. One is that if two people react to one another, each of them is transformed in some way. The second is that in some cases, there is no reaction at all, in which case there is no transformation. In this way, color is similar to both people and chemical substances. In most instances, the character of a hue is influenced by the hues around it. In fewer instances, there is little reaction at all and the affinity between them simply falls flat.

Your aim, then, is to put colors together that react with one another in a way that perfectly resonates with your inner artist. Simply choosing a color palette isn't enough to create a beautiful and supportive sanctuary. The hues on your ColorPrint must be chosen and arranged in a way that will create a personal alchemy nourishing to your spirit. That quality of synergy among your colors that proves to be your "sweet spot" is unique to only you.

Necessary and common to each of our color harmonies is that there is, in fact, *some* resulting reaction when individual colors are brought together. Otherwise, the space will be void of vitality. And when our surroundings have no life, they certainly cannot support and enhance our lives. To this end, let's look at a few more concepts that will guide you toward a sweet synergy of color composition.

By far, the simplest way to ensure dynamic color reactions that will buoy the spirit is with the insightful use of value. Consider a painting technique used in the late 15th century known as "Chiaroscuro." From the Italian chiaro, "light" and scuro, "dark," chiaroscuro uses widely varied values from the very lightest shade to the darkest. This creative use of value gives depth and dimension to a flat surface causing it to appear three-dimensional. Applied to your home, the richly varied use of light and dark within your ColorPrint causes your flat, lifeless surroundings to literally come alive. When the scope of your vision is full of life, this vitality of spirit permeates your entire being.

Look at the photo of the multicolored pinwheel. You know that the pinwheel isn't flat but has depth. We don't often wonder why our eye perceives three dimensions. However, artists know that three-dimensionality is most often depicted by using varied values of the same hue. Incorporating light, medium and darker shades of the same color in just the right spots conveys the direction from which the light comes making an object appear lifelike.

Look at any point on the pinwheel. Laid out perfectly flat, you would see that the each piece is, in fact, just one shade of color. But because the actual pinwheel is not flat, but three-dimensional, several shades seem to appear. In the same way, using varied values of the same color in your décor will provide interest, dimensionality and life to the spaces you create.

A much rebuffed ingredient in the practice of using varied values of individual colors, is the inclusion of darker hues. Recall that painting a dimly lit room white or a very pale color neither ensures that it will appear any brighter nor any larger. The lack of natural sunlight results in a grayish cast. The light walls simply act as a "movie screen" on which to project the dim light. On the other hand, painting the walls a rich, saturated color, say fresh green, overpowers the gray light. What you see then, is your favorite green.

Vinny Lee, author of <u>Mood Indigo</u>, an interesting book about using deeper hues, considers color in terms of musical notes and says that darker tones are similar to the bass notes in a composition. He continues, "They contribute a grounding influence to a scheme and create balance against which light and bright notes will sound or appear all the more brilliant." [21]

21. Vinny Lee, <u>Mood Indigo</u>, 11

Most people are apprehensive about using deep shades because they tend to consider dark values in complete isolation. Imagine for a moment a deep, rich eggplant color. An initial reaction may be, "lovely shade, but not on my walls!" Before deciding, think about what the richness of a dark violet can do for that which you place in front of it. Remember luminescing? The color and finish of the backdrop has the power to elevate a pleasant piece to the status of art. If your upholstered furniture is a very light value, then deep, rich walls may be a dramatic enhancement. On the other hand, light furniture against a rather light background may appear thin and anemic.

Whether you prefer a lighter or darker value background for your furnishings is merely a matter of individual artistic chemistry. Whatever the case, don't categorically dismiss more saturated walls. You may be surprised at your authentic preference. The only constant is that the greater the contrast, the greater the color reaction. With this in mind, at least explore the reaction that would be created should you choose a darker shade. Frequently, dark colors can be used with breathtaking results if only we would give the idea a chance.

Also, keep in mind that at first sight, dark painted walls may appear strong and even overwhelming. However, once carpets, furniture, pictures, lights and soft furnishings such as window dressings are returned to the room, the amount of visible, dark space is dramatically reduced. It is the same effect as when we visually lightened the dark green sofa with the addition of pale colored pillows. The walls essentially become less "weighty" as their surface area decreases. Here we use the ColorFlow Scale of Visual Weight not to solve a problem, but expressly to create a gratifying balance.

After detailing the virtues of using contrasting values to create appealing color reactions, I'll add a word of caution. In good design there can absolutely be "too much of a good thing." First, contrast creates tension. With no tension, your design will be flat and uninteresting. But with too much tension, it becomes busy and chaotic. So by all means consider various values of your ColorPrint hues by incorporating lighter and darker versions of your colors in the same way that you would add accessories to a simple black cocktail dress: one at a time until the balance of simplicity to ornament perfectly resonates with your artistic essence.

Then, borrow a trade secret known for the most part only to designers. They know that there is a distinctly different reaction between two colors depending upon their proximity in the space. Although the phenomenon bears a fancy name, the concept is easy. The "Law of Simultaneous Contrast of Colors" was discovered by French chemist M. E. Chevreul. It states that placing any two hues of different values side by side causes the lighter valued color to appear lighter and the darker one to appear darker. In other words, when positioned in close proximity the *contrast* of values is intensified. Hence, greater tension is created.

The converse is also true. If the same two hues are separated, or moved to opposite sides of the room, the eye perceives them as more similar. Use this to your design advantage. For instance, reds are notoriously difficult to match. Say you have a red sofa and a printed lounge chair with an abundance of red. Unfortunately, when placed side by side, the red of the sofa and that of the chair may create a bit of a clash. Move the chair to any other wall. Now, enjoy the interest and depth afforded by varied color values without the discordant note of quarrelsome reds.

The next chapter rounds out the discussion of our inner color spectrum and solves a mystery or two. You will discover that although your authentic ColorPrint palette makes up the greater portion of your space, the lusciously full spectrum of colors remains at your disposal. Explore this and more as you journey ever closer to your sweet, natural state of flow.

"You don't get harmony when everybody sings the same note."
Doug Floyd

Chapter 9

A GOLDEN MYSTERY
Your Inner Color Spectrum

It has been a particularly wintry January as I settle in to write this chapter. But today is a rare, perhaps record breaking, warm day for this time of year in the northeast. I am just in from the garden where I've clipped a generous bunch of tightly budded, yellow forsythia branches for indoor forcing.

This is an early spring tradition for me. I lust after the clear, brilliant yellow of the starry forsythia blooms. It is not something I need to put on my calendar or be reminded of in any way. This yearly gathering of golden treasure comes naturally to me with the same regularity that geese fly south in winter.

At Christmastime, too, I savor the yellow glow emitted from creamy white candles nestled among greenery all around the house. And just weeks before the blessed holiday, sprays of yellow chrysanthemum dance in autumn's winds of changing seasons. The claret, the purple and the white, all lovely, but it is the yellow, the last warm blaze of summer, that transfixes my gaze. These are among my cherished color treasures.

Surely then, yellow must be part of my "color fingerprint," my personal ColorPrint palette. The neutrals, so elevating to my spirit, are creamy white and brown. My nourishing colors are red-violet, violet, yellow-green, green and blue. Amazingly, nowhere on my Print is the primary yellow of the forsythia, the candle's glow or the chrysanthemum. The absence of primary yellow is the "golden mystery."

To solve the mystery, consider the components of my Print hues. Although yellow doesn't appear on its own, it is an ingredient of green. Our finger-painting days remind us that blue and yellow make green. And there is an even greater portion of yellow in my yellow-green. It's comprised of one part blue to multiple parts yellow. And this is precisely the amount of warm yellow I need to satisfy me through most of the year. But in late November, December, and early January I crave pure, saturated yellow. At those times I satiate my color appetite with mums and candle glow and forsythia.

Let's examine what this means when applied to ColorFlow. Simply stated: To achieve your ultimate life flow, it is necessary to consider both short-term and lasting color affinities. The permanent ones are your ColorPrint hues. Those for which your yearnings appear only to disappear later are most often among the component parts of your Print. Identify these by breaking down the secondary and tertiary colors on your Print into their component parts. These parts will in all cases be some combination of red, yellow and blue. Using the concept of *core component parts* aids in seeing hues obscured by the mixture they are within. The following chart illustrates this concept.

ColorPrint Hue	*Core Component Parts*
Yellow-green	*yellow – yellow – blue*
Green	*yellow – blue*
Blue	*blue*
Violet	*blue – red*
Red- violet	*red – red – blue*

By examining the component parts of my authentic colors, it becomes clear that yellow truly is one of "my colors." However, for most of the year I need merely the warm essence of yellow that lies within my green and yellow-green. In the same way as I may crave a cup of hot soup on a chilly winter's day, I seek pure primary yellow only during the coldest time of year.

Recall that in a previous discussion, I pointed out that one's authentic ColorPrint hues never vacillate. The cause for tiring of a once loved palette in many cases is that those hues were never authentic choices. Mindfulness of the *Core Component Parts* of Print hues deepens our understanding of such color missteps. Broaden your artistic wisdom to include the possibility that a "color misstep" may in reality be no more than a momentary need to seek a greater or lesser portion of a particular quality of color. In the case of my winter yellows, it is merely the inner desire to turn up the heat on the yellow that already exists on my Print.

Perhaps you, too, have experienced a phenomenon which initially appears to be a fluctuation of color preferences. When this occurs, consider distilling your ColorPrint to its component parts. This simple exercise may uncover the underlying cause of your seemingly "new" attraction. Just for practice, see if you can name the core colors of this hypothetical ColorPrint. The answers appear at the end of the chapter.

Color Print Hue	Core Component Parts		
Blue	_____		
Violet	_____	_____	
Yellow-orange	_____	_____	_____
Blue-violet	_____	_____	_____
Yellow	_____		

When expressing your ColorPrint in terms of its component parts, the results are always conveyed in terms of the three primaries: red, yellow and blue. That's because the primaries are the only hues on the wheel not comprised of at least two other colors. Further, these primaries are the components of every color on the wheel. With this in mind, consider the viewpoint of Owen Jones, author of <u>The Grammar of Ornament</u>. I concur with Jones when he says, "No composition can ever be perfect in which any one of the three primary colors is wanting, either in its natural state or in combination." [22]

Consider Jones' statement as further guidance in the discovery of the final hue or hues on your ColorPrint. If, for instance, you have identified only blue-violet, blue and green as colors that effortlessly vibrate in sync with your inner artist, you might explore a color on the opposite, warmer side of the wheel. This is so because the three initial colors lean heavily toward the cool side. The addition of a warmer hue will balance the palette. Since specific color choices are deeply personal, only you can determine whether it might be a deep persimmon orange, pale yellow or any other toasty shade.

The desire to balance our surroundings with shades from both the warm and cool sides of the wheel is universal. Additionally, expanding a basically warm palette to include a cool accent or a cool palette with a dash of warm provides a lively, accentuating twist to your color plan. I like to think of it as the "yin and yang" of color.

The sum and substance of this book has centered around my belief that each of us has a specific, limited set of innate colors that cultivates our spiritual contentment. Here I've asked you to accept the notion that in addition to these hues, one may extract a component part of a Print hue to satisfy interim emotional needs. This is what happens when I seek the warmth of pure yellow in wintry weather. Now, before revealing my final view on the topic, you'll need to recall the existence of amazing and powerful paradoxes in our creative realm. One such remarkable anomaly comes to the forefront here.

22. Owen Jones, *The Grammar of Ornament*, 26

You are nearing the end of a long journey of discovery. Specific hues have revealed themselves as being uniquely supportive and nurturing to your emotional essence. You have, in fact, *limited* your color choices to include only those hues that speak most resolutely to your authentic design voice. Just as you are relaxing into the notion that your number of genuine colors is finite, I want you to consider the idea that each one of us needs a *full spectrum of color* to be so nurtured as to experience the full potential of life's flow. In other words, I believe that we seek *both* a limited color palette *and* one that is complete with each spectral hue.

The greater my immersion into color exploration, the stronger my conviction to the notion that living amidst the entire spectrum of hues draws us nearer to the rich, deeply gratifying life we deserve. I have begun to see color, all color, as a miraculous, even magical gift from the Universe. Surely, a prize of such enormous beauty and inexhaustible abundance is offered with no less than the promise of unrestrained use.

In order to fully understand the role played by a "full spectrum of colors," one must first realize that this rainbow of color exists in two distinct forms. First, consider a single color. Let's take gray, for instance. If you had a can of black paint and a can of white, they could be mixed in any proportion to make gray. However, once applied to the walls, you would notice that your gray is stark, lifeless, almost two-dimensional. And even if gray is on your ColorPrint, you are likely to soon tire of this lackluster, slate colored room.

The antithesis of this undesirable gray is one that is lively and appears multi-dimensional. It changes with changing light. This gray has personality and character and soul. It has these appealing qualities because it is a complex mixture of all three primaries. In fact, it may even be comprised of red, yellow and blue along with some of the secondaries. Using a mix of many colors to make gray adds a depth and complexity that can't be simulated with the simple combination of black and white.

And although at first glance, the "black and white" gray and the "full spectrum gray" may look similar, they speak to our emotions in markedly different ways. The simple gray may be pleasing for a brief time. But in reality, the attraction is more likely to the *change* rather than to the color itself. Recall that change, almost any alteration in décor, is uplifting at least for the short-term. Soon, however, the flirtation with your newly painted walls will prove unstimulating. The more complex gray, the one made from a rich, full spectrum, is more alive because it replicates the nourishing balance we see in nature. This gray will satisfy for years, perhaps indefinitely. In actuality, as you come to know your gray in different seasons and different lights, fondness for your color choice will deepen over time.

If you have the opportunity to purchase a custom paint color at the local hardware store, notice how many colors are mixed to yield your chosen hue. If it is no more than a light or dark base and a couple of colors, you may not have to concern yourself with the paint warranty. I suspect you'll tire of the color long before the space actually needs repainting.

Farrow & Ball paints, on the other hand, use up to 18 pigments to blend a single color. Yet another difference between the lower priced store brands and the more expensive, full spectrum paints, lies in the method used to adjust the value of the color. The less costly paints normally add white to make a color lighter and black to darken it. Full spectrum paints rely on the addition of a color's complement to change the shade. For example, red can be made darker and richer by adding a dark value green instead of black. And the addition of a pale green will lighten the red in a more pleasing way than simply adding white.

Take advantage of the increasing availability of the luscious, complex colors of full spectrum paints. Although not an all inclusive list, companies that offer full spectrum paints are Citron (www.citronpaint.com), Anna Sova (www.annasova.com), C2 Color (www.c2color.com), Donald Kaufman (www.donaldkaufmancolor.com), Farrow & Ball (www.farrow-ball.com) and Ellen Kennon (www.ellenkennon.com).

Ellen Kennon offers a particularly breathtaking range of hues. Before I began painting parts of my interior with Ellen Kennon paints, I sent for her carton of paint swatches. On the back of each card is a wonderful disclaimer that sums up all one needs to know about these full spectrum colors. It reads as follows:

> *"PLEASE NOTE: Should another paint manufacturer attempt to copy this color, his computer will create a formula using only 2 to 3 pigments. The result will not contain the luminous, healing qualities of our Full Spectrum Paints."*

So when Owen James said that all three primary colors either in their natural state or in combination must be present to create a perfect composition, he could have been speaking about the composition of a single hue or of more encompassing compositions such as the mix of colors in a print fabric or perhaps those in an entire room's décor. We've discussed how a nourishing, full spectrum can exist within a single paint color. Now let's consider how a full spectrum of hues within an entire room can work together with your ColorPrint to create surroundings that support your dreams.

One could argue that interior design using both the limited palette of your ColorPrint and the unlimited palette of the full spectrum is mutually exclusive. In other words, you can't have it both ways. But you can and should. The magic is in the quantitative relationships among the colors.

Recall that each color on your ColorPrint is not necessarily used in the same quantity. There are comfortable large surface colors that lend themselves to sizable surfaces such as walls, floors and large-scale furniture. Edgy limited surface colors function more appropriately on compact surfaces such as accents and accessories. And all of us need a palette of neutrals to give the eye a rest. The quantity of neutrals is a matter of personal preference. Additional colors drawn from the full spectrum account for the smallest portion of color in the space. Study the following bubble charts for workable, quantitative relationships among each distinct group in your color rich, healing space.

Sample of a Successful Quantitative Color Relationship

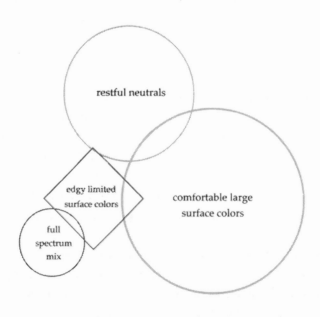

Sample of an Alternative Successful Quantitative Color Relationship

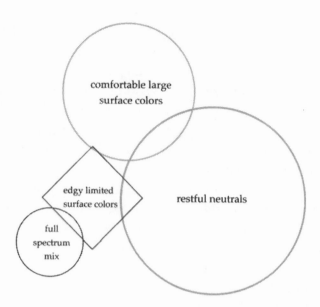

Depending upon your personal preferences, there are several configurations of the color relationship bubble chart that can yield an effective palette. The single constant is that the full spectrum mix represents the smallest surface space. This allows for your ColorPrint harmony to take the spotlight. At the same time, the varied spectrum of colors and their diverse vibrations provide support for life's natural ebb and flow.

Key to the understanding the role of the full color spectrum mix is that these small quantities of color are just as potent as any other hue in the space. Your sentient, artistic spirit has the ability to seek precisely what it lacks. Each autumn when I experience a subconscious longing for greater warmth, I notice a renewed interest in the abstract painting over the sideboard. It's a painting I've enjoyed for decades. At this particular season, however, I'm magnetically drawn to the small, yet compelling amounts of radiant yellows throughout the piece. This artwork, for me, has dynamic, vital energy.

Keep in mind that even though from a scientific standpoint, a full spectrum signifies the presence of all colors, it is popularly used to simply suggest many colors. ColorFlow's interpretation is that any and all hues have equal possibility for your selection. Although infinite selection is yours for the taking, it is not necessary, possible or even advisable to use *every* color outside of your ColorPrint. Further, the selection process for these items is less contemplative than the unearthing of your authentic ColorPrint. If you love the style, line and color of an accessory and the item harmonizes compatibly with your Print colors, then by all means incorporate it into your design.

With a little practice at selecting full spectrum hued accessories, you'll soon discover certain *shades* of colors that are clearly compatible or incompatible with your surroundings. Whether or not a particular shade has an affinity for your Print palette is determined by the value, intensity and ratio of component parts of each hue on the wheel. Said another way, there are no colors that "clash." There are only values, intensities and component part ratios that make bad color marriages. This concept will become more clear as we move to the topic of matching in the next chapter.

Perhaps the most spirit lifting accessory that is likely to bring myriad colors of the spectrum to your space is wall art. This is because paintings, photographs and wall sculpture not only have color, but the additional message of a personal story. A good example is a collectible poster that hangs in my living room. The colors include brilliant yellow, gold, soft peach, orange, several shades of green and blue, chartreuse, eggplant and black. This combination of colors does two things. First, nourishing vibrations of hues outside of my Print (yellows and oranges) are brought to the space. And second, those colors of the poster that repeat my personal Print (blues, greens, violets) link it to my design.

And wall art imparts your unique experience to the decor. My poster is one that was commissioned to Danish artist Bjorn Wiinblad to commemorate the 1987 Royal Danish Ballet season. It depicts a whimsical ballerina on toe. In my youth and early adulthood I danced and have had a lifelong love for the ballet. So for me, this piece melds my ColorPrint, additional colors from the full spectrum and a heartfelt connection to the essence of dance that forever lives within. What an inspired design element!

A full spectrum of hues can also be incorporated into your design through printed fabrics, patterned rugs, books on a shelf, a cherished vase from your favorite aunt or any other accessory that speaks to your color essence and to your authentic design voice. Your ColorPrint colors remain the ones with which you will create a basic decorating theme. Then, as you become increasingly intimate with your inner artist, traces of other colors will spin effortlessly into the space balancing your interior across the full spectrum just as nature intended.

Imprint
Sipping in the Rainbow

Find a quiet time and place. Sit upright and notice your straight, vertical spine. Lift your legs and stretch them in front of you. Point your toes forward and hold. Now point your heels forward and hold. Let your feet drop gently to the floor. Closing your eyes, drop your head toward your left shoulder. With your head to the side, draw in a deep, belly breath. Recall that your belly rounds as it fills like a balloon When you can comfortably hold the breath no longer, slowly release the air. Continue pushing your breath out until you can feel a reassuring tug in the area of the hara. The center of your being, or the hara, is located 1 to 2 inches below your naval. Now drop your head over to your right shoulder. Feel the elongation of your neck muscles. Again, take a restorative hara breath.

Mentally count with me slowly and rhythmically from ten to one. Breathe in the raw, life force energy that comes most prolifically with hara breath. Ten nine eight seven six five four three two one. Imagine now that it is March. In the air there is the antithetical mix of both winter's chill and the scent of spring's promise. The quality of light in the woods where you walk is dusky and gray. The winter weakened light will remain at least until April's lamb ushers in the shimmer of spring. And it's due to the contrast in light that your eye is drawn to an area of unusual brightness. Since the beginning of time, we have all been magnetized to light, the light of a fire, of the sun and of the moon.

Instinctively, move from the darkness of the woods to the light of a clearing. The treetops have sheltered you from a late winter's rain. Now the sun's rays refract in the misty droplets creating a multicolored arch overhead, a rainbow. The lure of clear light alone is trifling when compared to the seduction of bending light separating into every color of the Universe.

Face to the sky, lie down on the moist grass beneath the curvature of color. With no thought in mind, with no feeling but serenity in your viscera, drink in this nutritionally charged, prismatic juice. The hues of the rainbow permeate the mist that now wets your lips, your mouth, your throat. It is a satisfying quench for a long-standing emotional thirst.

The color of the longest wavelength is red and it is first to reach you. In your mind's eye, see the droplets of vermilion enter your body. They energize you in mind, body and spirit. Bask in the atmosphere of this gentle rainbow energy and take a deep, hara breath.

The qualities of orange are such that they form a concentrated liqueur that moves through millions of raindrops. Orange imbues the body with the energy of achievement without struggle. The saffron cloud evanesces leaving behind only the knowing that your authentic path is one of gentle flow. And when the waves of yellow reach your still thirsty lips, love and acceptance for all the unseen beauty in the Universe swells within you. Savor yet another vitalizing hara breath.

Drink in the splashes of blue for contentment. It is an elixir flavored with patience, freedom from envy and gratitude. You feel energized and happy. Can this rainbow offer yet more? You know that it can as you sip now from the mist of health sustaining green. Within each verdant cell is a world of strength, vigor and vitality. Breathe.

Finally there is violet, the last visible color in the spectrum, the symbolic boundary that bridges the known to the mystical unknown. Violet is a fluid rich in creativity and personal growth. Its position reminds us that we learn by going from the familiar to that which we have yet to imagine. A tonic that transports to unexplored realms, the purples are inventive and exotic.

Take several hara breaths drawing in the full spectrum of rainbow colors. Each hue of this illusory talisman of hope is necessary to reach a perfect state of flow. With a balance of color, our natural vitality, weakened by our frenetic lives, rushes back into body and soul.

Mentally count with me slowly and rhythmically from one to ten. One two three four five six seven eight nine ten. Return from your Imprint mentally refreshed and eager to experience the flow.

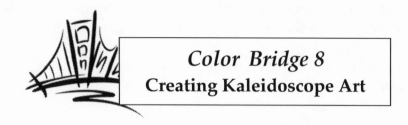

Color Bridge 8
Creating Kaleidoscope Art

Recall that the actual physical manifestation of everything in your life and in your home begins in the form of thought. This chapter's discussion of a full spectrum of colors will serve as your thought rich beginning to a home that includes both your ColorPrint palette and a kaleidoscope of additional hues.

As you work through the Bridge, keep in mind the size of the relative surface area that will ultimately be represented by this rainbow of colors in your environment. Although actually very small, these hues will add great vitality to your space. Colors from the full spectrum will appear in accessories such as wall art, porcelain and glass collectibles and patterned fabrics. Refer to the bubble charts on pages 194 and 195 to see a visual representation of the surface area given to what we have called the full spectrum mix.

The simplest of thoughts may manifest into reality in a single step. For instance, you think about being cold, so you put on a sweater. However, thoughts of incorporating myriad hues into your design to complement your unique ColorPrint are a bit more complex. An endeavor such as this requires some practice and beginning steps of self-discovery. Hence the Color Bridge, *Creating Kaleidoscope Art*.

Open your Studio to the next clean page. Label it, "Color Bridge 8, Creating Kaleidoscope Art." Using a template such as an appropriately sized plate or bowl, draw a circle about 8 inches in circumference on a piece of black construction paper. Cut out the circle and paste it into your Studio. The circle represents the background of the multi-hued, mirrored end of your kaleidoscope. Do this before you have considered any color choices to place on it. It is a clean palette, a signal to the Universe that you are a ready and receptive partner for yet deeper artistic discovery.

On your kaleidoscope you will be affixing small, multi-hued slips of paper stock cut from paint chips gathered from your home improvement superstore. The background is black because the deep richness of black both emphasizes and connects the characteristics of the colors it surrounds. Recall that white tends to separate and dilute the lyrical synergy possible among hues.

Note also that your kaleidoscope colors will include only saturated hues. There will be no neutrals or popular neutrals. Again, consider the balloon chart where neutrals are given their own space. Your kaleidoscope piece should be a melange of vibrant color. Here there will be no need for the eye to rest with the help of a neutral. Study the example of kaleidoscope art.

Kaleidoscope Art

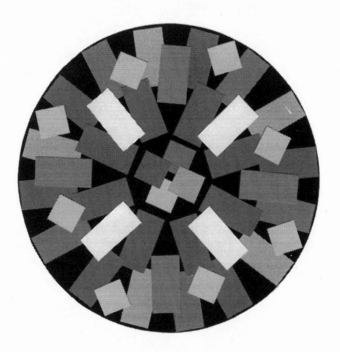

The kaleidoscope you create is meant to represent a design element in your room colored with a burst of multi-hues from the full spectrum. As you work, remember that although technically a full spectrum signifies the presence of all colors, it is popularly used to simply suggest many colors. Your art piece should ideally include a few hues from your unique ColorPrint palette plus several additional colors to make it a full spectrum design.

In the example above, the ColorPrint colors are violet, blue and green. Notice that two values of green were chosen. Additional colors outside of the ColorPrint are red expressed as medium and light pink, orange and yellow.

Let's get started. First, gather paint chips. If you get the larger sized samples now carried by many stores you'll only need one or two of each color. Certainly you'll want one to represent each saturated hue on your ColorPrint. Later you'll choose which ones to use in the final design. Now, suspend your judgmental mind and simply grab other colors that draw your eye. These are the hues *not* on your ColorPrint.

Even though I want you to be completely non-judgmental, to let your mind float and wander, I do have a word of caution here. Because you are so attracted to your Print colors, you may unwittingly choose hues that are very close to your unique palette. For instance, if violet is on your ColorPrint, you may be tempted to choose a red-violet that is nearly violet. If blue-violet is on your palette, you may select a very similar blue. Try instead to choose hues that are different than your Print colors. In our kaleidoscope example, the pinks, yellows and oranges were quite a departure from the ColorPrint hues of violet, blue and green.

Gather many more colors than you think you'll need. The more hues you collect at the outset, the more possibility there will be for creative trial and play later. Remember that you are always working to expand your design repertoire rather than working within its existing confines.

Once all of your color chips are gathered, find a quiet time when you can simply explore the possible combinations. I suggest that you spread the colors out on a table. On one side, place your ColorPrint hues. On the other place the multi-hued, full spectrum colors you will add to make a vibrant kaleidoscope. Creating this physical separation reinforces the objective of this Bridge. You are learning to artfully infuse pieces of the lavish treasure trove of colors offered by the Universe onto your unique ColorPrint palette.

Remember that there are no colors that clash. There are only values and intensities of particular hues that don't work well together. Additionally, there are certain colors that you personally may not care to see paired with one another. But, in fact, for every red there is a yellow that harmonizes beautifully. For each blue in the spectrum, there is an orange, a violet and a green that make it sing. It is only a matter of selecting the multi-hued, full spectrum colors that when married with your unique ColorPrint resonate with your authentic design voice in the deepest, most genuine way possible.

A selection of three to four ColorPrint hues plus another three to four multi-hued, full spectrum colors seem to make the most appealing kaleidoscope.

After choosing these, you'll need to cut the paint chips into smaller pieces to represent the tiny glass chips of a kaleidoscope. The rectangles in the example were cut to 1½ " by ¾." The squares were simply made by cutting those rectangles in half, thus making them ¾" by ¾." Each of the larger paint chips makes several rectangles. Depending upon the design you wish to create, you may need several store chips of each color.

Begin placing your "glass kaleidoscope chips" on the black background in a symmetrical design until you find an appealing pattern. Carefully paste down the design. When finished, take a break and enjoy your kaleidoscope for a few days before completing the analysis and summary that follows.

Color Bridge Analysis
Creating Kaleidoscope Art

With your vibrant kaleidoscope art in front of you, consider the following.

1. Using names from the twelve color artist's wheel, what colors did you use from your unique ColorPrint palette?

2. What colors did you use that are not from your palette? These are the hues that make your kaleidoscope a multi-hued, full spectrum piece.

3. Is the attraction to any of the hues outside of your Print surprising to you?

4. Perhaps more importantly, is the attraction to any of the color harmonies among your Print and the additional hues particularly surprising to you?

5. Were you able to identify any color or colors for which you have a distaste, that you do not want in your interior?

6. Do you think a single item having a similar melange of colors would fit comfortably into your room?

7. Can you imagine an attractive item having a similar color palette? (e.g. a painting, a rug, a pashmina, a mosaic, a piece of art glass or pottery, a flower arrangement)

8. What would the addition of a full spectrum mix to your room's limited color palette do for the pervading atmosphere of the space?

Color Bridge Summary
Creating Kaleidoscope Art

Following is a sample written summary. Use the eight questions in the Bridge Analysis as a general guideline. However, you won't need to answer each question word for word. And you may have made other discoveries not highlighted by the questions. Include in your summary any pertinent information that has bubbled to the surface.

ColorPrint hues on my kaleidoscope are violet, blue and two values of green. Colors not from my Print making it a full spectrum piece are two shades of red expressed as pale pink and a brighter hot pink, orange and yellow. Pale pink has never been one of my colors either for the house or for clothing. But since my discovery of red-violet as one of my authentic hues, I have been noticing the spectrum of pinks. I tried the kaleidoscope with and without the paler pink and had no trouble choosing the one with. I may rarely use a light value pink on its own, but in harmony with all the hues in my creation it's very attractive to me.

There are two hues that I would like for the most part to keep out of my spaces. The first is pure, saturated red. Just to keep an open mind, I brought a paint chip of primary red and experimented with it in my kaleidoscope art. It simply doesn't resonate with my authentic design voice. Another hue that for my artist's eyes doesn't "go" with my palette is anything in the blue-green to turquoise range. I guess you just can't assume anything. I love the blues on my ColorPrint and I adore the green. Obviously that doesn't necessarily mean that I'll love the blue-greens. And it's such a popular shade right now. It's almost unpopular to say you don't really want it in your surroundings!

I would love to have one or perhaps a few full spectrum mix objects in color harmonies similar to this kaleidoscope in my space. I have a strong aesthetic connection to artisan made objects. In some cases these are made by more primitive peoples deeply connected to the earth and tend to be decorated with detailed, folkloric designs in rich multi-hues. I can think of a hand loomed rug in one of my picture files that would bring in both a full spectrum of hues and the artisanal atmosphere that I so crave.

The addition of a full spectrum mix of hues to any room's palette of comfortable large surface colors, neutrals and edgy accents, can turn a pretty room into an inspired one. Our authentic ColorPrint palette provides nourishing support, while the dashes of a full spectrum mix add energy and panache. Keep in mind that too much harmony can become boring. A full spectrum mix uses hues from the ColorPrint to anchor it to the room while the newly added hues add a richness of character thus avoiding the antiseptic feel of "hotel-like" matching. After spending much time and effort to unearth my authentic ColorPrint, I almost couldn't believe that now we were being asked to add the rest of the spectrum back into the mix. But it's all one beautiful, artistic paradox that now makes perfect sense. And so it flows...

CLEANSE
Birdwalking is for the Birds

Many years ago when I taught in the public school system, we were required to take a class to improve teaching skills. At this point I recall almost nothing about the training except the details concerning a concept called "birdwalking." The most important life lessons are many times simple and consist of little more than common sense. And *birdwalking* was no exception.

If you're a birdwatcher like me, you've seen the frenzied dance done by a tiny bird as he scavenges for food. He will stop just long enough to sample something tasty before darting in another direction. This choppy, zigzag cavort that we'll call *birdwalking*, continues until he's satisfied. Hence, *birdwalking* as it applies to teaching is the veering off course to topics that are at best, on the periphery of the main objective. Most times, however, *birdwalking* takes teachers and students to completely unrelated subjects.

Applied to the decor, *birdwalking* occurs when we frequently jump from one style or color palette to another in a fevered search to discover the look that truly speaks to us. But keep in mind that life enhancing design does not materialize overnight. Rather it is patiently built in measured steps over time. During this period of incubation, the components of our composition may remain underdeveloped and in all likelihood appear less seductive than we had hoped. Oftentimes, however, before allowing ourselves the blissful intoxication of experiencing the emergence of an atmosphere rich in our authentic spirit, we become magnetized to something "newer and better." In reality, what we need is not a new direction, but the patience to allow the design that aligns with our deepest artistic essence the time and freedom to evolve and mature.

It is at the stage when we are just beginning to know our aesthetic selves that we may be quite vulnerable to the myriad and alluring options afforded us by ever present design chatter. It is interesting to me that in other areas of our lives, we fully understand the concept of incubation and development. We don't pull a turnip out of the earth to check its growth and we understand why after only three piano lessons our children don't play a concerto at the Met. Is it such a leap to fathom the patience required to create a home rich in our authentic spirits?

I have often viewed this as a good news, bad news situation. In our fast paced, instant banking, drive-thru dinner society, having to wait for our décor to metamorphose and mature is most probably viewed as bad news. However, the good news or in this case the pay off for patience, is *enormous*. As you slow down and mindfully build a nurturing personal space adagio style, there will come a point in the design when a "critical mass" is reached. It is this tipping point when there is a precise proportion of authentic design necessary that you cease to be so easily vulnerable to the allure of the latest trends. In other words, your most profound personal style begins to shine more brightly than elements that don't belong.

It is important to understand that critical mass is neither likely nor necessarily reached when a simple mathematical half of your space has been refashioned to align with your innate artistic essence. We are not weighing fruit on a grocery scale. Further, the Universe rarely chooses the clear cut, "logical" path as we are apt to assume. Continue to observe your surroundings with sharp artist's eyes. Additionally, remain attentive to your emotions both conscious and just below consciousness. Eventually, you will see and feel this soul soothing shift.

Once the transposition begins, you will notice an overall calming of the spirit. This is the flow that comes with living in a soul-nurturing retreat. Further, you will be blanketed in the peacefulness brought about by the acceptance of your true artistic essence. There will be no more scraping wallpaper that you've grown to despise, no more giving away furniture that looks outdated and perhaps best of all, no further feeling as if your décor just isn't you. In short, coming home begins to feel like clean, dry clothes when the world beyond is a stormy day.

You will notice a complete about-face in the way you see your surroundings. In the past, you experienced delighted anticipation when purchasing a new item for your décor. Once at home, this latest addition proved breathtaking.

However, after a year or so the charm faded and the once loved piece seemed to virtually disappear into the mundane familiarity of the background. Several years later, you perceive it once again. This time unfortunately, it stands out at very best as an element not compatible with your current taste and at worst, as a distasteful piece that robs vital energy from your very spirit.

You have chosen to expand your existing design repertoire and discover your true inner artist. You patiently await the critical mass that allows the first delicious taste of the sweet state of flow. In stark contrast to the scenario above, each addition to your space perpetually remains an uplifting art piece. Its form, color and texture soothe your world weary psyche. In fact, instead of weakening in aesthetic and energetic impact, its effect when viewed within the context of the room is magnified over time. When entering my living room, for instance, I invariably experience the dynamic design as if I'm seeing its beauty for the first time. It lifts my spirit and elevates my mood.

As if all this isn't enough, the lavish generosity of the Universe has even more in store for you. Recall that beauty begets beauty. This is part of the law of synchronicity. When we are tuned into the lasting splendor that surrounds us in our homes, we are more apt to perceive the beauty in others, in the events around us and most significantly deep within. And when we love and accept ourselves, the world becomes an ever more peaceful place in which to thrive.

And so in this Cleanse, you have three crucial jobs. First, become hyper-conscious of the integrity of every design decision. This keen awareness helps to keep *birdwalking* at bay. Second, trust that a most enchanting critical mass will occur in perfect time. Finally, realize that beauty begets beauty. Once you fully embrace true beauty, which is nothing more than the visual splendor authentic to your most primal essence, unlimited beauty will enter your life in a swelling spiral. With that said, this may be the most beautiful, flowing Cleanse ever!

Color Speak

Birdwalking: Occurs when we frequently jump from one style or color palette to another in a fevered search to discover the look that speaks to us. There is little chance that this will eventuate in authentically personal surroundings. Rather, *birdwalking* manifests in a hodgepodge of styles that remains unable to meld into a pleasing whole.

Core Component Parts: The separation of secondary and tertiary colors into their component parts. These parts will in all cases be some combination of red, yellow and blue. Using the concept of *core component parts* aids in seeing hues obscured by the mixture they are within.

Color Study
Color Marriages

"The whole world as we experience it visually, comes to us through the mystic realm of color."
Hans Hofmann

There is no doubt that color in and of itself is magical and mystical. But when single hues enter into color marriages, the mystery of color can become a real thriller. Let's begin by taking a look at the traditional color schemes we have yet to discuss.

Recall that a complementary scheme is comprised of any two hues opposite one another on the artist's wheel. Possible complementary schemes include:

yellow and violet	*yellow-green and red-violet*
green and red	*blue-green and red-orange*
blue and orange	*blue-violet and yellow-orange*

Expand the concept of complementary colors and consider a **double complementary** harmony. This is simply any two sets of opposites on a 12 hue color wheel. Hence, any two sets from the above list together form a double complement. At first, a four hued combination such as this may seem garish, but remember that it is unlikely that anyone would use equal parts of all four colors. Two hues, for instance may be larger surface colors, while the remaining two act as accents. Intensity, also, may be moderated for a richer, more subtle appearance.

A **tetrad** is a particular kind of double complementary. Instead of two sets of *any* complementary pairs, a tetrad incorporates two complementary sets that when viewed on the 12 color wheel are equidistant. This combination will always be comprised of one primary, one secondary and two tertiary hues. An easy way to visualize a tetrad on the wheel is to think of the four directions of a compass rose: north, south, east and west. Turn the wheel so that any color is at the top and the directional image will consistently show a tetrad scheme.

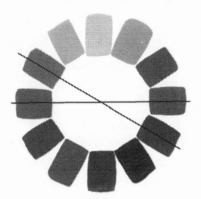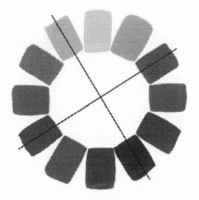

Look at the color wheel above. The lines that form an "X" show a **double complementary scheme**. The color pairs that make it a "double," are orange with blue and red-orange with blue-green.

The "X" here is formed by lines that are equidistant creating a cross that resembles a compass rose. This is a **tetrad scheme**. The colors are red, green, yellow-orange and blue-violet.

The final artists' combination is a **triad** comprised of three equidistant colors on the 12 color wheel. In other words, a triad forms an equilateral triangle. Examples of such a scheme include red, yellow and blue and red-orange, yellow-green and blue-violet. As with any harmony, it is advisable to vary the qualities of value and intensity. And perhaps more importantly, the quantities of the three colors should not be equal. One dominant hue with two supporting accents is more pleasing to the eye. Finally, a triad made up of secondary or tertiary hues expresses a subtle elegance not as easily achieved with the primaries red, yellow and blue.

In addition to the complementary, split complementary, analogous, double complementary, tetrad and triad combinations, there is, of course, a simple one color or **monochromatic scheme**. I illustrate this last so that it follows our comprehensive discussions of value and intensity. In a monochromatic space, the major surfaces are dressed in various values and intensities of a single hue. For instance, you may choose a range of violets. Changing the color's component parts, however, to include red-violets and blue-violets transforms it from a monochromatic scheme to an analogous harmony. Additionally, at least one neutral is necessary to give the eye respite from saturated color.

A monochromatic scheme is serene and often appropriate for small spaces such as a powder room or foyer. Remember that incorporating even a dash of the darkest values has a wonderful grounding effect. Use deep grays with an essence of the featured color to black in a cooler space or shades of brown in a warmer one. Since the element of color in a monochromatic space is significantly less lively, interest can be injected through the use of pattern and texture.

Now having examined each type of color harmony, relax in the knowledge that it isn't vital to memorize each one. What is of significant value is twofold. First, you must be thoroughly acquainted with the color wheel. And second, a full understanding of the concepts that define both analogous and complementary combinations provides the most beneficial tool for creating the expressive color schemes you crave.

A novice at the color game will most times review each of the artists' color harmonies and set out to choose *one*. In other words, he or she will consider, "Do I prefer the serenity of an analogous scheme or the liveliness of a complementary one?" Or, "Would it be better to attempt a tetrad for its subtle complexity or settle on a triad so the space doesn't become too busy?" The answer is that no scheme is an "either or" proposition. Use what you know about analogous colors which are those that live on the same side of the wheel. Add what you have learned about complementary colors which are those that live roughly on opposite sides of the wheel. Then build a color harmony. Once finished, it may be fun to try to identify your chosen combination as one of those listed above.

Your thought process may go something like this:

"Blue is on my ColorPrint and I have at least a bit of it in every room. In my bedroom, I know that I want lots of blue. For me it's soothing and peaceful, like bringing a piece of the sky earthward. Violet is also on my Print, but I don't want my other main color to be even that contrastive. I believe I'll go with a blue-violet. It is serenely analogous

in nature and the violet lends a bit of warmth to the totally cool blue. To add even more coziness without the addition of a third saturated color, I'll use metallic accessories in brass and gold tones. This will also add some bright, smooth textural interest. Finally, an element or two of charcoal gray will ground my light to medium value space."

Instead of choosing colors according to prescribed schemes, current trends or existing design repertoire, each color in the above harmony is added one by one in response to specific, deeply personal needs. Further, a firm knowledge of the color wheel works in tandem with personal preference for a successful, long lasting result. The colorist in this instance embraces the theory that generally speaking, analogous combinations are restful, while complementary ones are livelier. The serenity of analogous hues is expressed in the pairing of blue and blue-violet, while the effervescence of complements manifests in the pairing of the blues and gold tones.

A second example further illustrates the point:

"Since childhood I have always loved orange. Deep burnt orange, peach or a mid-value tangerine, it really doesn't matter. Since embarking on a journey for my ColorPrint, I have confirmed my sentiment about orange, but have been surprised to discover that there are a few other colors that speak with equal resonance to my authentic design voice. These hues not only nourish me emotionally but enhance the orange more than using it alone.

For instance, I love the combination of yellow-green and orange. And that's why I chose to pair these in my new sunroom addition. Higher intensities than I would normally consider can be brought into play to stand up to the abundance of natural light. Pale peaches and subtle lime greens would simply wash out under the intense sunlight.

A batik-like fabric that I selected for the sofa and chaise is made up mainly of brilliant orange, green and yellow-green ferns and tropical foliage. Making the print even more appealing is that it is set on a background of a small-scale, pale blue and red-violet geometric print. This cooler backdrop serves to highlight the warm, island motifs. I became so enamored with the print that I chose watery blue pillows to echo the cool elements in the fabric."

In this case, the colorist begins with her personal preference for orange and yellow-green. The scheme is further developed by borrowing from the skills of the fabric artist responsible for the batik-like print. This textile artisan had serendipitously paired the colors of preference with the concept of complementary hues creating a lively, multi-colored design. The touches of blue and red-violet speak to the idea of surrounding oneself with a fuller spectrum of color thereby avoiding an aura of sterility in matching.

Upon closer examination, we see that this color harmony is actually a tetrad. It consists of orange with blue and yellow-green with red-violet. Had the colorist chosen the tetrad first, the resulting design would have been quite different. Instead of free thinking, intuitive selections, he or she would have set out with predetermined rigid guidelines regarding color. This method is akin to fitting a square peg into a round hole in place of allowing for the discovery of the perfect shape into which you naturally fit.

Begin with your ColorPrint hues, as these will serve as the main colors in the space. Mindfully build on this foundation, shade by shade, color by color. As you do, use the characteristics of both analogous and complementary relationships to achieve a uniquely uplifting and nourishing atmosphere. Building a color harmony for a particular room should never be a matter of choosing *either* an analogous scheme *or* a complementary one. Your outcome will be far more satisfying and personally expressive if it incorporates the merits of both associations together with the deeply personal color intimacy you've developed through your ColorFlow experience.

Journey now to the final chapter, as we delve further into the profoundly gratifying endeavor of building a color scheme. You may begin to think about matching in an even more deeply satisfying way.

Recall that you were challenged to distill the following hues into their *core component parts*. Below are the correct answers. I know that you did well!

ColorPrint Hue	Core Component Parts
Blue	blue
Violet	blue red
Yellow-orange	yellow red yellow
Blue-violet	blue red blue
Yellow	yellow

"Color is the language of poets. It is astonishingly lovely.
To speak it is a privilege."
Keith Crown, 20th Century Watercolorist

Chapter 10

WABI SABI AND THE ZEN OF COLOR MATCHING
A Relaxed Palette

"A priest was in charge of the garden within a famous Zen temple. He had been given the job because he loved all of nature, most especially the flowers, shrubs, and trees. Next to the temple there was another, smaller temple where there lived an elderly Zen master.

One day, when the priest was expecting some special guests, he took extra care in tending the garden. He pulled the weeds, trimmed the shrubs, combed the moss and spent hours meticulously raking up and carefully arranging all the dry autumn leaves. As he worked, the old master watched him with interest from across the wall that separated the temples.

When he had finished, the priest stood back to admire his work. "Isn't it beautiful?" he called out to the old master. "Yes," replied the old man, "but there is something missing. Help me to climb over this wall and I'll put it right for you."

After hesitating, the priest lifted the old fellow over and set him down. Slowly, the master walked to the tree near the center of the garden, grabbed it by the trunk, and shook it. Leaves showered down all over the garden. "There," said the old man, "you can put me back now."

On the surface, this popularly told Zen parable exemplifies common man's interpretation of perfection in contrast with nature's profound, yet unpretentious splendor. The story's simplicity, however, belies the broader, more scholarly lesson. It speaks to man's inability to create for himself anything comparable in genuine beauty to that which naturally occurs in the Universe. Further, it articulates the virtue of allowing oneself to dissolve into the fiber of the Universe thus becoming an integral part of it rather than master over it. Finally, this enchanting tale reveals a nearly perfect illustration of the relaxed manner whereby we can experience our surroundings through nature's intended lens of wabi-sabi. Let go. Unclench. Relax.

213

The elder Zen master in this charming allegory practiced the ancient art of "wabi-sabi." Although nearly impossible to define, according to Robyn Griggs Lawrence, author of an immensely interesting book called the wabi-sabi house, the Japanese art of imperfect beauty:

> *"Pared down to its barest essence, wabi-sabi is the Japanese art of finding beauty in imperfection and profundity in nature, of accepting the natural cycle of growth, decay, and death. It's simple, slow, and uncluttered - and it reveres authenticity above all. "* [23]

For me, wabi-sabi has much to do with allowing myself to perceive nature's beauty on a purely visceral level in broad impressionist strokes devoid of thought expressed in words. For instance, I recall a particular occasion in late spring when I was struck motionless by the stunning hues on a woodland floor. The beauty of nature's palette touched me inside of a single heartbeat. It was unadulterated emotion and I reveled in the beauty of myriad, vibrant greens of the moss, a wonderful foil to the warmer yellows of the wild celandine. Had I considered the palette in words, analysis would surely have followed. It is this kind of analytical thought that inevitably blocks the indescribably luscious bliss that comes only when one is able to let go of all but pure gut sensation.

With regard to color, nature's wabi-sabi palette is relaxed while ours tends to be contrived. A wabi-sabi composition has effloresced into a subtle patina. Literally thousands of color nuances within a seemingly simple harmony of hues evidence each pigment's response over time to changing light, temperature and atmospheric moisture. It is from this aesthetically genius *imperfection* of nature's color palette that we learn much about creating our interior palettes. These wabi-sabi color marriages can make us feel an integral part of the natural world around us. And true flow comes only when we are perfectly at ease, at home in the Universe.

We appear to have internalized the idea that a chosen color scheme will look best if everything matches as precisely as possible. The notion is further solidified by the fact that we have discovered that perfect color (and for that matter, style) matches are safe. They are no fail. And wavering even slightly from a prescribed group of matched hues opens the possibility for missteps.

23. Robyn Griggs Lawrence, *the wabi-sabi house, the Japanese art of imperfect beauty*, 17

Realize, however, that there are significant limitations with the safely matched approach in which many of us endeavor to color our homes. Perhaps the most consequential of these is that if each color choice is a perfect match, the eye will read the composition in one fell swoop. As a matter of fact, the eye can register the artistic content of a space so rapidly that it even skips portions of the décor. This is because the hues becomes expected, even anticipated.

Imagine a room with a brick red sofa. A recliner is the identical rusty red and sage green plaid. The area rug is the same green. The valances above the sliding glass door are a companion tweed with flecks of green, brick red and gold. The metals in the room are brass. At the opposite end of the space is a table with a floor length cloth. But this piece doesn't even register. The eye is no longer curious because the message it sends to the aesthetic brain is brick red, sage green, brick red, sage green … Surely the table is brick red or sage green. And there must be some sort of brass lamp on that forgettable table. Our senses to a degree fill in what we expect or anticipate to be there.

A second drawback to these precisely coordinated combinations is that they significantly limit the available selection of furnishings and accessories. For instance, suppose that your chosen harmony for the bedroom is red-violet expressed as eggplant and violet manifested as blackberry. You have juxtaposed this rich color marriage against creamy ivories and in turn grounded everything with a warm chestnut floor. Beautiful!

Now when selecting a generous grouping of pillows for the bed, the precise eggplant and blackberry hues are very difficult to find. After several shopping excursions, you have custom pillows created that perfectly match your gorgeous palette. They were expensive but the match is exact. The downside is that those breathtaking fuschia, mulberry and hyacinth purple cushions and bolsters you had admired in the department store were not part of the very narrow color parameters you had set. And so, although captivating in their uniqueness, they were never a consideration for your space.

Why will fuschia, mulberry and hyacinth purple create such a strong aesthetic presence when paired with the existing scheme? It's because these hues that are slightly skewed from the main palette sumptuously *relate* rather than simply *repeat*. Let's look at the core component parts of the original harmony.

Color	Core Component Parts
red-violet	red-red-blue
violet	red-blue

215

Fuschia is a lighter value, high intensity red. Mulberry, although a bit darker, is also in the red family. These two hues relate to the main color scheme because each contains an essence of red. This is akin to pulling a color from a print and using it in a solid. The fuschia and the mulberry are mirroring the red which is a component part of both the red-violet and the violet. In the same way, the hyacinth purple is picking up some of each the red and blue. In place of an identical repetition of color, no more than the subtle essence of the hue is repeated. The core component parts have not varied. Only their ratios, values and intensities have changed. In ColorFlow we call this repetition and variation of hues that share a common essence a *Core Component Harmony*. It's a Color Speak term listed near the end of the chapter.

An excellent way to conceptualize the allure that can be created with a relaxed color palette is to liken it to eclecticism in design. Most of us are familiar with an eclectic style of décor in which a richness of character is achieved by bringing together a melange of furnishings and accessories. A sleek, modern sculpture on a farmhouse table, a silk covered chair on a coarse jute rug or a few ornate, heirloom antiques in an otherwise tailored traditional space . . . all of these cause the eye to remain curiously engaged.

The movement of the eye can be slowed as it makes its way through your room's composition by creating focal points of interest and providing rich variety and unexpected combinations. Consider once again the luscious, modern sculpture on the farmhouse table. Were we to replace the sculpture with a basket of hand carved wooden apples, the pairing becomes expected, even cliché. Now the eye sails past the arrangement because there is nothing extraordinary. In other words, there is no new aesthetic information to magnetize the viewer.

It is the same with color. In a perfectly matched room, the eye moves rapidly through the composition because there is nothing but repetition. All becomes expected. Further, any one item that doesn't precisely match stands out like the proverbial sore thumb. On the other hand, a space with a more relaxed color palette invites the eye to linger. The interesting medley of color variations draws the eye to experience a gently flowing impression of beauty. And if, for instance, you wish to display a cherished family heirloom that was not of your color choosing, it won't stand at attention shouting, "I don't belong." Instead, the treasured piece relaxes into a space that is already less than perfectly matched.

If each match in your space is precise, then all is assumed and the inherent joy that color imparts fades. Allow for watercolor imperfections to create a profoundly satisfying patina closer to nature than to Nordstrom's. Your home will exude a warmth not possible in a sterile, hotel-like environment. Such contrived, perfectly coordinated color schemes are at worst, blandly inoffensive and at best, pleasant. These palettes lack the depth of character and lyricism associated with freer color choices. And *matchy-matchy* spaces are easily taken for granted over time. Recall the manner in which the Zen master in the Taoist parable rendered the priest's garden splendidly relaxed and natural. You, too, can let compositions relax with regard to color and, for that matter, style. The results will propel you to spiritually and physically satisfying heights that you hadn't yet dreamed possible.

Imprint
The Japanese Bridge

With eyes closed, envision yourself moving toward the banks of a great river. Your stride is effortless as if in a wakeful dream. Upon reaching the banks you are awestruck by the crystal clarity of the water. The riverbed tilts ever so slightly and so is not dammed at any point on its course. For this reason, the river flows as naturally as it has for perhaps thousands of years.

The soothing sounds of the waterway hypnotize you into a deeply tranquil state. You are in perfect rhythm with the natural world around you. For the first time, Hara breathing engages in your solar plexus without conscious thought. Your muscles relax and you experience a perfect state of flow. Mentally count with me slowly and rhythmically from ten to one. Ten nine eight seven six five four three two one. Breathe in the life energy you garner from the enormous power of the river.

Picture now low hanging trees on either side of the river. They have grown prostrate as if bowing to the awe inspiring water channel. As you admire the tracery of the gnarled branches reflected in the clear water, notice a wooden bridge just a short distance upriver. It isn't a traditional bridge, nor is it the arched sort we might imagine in Monet's garden. Rather, it is a series of zigzags, regular diagonal turns, spanning from the nearest bank to the farthest. You are curiously drawn to the bridge, anxious to learn the serpentine nature of the structure.

Autumn has transformed the water-rich greenery of the trees into fiery reds, magentas, saffrons, caramels, plums and yellows. Poised to cross the bridge, picture in your mind's eye, each tree drenched in only a single, fall hue. Now just as you are about to take the first step, a breeze rustles through the branches. Leaves from each tree gently drop to float on the water's surface.

Walk the length of the first diagonal portion of the bridge. At this juncture where the surface turns creating the first "zig" followed by a "zag," a tree hangs over the water. In fact, at each successive turn in the bridge, a tree bearing a different color leaf suspends its branches over the water.

Pause near the first tree. Watch its amber yellow leaves spiral to the river's surface. Take a rejuvenating Hara breath. Now move to the next zigzag juncture and observe the second tree. Its brilliant orange leaves pool in the water below. The breeze strengthens. As it does, contemplate the design that nature creates on the river's surface. There are patches of yellow, of orange and of yellow-orange. The color melange created by the air movement is more nourishing to the spirit than either color alone.

As you explore further, notice a lightening of spirit. The branches of the third tree drip with flames of red. The breeze becomes a playful squall and claret leaves flurry to the water below. Although keenly drawn to this hue, even

218

more magnetic is the new combination that includes a scattering of oranges and yellows. With a lowering barometric pressure, these ambers and saffrons have broken ranks to journey upstream.

With nature's perfect color palette your impetus, continue traversing the bridge from tree to tree, zig to zag. The wind blows. Leaves fall. Grape purples now mingle with reds, and red-violets blend into orange. Single, nourishing hues fade one into another in a swirling patchwork. The effect is both stunning and inspiring. These are not the contrived color harmonies of man, but the splendid, lyrical fusions of nature herself.

Notice that a light rain has begun to fall. The already sumptuous medley of colors floating below, fade yet further one into another in magnificent, watercolor imperfection. Take several Hara breaths and become aware that the volume of energy once captured by this deep, natural breathing has become significantly greater. The spiritual and physical buoyancy you experience now is a result of your innate visceral connection with nature's perfect color palette. With this new discovery, you are prepared to bring watercolor imperfection to your palette at home. Together with your authentic ColorPrint, these color-rich divergences usher you the rest of the way into the most advanced state of flow.

With profound gratitude for discovering the secrets of using the dynamic force of color in the most personal way, mentally count with me from one to ten. As you do, return from your Imprint knowing the gifts of using color to achieve the sweet state of flow. Return now from the Japanese bridge as you count: one two three four five six seven eight nine ten.

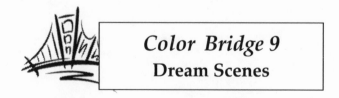

Color Bridge 9
Dream Scenes

"All life is vibration. You combine with what you notice, or you combine with what you vibrate to. If you are vibrating to injustice and resentment you will meet it on your pathway, at every step."
Florence Scovel Shinn

Recall both our discussion concerning creative visualization and the Color Bridge, Manifest Blessing, in Chapter 7. In the blessing for your home, you set down in words a clear mental picture of the aura you wish to create in your space. Having envisioned specific objectives that honestly portray your dreams, you drenched the images in positive energy that included a belief in their possibility.

In this, your final Color Bridge, you'll once again create a vision of your most nurturing space. There will be, however, a few key differences. For instance, this time you'll not conjure up only a mental picture. Instead, that which you'll visualize is first graphically expressed in pictures. The exercise is similar to the Treasure Maps first introduced by Shakti Gawain in her renowned book, Creative Visualization. According to this celebrated teacher of metaphysics:

"A treasure map is an actual, physical picture of your desired reality. It is valuable because it forms an especially clear, sharp image which can then attract and focus energy into your goal. It works along the same lines as a blueprint for a building. You can make a treasure map by drawing or painting it, or by making a collage using pictures and words cut from magazines." [24]

Gawain proposes the use of treasure maps to manifest goals related to health, career, relationships, family and even weight loss. Our "treasure maps," on the other hand, are specifically designed for the manifestation of our deeply authentic colors, styles and overall aura of space. To distinguish them from the all encompassing treasure maps of Gawain's book, the ColorFlow blueprints of interior dreams are called, Dream Scenes.

Open your Studio to the next clean page. Label it, "Color Bridge 9, Dream Scenes." Now look for any pictorial representations that convey the atmosphere you wish to manifest for your home. Use pictures from magazines or greeting cards, designs from stationery or swatches of fabric, photographs, words and drawings. Sometimes a motif that captures one's personal design spirit appears in the most unlikely of places. Once I found a colorful, paper party napkin that had both a design and color palette that profoundly resonated with my inner artist. Your Dream Scenes will spread over numerous pages. Instead of creating one large collage that is quite busy and difficult to mentally sort out at a glance, each page may become a single, simple "scene."

24. Shakti Gawain, *Creative Visualization*, 147

Previously you fashioned a Vignette for the purpose of creating an artistically nourishing composition. Now, as your design becomes increasingly reflective of your authentic essence, there most likely are mini-vignettes in several areas of your home. These are not staged, but real expressions of your genuine aesthetic. A photo of a real life Vignette such as the one shown here is a wonderful way to graphically encapsulate the ambience you desire in your Dream Scenes.

Because the real Vignette is an actual arrangement you've created, it solidifies the belief that you are capable of manifesting an aesthetically gratifying space. I chose this actual photograph from my home to include as one of my scenes.

Keep in mind as you work that Dream Scenes are not meant to represent specific furnishings or accessories you wish to have. Nor are they simply design ideas. Instead, they are depictions of any item, arrangement, pattern or composition exuding the sensory impressions that will support your natural state of being, your flow. The activity reminds me of an article I once read. In it a client gave her designer a richly hued, tapestry carpetbag she had brought back from India. When handing over the bag, she said, "Here, I want my home to *feel* like this." The carpetbag, like a Dream Scene, conveyed a complete aura. The exotic souvenir relayed more profound and useful information than would a laundry list of precise requests, likes and dislikes.

In other words, these are not simply wish lists. You won't be placing a picture of a seven foot, brown leather sofa with nailhead trim in your Studio and wish that it will magically come into your possession. Instead, this kind of dreaming is more of a free flow brainstorm of design *essences* that resonate with your aesthetic spirit. You are telling the Universe that you *wish to combine with certain vibrational aesthetics which are most natural and nourishing for you.* It is, in fact, a wabi-sabi way of creating design. You are choosing to relax your grip and become a co-creator with nature and the Universe. Consider the Dream Scene that follows. It is quite clever.

This page was created by a friend who collected magazine clippings that resonated with her authentic design voice in a small gift bag. The cheerful, chintz motif of the bag expresses just the mood she wishes to convey in her home. And even better, the colors look as if they have been taken directly from her personal ColorPrint. Could this be synchronicity at work?

My friend simply made a color copy of the gift bag for her Scene. The actual one was her design spirit goody bag where pictures were collected to be used later where they best fit. I like her idea of keeping a ready supply of pleasing design examples to be revisited in quiet times of aesthetic self-exploration.

By collecting and displaying graphic representations of your design spirit, you are sending your intentions out into the Universe. Any basic metaphysics or Feng Shui text will tell you that energy flows where intention goes. In other words, the vibrational energy of your Dream Scenes magnetizes similar essences. You get back that which you send out. Dream Scenes are about projecting intention into the Universe and then letting the energy form.

There is a two-pronged requirement essential to attracting that which you desire. The first is that once your intention is created, you must relinquish any tight grasp on the idea and release it. Only then can your intention float freely in the Cosmos gathering like vibrations. The second is that you allow yourself to experience no aversion to that which eventually manifests. In Feng Shui, we call this "no attachment, no aversion." Although either can be tricky, for many of us the "no aversion" piece is a bit more difficult to follow.

Say, for instance, that your intention is to have a space filled with pastel hues in a variety of floral patterns. The furnishings and accessories you find, however, tend more toward small geometric prints, heavy textures and solids. Since the pastels you wanted are generously represented, you decide to divert any lingering aversion and accept what the Universe has in store for you.

Several months later, a friend calls to say that she is downsizing to a small condo. Knowing how much you adore gardening, she asks if you would like to have several of her floral paintings. You enthusiastically accept and hang the artwork in your space. It quickly becomes clear that solids and small patterns acting as an enhancing backdrop to the floral artwork is much more in rhythm with your authentic design spirit than the specifics of your original intentions. Once again, co-creation with the Universe yields far more gratifying results than flying solo.

To borrow a cliché, the creative sky is the only limit when creating Dream Scenes. Once you begin, you'll be surprised at the innovative compositions you dream up. Of equal importance, however, is the way in which you ultimately use your Scenes. Recall making your Manifest Blessing part of your daily mental commentary in order to engage the energy that swirled about your ideas. Now, in place of words, there are actual images of your desired essence. Simply page through and quietly focus on your Scenes daily. Soon they will integrate naturally into your consciousness becoming a permanent part of that which you visualize for your space. With this ongoing meditation, there is no need for a written summary.

With this your final Color Bridge, your Studio should not be stored away. Instead, this valuable book now changes course slightly from a workbook of self-discovery to a continuing journal of nourishing colors and designs. You may wish to repeat selected Bridges, create your own, collect pictures or record additional insights. It's even fun to go back to the beginning and leaf through each activity. You'll be amazed at just how far you've journeyed. Your ColorFlow Studio has guided you to replace that incessantly noisy design chatter with your own soothing, authentic design voice.

Color Speak

Core Component Harmony: Distill the hues in a palette to their Core Component Parts. A common color among the parts makes a *Core Component Harmony*. For instance, a touch of yellow in a room with a palette of green and blue-green works because each of these contains yellow as a Core Component Part. Therefore, yellow makes a lovely *Core Component Harmony* with green and blue-green.

Watercolor Imperfection: Rather than utilizing a precisely uniform color composition throughout a space, *watercolor imperfection* both allows and encourages a more relaxed palette. Colors used, although basically from your ColorPrint, have interesting variations and tonal gradations that mimic those found in nature.

CLEANSE

Gilding the Lily

Your authentic ColorPrint has now become an essential part of your design repertoire. It is just about this time when you begin to feel the giddiness often associated with falling in love. In fact, you have fallen into a natural, rhythmic sync with your core design spirit. That which you experience is the love that naturally accompanies an intimate knowledge of self. This love comes complete with a familiar scintillating tug in the pit of your stomach. Having felt it before, you know that it affirms your selection of the right path. And in these final steps of your journey, you are confident that true north exists nowhere but deep within.

Because of the awe inspiring, yin-yang nature of the Universe, that which is blissfully light of spirit is always balanced with a heavier, darker underside. With regard to this newfound love affair with your aesthetic core, this means that there is a bit of caution to be heeded as you enthusiastically plunge into your authentic redesign. In the first chapter, I asked that you stop acquiring any new elements for your décor. Gratification would simply be delayed. Once your authentic design voice could be clearly heard, shopping would be an amazing experience. There would be no more confusion, buyer's remorse or purchases that once at home surprisingly didn't harmonize with your vision. Now, at journey's close, you unerringly recognize visceral attractions. This occurs because the vibrations of your genuine design essence have become so familiar that identifying like vibrations is effortless.

And the dark side? Authentic home décor possibilities appear so easily that you may actually bring in too much of a good thing. One of life's valuable lessons is that an overabundance of almost anything perceived as rewarding will begin to lose its allure. With even the most wonderful furnishings and accessories, a space can become a confused jumble. I think of it as "gilding the lily." The lily is beautiful in and of itself. Gilding, or embellishing it further, serves only to diminish its inherent splendor.

Become mindful of two distinct types of gilding. The first occurs when a single item is so adorned that its initial charm is obscured. A good example of this is what many of us have seen done to lampshades. Imagine a space with an exotic African aura. The homeowner is delighted to find a lamp with an earthenware jar for its base. The shade, covered with a richly textured, grasscloth, is simple in design.

Once in place, the lamp works beautifully with the existing décor. The zealous decorator, however, experiences such delight by this ideal addition that she wants to do even more. Armed now with ceramic beads, leopard printed faux fur and a glue gun, simple lampshade perfection turns to unfocused confusion. The animal print and beads are an interpretation of a theme that has become overly literal. The earthenware and grasscloth had on their own, perfectly distilled the theme to its bare essence. Bear in mind that a literal interpretation is one that we tire of quickly, whereas the abstract choice nourishes our artistic core for the long term.

One of the rewards for having invested your time and focus for the deepest of artistic exploration, is that you can stop trying so hard. Begin to experience the relaxation that comes with confident restraint in design. Instead of fussing with baubles, ornament and embellishments of all sorts, indulge in some restorative quiet time in the already nurturing refuge you've created.

A second kind of gilding applies not to a single item but to an entire space. Here again, restraint is key. By now you are cognizant of the aura or mood that is most revitalizing and balancing to your unique nature. Although mood is largely expressed through color, pattern and style, it is not uncommon for some sort of theme to have emerged.

Say you are a passionate gardener and wish to bring the refreshing vibe of the garden into your home. A sumptuous floral chintz on a single chair certainly brings life indoors. An occasional table fashioned from cement statuary topped with glass further expresses the room's botanical character. However, it is unnecessary and unadvisable to believe that every item in your room should have a literal connection to the garden.

In this same room with the chintz chair and the statue based table, it would be easy to add a wallpaper border depicting antique garden implements, a chandelier with tole painted greenery, clay pots to hold pencils and real lattice on the ceiling. Each piece on its own is special. However, with so many specialty items in a single space, focus on any one of them is lost.

We most likely have all heard to simply buy what we love and somehow it will all work. I finally realized that this advice has a big catch. Each item of beauty you choose must be one that you love *and* it must have a *purpose*. In the example above, the chintz chair and the themed occasional table both with botanical references were chosen for the purpose of creating focal points to carry the eye around and through the space.

Each additional item with a literal garden theme dilutes the impact of the specialty pieces. The eye is no longer pleasantly guided through the composition, but bombarded with the theme. Replace heavy handed cliché with a subtlety expressed design thread allowing focal points to gain impact. Think about what initially attracted you to the garden. It may have been the smell of newly turned earth, the ever spinning cycle of life or the grandeur of trees. Select the greater portion of furnishings with form and function as the priority accompanied by no more than the delicate essence of these joys. You might, for instance, use organic shapes, brown and green hues, faux bois and natural stone. Now, everything quietly relates but doesn't overwhelm.

So my old excuse, "Beauty for beauty's sake," for purchasing every gorgeous accessory and tchotchke, really doesn't stand up. Even beauty must have purpose. It can soften the utility of a space while drawing the eye in rhythmic motion through the room. Use beauty with sophisticated restraint and you'll be rewarded with profound artistic fulfillment. From this point on, when you feel the urge to be creative in your space, know that additions to what you already have isn't the only option. Sometimes, editing the layers of gilding to uncover pure, unadulterated beauty awakens our aesthetic spirits. Lighten your decorating hand. Rather than amassing more flourishes and frills, revel in the simple beauty of form and functionality.

YOUR COLORPRINT

Congratulations! You have completed the portion of your ColorFlow journey that lies within the pages of this book. I have loved traveling with you. As your exploration continues, know that you are not alone because in all matters of genuine artistic expression you co-create with the Universe in a never ending dance with the starfires of the night sky.

Envision the silvery artist's palette from our first Imprint. It was the palette from where one day your treasured ColorPrint would emerge. On the palette that follows you will place the authentic colors and neutrals unearthed during your ColorFlow journey. At last, you are documenting the results of your self-exploration in the form of an authentic color palette, your ColorPrint.

Even though this isn't a Color Bridge per se, open your Studio to the next fresh clean page. Alternatively, you may wish to place your palette at the end of your Studio leaving all pages in between for further dabbling, dreaming and bridging.

Make a photocopy of the blank palette below for pasting into your Studio. If your pages are 9" X 12," enlarge the palette by about 300 %. Now it will fit nicely onto your page in the landscape position and be a bit easier to work with. On the blank palette, place a representation of each color and neutral on your ColorPrint. Use a dab of paint, colored pencil, a paint chip, a tiny swatch of paper or fabric or really any combination of materials you can find that best shows each hue on your Print.

As you search for colors, keep in mind that you will be using a variety of values of each hue. Intensity, on the other hand, will vary less. If your authentic aesthetic is one that tends toward muted, grayed hues, this should be apparent on your palette. And if your genuine preference is for brighter, clearer colors, this, too, should be evident on your final ColorPrint.

Once your color swatches are in place, label them in two different ways. First, identify each color using one of the names from the twelve color wheel plus black, white, gray, cream or any of the browns. Second, identify each color with the authentic aura name you've chosen. Recall that this is a name that reminds you of the mood or aura you wish to express in your space. To review this naming process, go to the sample ColorPrint on page 40. Additionally, a labeled 12 color artist's wheel appears on page 22.

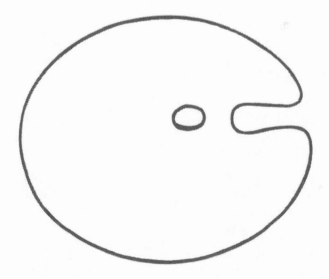

Copy and enlarge this blank palette. Paste it into your Studio. Then create your ColorPrint palette . . . the unique combination of hues sparking the gentle rhythm of life's sweet flow.

FLOW

"I am working with the enthusiasm of a man from Marseilles eating bouillabaisse, which shouldn't come as a surprise because I am busy painting huge sunflowers."
Vincent van Gogh

Science has proven that we live in a world where everything is moving energy. Rely only on your five senses and it appears that some substances are quite solid and have no movement whatsoever. In reality, though, anything that is perceived as solid matter is vibrating energy that has been captured in a form or matrix. It is still moving. And it is still energy.

Because we are so strongly conditioned to the notion that seeing is believing, it may be difficult for some to fully accept that seemingly solid matter isn't solid at all. It may help to consider that the energy that makes up matter is vibrating extremely fast. Imagine the strings on a guitar vibrating so rapidly that individual vibrations cannot be detected. Instead, there is only a blur. Initiate a shift in perception by adopting the notion that there is stationary energy and fluid energy. Add to this the fact that all energy is magnetic.

Each of us conducts, absorbs and radiates waves of energy. These internal vibrations of energy are colloquially called our "vibes." Whether we've explored them or not, they are there. And when we embark on a journey of self-discovery, our connection with the distinct qualities of vibrational energy radiated by our spirit is strengthened.

Once we know ourselves at this deeper energetic level, we begin to understand the importance of creating surroundings that will nurture and support this unique, living masterpiece of nature we know as self. Our journey of ColorFlow guides us to unearth the forms, patterns, mood and colors that resonate in perfect harmony with our aesthetic vibes. What results then, in essence, is a magnification of our unique energy field. At the outset we were as a tight bud, our beauty obscured within. As our intimacy deepened, petals unfolded and our energy unfurled into a lustrous, radiating field outstretched to the Universe.

Now open to the vast riches of the Universe, our energies emanating in a strong aura, we attract with ease all that is necessary for an emotionally fulfilling, abundant life. Everything that is potent in vibrational energies similar to our own seeks to share our life's journey. People with whom we can build lasting intimacy, careers in which we can make a significant contribution, abundance in health and finances; all that honestly befits us falls into rhythm with our natural step.

Initially, it may be hard to accept that our natural path is meant to be so painless, so gentle. We have been reared on the notion of toil and arduous work to get to the top. This is not to say that life is nothing but sipping tea on the veranda, but there is a significant difference between challenging and backbreaking, between fulfilling and frustrating.

If a goal is one chosen with integrity, then the laws of attraction will be in play. Consider how a paperclip is pulled to a magnet. Because your desired goal resonates with your inner vibrations, you no longer tow the line solely on your own power. You work in partnership with the Universe, a benefactor of its compelling magnetism. Said another way, an endeavor that becomes overly burdensome may indeed not be your true path. The struggle is to the psyche as disease to the body. It is the cosmos telling you to change course.

In the quotation above, Van Gogh "works with the enthusiasm of a man from Marseilles eating bouillabaisse," because for him, painting was an authentic dream. When creating his beloved sunflowers, he was fully immersed in the endeavor and experienced an energized focus. Today we hear phrases like "in the zone" or "in the groove." Marked by total immersion, enthusiasm and intense focus, the state of flow is also characterized by an ability to enjoy the present moment. While in the zone, we neither fret over the past nor worry about the future. And every ounce of our sparkling energy is directed toward the manifestation of true aspirations.

Each of you has a unique perception of beauty. The silver artist's palette you imagined at the outset shimmers with your authentic hues. Your surroundings vibrate in unison with your aesthetic essence. Bask in this charged atmosphere where genuine dreams now flourish. Everything, your cycles of work and rest, your creativity, your thoughts and dreams pulsate in perfect rhythm. Your space is brimming with nourishment both spiritual and physical. The authentic beauty you've created transfuses you with energy and lightness of spirit. Color is a joyous miracle of light bringing radiance to your life. It is the pursuit of your genuine dreams revealed only in the luscious state of flow that is the secret to living the rich life you truly deserve.

List of Color Speak Terms

*The number after each definition refers to the chapter in which it was introduced.

Adagio: The feathering of our nests in partnership with the Universe with emphasis on authentic desires and genuine preferences rather than tradition and expediency. It is what we notice perhaps synchronously rather than what we seek in a prescribed time frame. The adagio method of design emphasizes a gently paced and well controlled layering over time. Colors are unusual and combine in breathtaking melanges. They are unique to the individual, but do not precisely match. Fabrics and furnishings need not be in perfect, showroom condition. Timeworn elegance is welcomed. (5)

Artist's Eyes: One who uses his or her *artist's eyes* observes the environment without judgement or bias, using the visual sense to its fullest in a joyful, child-like manner. When our eyes are freed to become *artist's eyes*, the viewed object is actually seen for the first time. Hence, limitations are removed and possibility becomes boundless. (3)

Authentic Design Voice: That visceral or gut feeling that draws us to particular colors, patterns and styles, regardless of current trends, fashions or opinions of others. Our design voice is innate and unchanging. (1)

Birdwalking: Occurs when we frequently jump from one style or color palette to another in a fevered search to discover the look that speaks to us. There is little chance that this will eventuate in authentically personal surroundings. Rather, *birdwalking* manifests in a hodgepodge of styles that remains unable to meld into a pleasing whole. (9)

Bridge Summary: A handwritten paragraph that sums up discoveries, clues, patterns or any additional significant bits of information with regard to your ColorPrint and genuine design style. A *bridge summary* is written directly into your Studio after most Color Bridge exercises. Content, not spelling or grammar, is most important in a *bridge summary*. (2)

Clarity Marker: You are rather certain of your ColorPrint palette. You are attentive to your authentic design voice and have settled into the gentle layering of adagio. With these principles in place, a subtle clue to a yet unconsidered design direction or solution materializes for any decorating perplexity. The idea promises to be the most uplifting and life balancing solution for your environment. This creative signal from the Universe, a *clarity marker*, portends genuine, aesthetic clarity. (7)

Clutter: Anything that does not bring comfort, convenience or joy on a regular basis. (1)

Color Bridges: Design activities completed with your most creative, playful, non-judgmental mind. The purpose of a *Color Bridge* is to discover the unique ColorPrint that will reawaken your spirit enabling you to celebrate life's bounty. (2)

Color Chain: Imagine cutting a color wheel on the line between violet and red-violet. Open up the wheel first so it looks like the arc of a rainbow. Open it further until the colors are in a straight line from red-violet to violet. You have created what is referred to in ColorFlow as a *Color Chain*. (6)

Color Essence: Any color that is actually a blended hue containing a greater amount of neutral than pure color is a popular neutral. The color within the popular neutral is its *color essence*. (6)

Color Family: A primary color on the 12 color wheel and its neighbor on either side make a primary *color family*. A secondary color and its neighbor on either side make a secondary *color family*.   An example of a primary *color family* is red, red-orange and red-violet.   An example of a secondary *color family* is green, yellow-green and blue-green. (2)

ColorFlow: A mindful creation of interior design that incorporates your ColorPrint together with styles and arrangements unique to your personality and lifestyle. This genuine atmosphere clears your mind, exhilarates your body and lightens your spirit transporting you to your most natural state of flow: *ColorFlow*. (1)

ColorFlow Scale of Visual Weight: A sketch of key pieces of furniture made with the intention of balancing the décor with regard to color and visual weight.   Briefly describe each piece considering value and intensity. This information will reveal to which side of the room the imaginary scale of visual weight is tipping.   Appropriate adjustments to achieve a more pleasing balance can then be made. (8)

ColorPrint: The specific colors and color harmonies which when used in our homes act to nourish our spirits creating an environment that enriches our lives with unimagined abundance and ever diminishing stress. (1)

Color Restraint: The use of color in interior design is readily noticed, frequently discussed, inexpensive and easy for even the novice designer to manipulate. However, in addition to color, we all need to create contrast and interest by bringing into play other design elements thus emphasizing the stunning subtleties of color. Spark visual interest by placing equal attention on texture, pattern, shape, style and proportion. Self-expression through design becomes more personally meaningful by restraining the use of color while supporting your design with these additional elements. (6)

Color Sophistication: The discrimination of colors based not simply on the color wheel hue, but additionally on its intensity, value, quantity and the environment in which it is used. (3)

Comfortable Large Surface Colors: Colors that can be comfortably envisioned on large surfaces such as walls, floors and sofas. These hues have become familiar simply because each of us has had to cover large surfaces. Therefore, practice in choosing colors for these spaces has been frequent. (8)

Core Component Harmony: Distill the hues in a palette to their Core Component Parts. A common color among the parts makes a *Core Component Harmony*. For instance, a touch of yellow in a room with a palette of green and blue-green works because each of these contains yellow as a Core Component Part. Therefore, yellow makes a lovely *Core Component Harmony* with green and blue-green. (10)

Core Component Parts: The separation of secondary and tertiary colors into their component parts. These parts will in all cases be some combination of red, yellow and blue. Using the concept of *core component parts* aids in seeing hues obscured by the mixture they are within. (9)

Creative Paradox: A design phenomenon wherein projects or ideas come to fruition with the greatest artistic success if approached in the exact opposite way than one would normally believe to be most logical. (2)

Deeply Genuine Place: A particular place created by one person or family who resides there. This space is saturated in authentic colors and styles creating an environment steeped in life-giving energies which brings lasting contentment, joy and abundance to those embraced by the space. (1)

Design Chatter: The ever changing plethora of colors, patterns, styles and opinions that bombards us on a daily basis consciously or unconsciously deafening our own authentic design voice. (1)

Design Venue: Your affinity for any design element whether its color, style, pattern or texture may be obscured by the environment in which it is viewed. The element in question may lack any surroundings to enhance it. Conversely, the existing surroundings may heighten its beauty. *Design venue* is a key component to your ever increasing color sophistication. (5)

Domestic Patina: The results of a gradual layering of elements over time in partnership with the Universe. A fine antique as a result of gentle wear, loss of moisture and exposure to light over time has naturally formed a surface patina, subtler, richer and full of character. Perfection in color match has been lost to the years. In the same way, your décor will possess the luminous beauty of a personally expressive accumulation. Spaces with *domestic patina* are characterized by lyricism and a depth of artistic expressiveness that cannot be achieved by any other manner. (5)

Edgy Limited Surface Colors: Colors used in relatively small doses as accents. These hues tend to be edgy, offbeat, anything but neutral hues. They are many times unfamiliar to us because we have been too timid to experiment with supporting hues. Once the larger surface colors are chosen, we believe our palette to be complete. It is the *edgy limited surface colors* that when added to our yet thin color harmony will cause the *comfortable large surface hues* to literally sing. (8)

Energy of the Process: Hidden, untapped stores of energy locked deep within the process of gentle, mindful and reflective cleansing. This energy is a necessary component of the flow that becomes part of your life during the ColorFlow journey. (3)

Existing Design Repertoire: Any design knowledge, experience or expertise that is currently part of your consciousness is your *existing design repertoire*. It is the intent of the ColorFlow course to help expand your aesthetic sensibilities, free your flow of natural creativity and ensure intimacy with your innate sense of personal taste and unique style thereby expanding your *existing design repertoire* many fold. (2)

Genuinely Limited Field: When a color or quality of color including intensity, value and quantity is discovered to be deeply genuine, this particular field becomes limited and can be placed on the ColorPrint. (4)

Imprint: Connection to the pliant, subjective mind easing acceptance of alternative or unfamiliar concepts into our personal realms while in a deeply relaxed yet mentally alert state. (1)

Infinite Selection: Literally every color that we can perceive expressed in all ranges of value and intensity. It is available only to those who are able to fully suspend judgement whether favorable or unfavorable of all hues. (1)

Luminesce: The color and finish of the backdrop has the power to elevate a pleasant piece to the status of art. In Color Flow we call the transformation of an object from satisfying to stunning by doing no more than changing its backdrop, *luminescing.* (3)

Seed of Color Truth: A color can be made up of at least some qualities that elevate our mood and balance our emotions while it simultaneously possesses at least one quality or characteristic that doesn't align with our innate color desires. Whatever nourishing quality this color has that attracts us to it is the *seed of color truth.* It is this seed that needs to appear on our authentic ColorPrint. (4)

Simply Beautiful Space: Any space in which all design elements including furnishings, color, pattern, scale and light are at least pleasing and balanced, but may be breathtaking. (1)

Studio: The artist's sketchbook for making lists, writing thoughts, creating color schemes and collecting magazine pictures. The sketchbook from where the final ColorPrint will emerge. (2)

Watercolor Imperfection: Rather than utilizing a precisely uniform color composition throughout a space, *watercolor imperfection* both allows and encourages a more relaxed palette. Colors used, although basically from your ColorPrint, have interesting variations and tonal gradations that mimic those found in nature. (10)

Word Stylings: Your own collection of words that gently guides you in the creation of a unique environment manifesting in marvelous, free flowing energy. A list of Genuine Words, a name for your home and a Manifest Blessing are the key components of *Word Stylings.* (7)

Made in the USA
Lexington, KY
10 May 2014